Sociology and Socialism

Sociology and Socialism

Tom Bottomore

Professor of Sociology
University of Sussex

DISTRIBUTED BY HARVESTER PRESS

First published in Great Britain in 1984 by
WHEATSHEAF BOOKS LIMITED
A MEMBER OF THE HARVESTER PRESS GROUP
Publisher: John Spiers
Director of Publications: Edward Elgar
16 Ship Street, Brighton, Sussex

ⓒ Tom Bottomore. 1984

British Library Cataloguing in Publication Data

Bottomore, Tom
  Sociology and socialism.
  1. Sociology
  I. Title
301'.01   HM24

ISBN 0-7108-0230-7
ISBN 0-7108-0235-8 Pbk

Typeset in 11 point Times by P.R.G. Graphics Ltd., Redhill
Printed in Great Britain by
The Thetford Press Ltd, Thetford, Norfolk

THE HARVESTER PRESS PUBLISHING GROUP
The Harvester Press Publishing Group comprises Harvester Press Limited
(chiefly publishing literature, fiction, philosophy, psychology and science
and trade books), Harvester Press Microform Publications Limited
(publishing in Microform unpublished archives, scarce printed sources, and
indexes to these collections) and Wheatsheaf Books Limited (a wholly
independent company chiefly publishing in economics, international
politics, sociology and related social sciences), whose books are distributed
by The Harvester Press Limited and its agencies throughout the world.

Contents

1 On the Relation Between Sociology and Socialism

That a close connection exists between sociology and socialism is evident. The terms themselves came into use, initially in France, at approximately the same time during the 1830s, and the new ideas which they expressed were derived to a large extent from the same body of social thought, that of Saint–Simon. Their association, far from being a fortuitous historical conjunction, grew out of similar intellectual responses to the new economic and social conditions brought into existence by the rise of industrial capitalism. In both the socialist doctrines and the sociological theories of the early nineteenth century there emerged, as one influential strand of thought, the idea of a progressive development towards a conscious, rational regulation of human social life, expressed most fully, in its sociological form, in Comte's 'positive philosophy' and 'positive politics'.

This is not to say, however, that the socialist and sociological conceptions of the social world were at any time identical. In sociology there was an emphasis upon 'order' and continuity as well as 'progress', and Robert Nisbet has shown that the conservative critics of the French Revolution (most notably de Bonald) made an important contribution from the very beginning to the formation of sociology, for in

opposing the whole philosophy of the natural order the conservatives were led to rest their emphasis upon the institutional order. And in the process of *defending* on moral grounds a set of traditional institutions—family, religion, local community, guild, social class—the conservatives succeeded in *identifying* these institutions; that is, thrusting them into the foreground of intellectual contemplation where they could become the objects of liberal, even radical, intellectual regard and also . . . the empirical objects of sociology and other social sciences.[1]

Comte himself was greatly influenced by the conservative thinkers, and his sociology eventually assumed the character of a theory of the new scientific–industrial society in its capitalist form, and an advocacy of reforms deemed necessary in order to overcome the confusion and crisis in the European societies and to consolidate and regulate the post-revolutionary social order.

On the other side, from the middle of the nineteenth century, socialist ideas attained their most comprehensive sociological expression in Marx's thought, which depicted and analyzed an ongoing process of revolutionary change. Some later Marxists, however, in concentrating upon the relation between Comte and Marx, have seen the contrast between their theories as one between 'sociology' and 'Marxism'. Marcuse, in particular, rejected the 'positivist sociology' inspired by Comte, which 'was to be a science seeking social laws', having as its consequence that 'social practice, especially the matter of changing the social system, was herewith throttled by the inexorable'; and he opposed to this positive science a rationalist 'critical theory' derived via Marx from Hegel.[2] Others also invoked the name of Comte in order to establish a fundamental distinction between Marxist thought and sociology. Thus Korsch, in a study of Marx contributed to a series on 'Modern Sociologists', argued that sociology is

'the opponent of modern socialism . . . For later "sociologists", up to the present day, just as for Comte after his break with Saint–Simon, it has been a matter of opposing to the theory, and hence also the practice, of socialism a different theoretical and practical discussion of the questions which it initially posed'

and he went on to suggest that Marx's thought stands in a much closer relation to

the social inquiry of that revolutionary period of development of the English and French bourgeoisie in the seventeenth and eighteenth centuries, when indeed the name 'sociology' had not yet been invented but 'society' had already been discovered as a distinct and independent sphere of knowledge and action, and its full significance had been recognized.[3]

But this is an inadequate account of the relation between sociology and Marxism for several reasons. First, Comte's thought had little direct influence, even in France, upon the formation of modern sociology later in the century, and was for the most part ignored or rejected, so that it is a manifest absurdity to identify sociology with Comte's theory. Second, when sociology became established as an independent academic social science towards the end of the nineteenth century it was by no means uniformly or consistently 'positivist' in orientation; in this respect too it owed little to Comte.[4] Thus, while Durkheim has often been regarded—though always with many qualifications—as a positivist, he has also been treated as a thinker who attempted to provide the foundation of a non–positivist, scientific sociology.[5] Max Weber was quite clearly not a positivist, and his thought has been interpreted either as a 'transcendence of positivism and idealism',[6] or as containing an unresolved antinomy between two distinct methods of social enquiry; on one side, the 'understanding' of meaningful human action, and on the other, causal explanation of social processes and events, with a particular emphasis given by many later writers to the method of 'understanding'.[7] On the other hand, Marx's theory can well be interpreted, and has been interpreted, as an attempt to construct a general science of society with a strongly positivist cast;[8] and one important school of Marxist thought, Austro-Marxism, presented the theory as a rigorous scientific sociology.

The continuing debates within Marxism about its nature as a social science in relation to sociology are considered more fully in a later essay in this volume (see pp.31–73 below)[9], and here it need only be remarked that the real historical development of sociological thought is more varied and complex than some Marxist critics of sociology have supposed. But this does not exclude the possibility of drawing major distinctions between Marxist and other specific sociological theories, as I endeavour to do in several of the following essays. One earlier attempt to establish such a contrast is that of Löwith in his study of Weber and Marx, where it is argued that:

'Like our actual society, which it studies, social science is not unified but divided in two: bourgeois sociology and Marxism. The most important representatives of these two lines of inquiry are Max Weber and Karl Marx. But the sphere of their investigations is one and the same: the "capitalist" organization of a modern economy and society.'[10]

Löwith's study is based on the view that both Marx and Weber were guided in their researches by a philosophical 'idea' of man, and by an underlying concern with the fate of human beings in the modern capitalist world, expressed by Marx in the notion of 'alienation', by Weber in that of 'rationalization'. From this standpoint the difference between their respective accounts of the nature and tendencies of modern western society is seen as arising from a fundamental divergence of value orientations: in Weber's case a commitment to defending individual freedom and autonomy in the face of growing mechanization and bureaucratization, and in Marx's case an allegiance to the cause of the proletariat as the agent of a general human emancipation and the bearer of a new civilization. At the same time these value orientations can be seen as related to the interests and aspirations of particular social classes, more especially if we take account of Weber's equally fervent commitment to strengthening the German nation state in its effort to become a world power; a theme which I explore more fully in a later essay (pp. 123–35 below). Conceived in this broader way Löwith's interpretation obviously has affinities with Marxist accounts, such as that of Korsch, which regard the emergence of academic sociology as a response to Marxism, in the form of an intellectual defence of bourgeois society against the revolutionary ideas of the socialist labour movement.

Such accounts, however, related most convincingly to a period—roughly from the 1880s to the 1920s—when Marxism and sociology were profoundly separated, in the sense that Marxist theory was expounded and developed almost entirely within socialist parties and movements, while the sociology which became established as an academic discipline was overwhelmingly non–Marxist or anti–Marxist. Subsequently, and notably from the 1960s, this situation changed significantly. It is true that the opposition between Marxism (historical materialism) as a 'proletarian social science' and sociology as a 'bourgeois social science' has been upheld throughout most of this period—though with diminishing intellectual conviction and persuasiveness—in Marxist–Leninist orthodoxy; but in most of the world, and notably in Western Europe, this ideological and dogmatic view has long since been abandoned and Marxist theory has established itself as a major sociological paradigm, necessarily involved in confrontation and debate with other paradigms. In this contestation the growing influence of Marxist thought in anthropology, history, economics and other disciplines has brought clearly into view that Marxism has so far been unrivalled by any other theoretical scheme in the social sciences in its capacity to stimulate thought and research in so many different fields of inquiry and to integrate them in a systematic conception of social life as a whole.

The rise of Marxist sociology in the past two decades has altered, in certain respects, the terms in which the relation between sociology and socialism should be conceived. All the essays in this volume are written from a socialist (predominantly Marxist) perspective, but they do not express only a particular value orientation; they are also, and even mainly, concerned with the validity of different concepts and theoretical schemes, and with the truth of specific explanations or interpretations. What is at issue in these studies is whether Marx's theory of history provides (and within what limits) a good account of the principal stages in the development of human society; whether his analysis of the capitalist mode of production and of class relations and class conflict in this form of society explains adequately the broad trend of events within it; whether the quite different conceptions of capitalism and the modern state in the works of Durkheim and Weber qualify in important ways, or supersede, or can be refuted by, the Marxist theory. More generally, with respect to Marxist and non–Marxist sociological paradigms, the question has to be raised (and is considered in several of the following essays) about the relation between social, i.e. 'structural', determinants of actions or events, and human 'agency', i.e. the intentional, knowledgeable actions of individuals or groups. Much recent debate in sociology, on the terrain of the philosophy of science, has been centrally concerned with this question, but, notwithstanding some useful clarification of the issues, I think it has to be said that we still lack a comprehensive theoretical reformulation which goes beyond what was expressed by Marx in his argument that 'Men make their own history, but they do not make it just as they please' (*Eighteenth Brumaire*), or by Simmel in his conclusion that the individual's existence

is not only partly social and partly individual, but also belongs to the fundamental, decisive and irreducible category of a unity which we cannot designate other than as the synthesis or simultaneity of two logically contradictory characterizations of man—the characterization which is based on his function as a member, as a product and content of society; and the opposing characterization which is based on his functions as an autonomous being, and which views his life from its own centre and for its own sake ('How is Society Possible?')

In recent Marxist sociology a clear distinction has emerged between a rigorous structuralist conception, inspired by Althusser, which treats the individual only as a 'bearer' of structures, and versions of the theory which emphasize human agency, above all in political struggles, though there have also been attempts to bridge the gap.[11]

Marxism has been a focal point in discussions of the relation between socialism and sociology largely because of the claim made on its behalf—though less frequently in recent years—that it is at the same time, and in some unitary way, both a science of society *and* the necessary form of political consciousness of the working class; a claim most extravagantly expressed in the once widely used term 'scientific socialism'. But Marxism as a science cannot be equated with socialism, even though, for reasons which are easily understandable, it has a close historical affinity with it.[12] There are many forms of socialism besides Marxism, and in all its diverse manifestations socialism, as a doctrine and a movement, expresses distinctive interests and values which culminate in the idea of, and the striving for, a new civilization, morally superior to the old. In this context Marx's great achievement was not to present any new image of the future form of society (an aim which he explicitly disavowed) but to reveal, through what he conceived as a rigorously scientific analysis, the mechanism (or 'law of motion') of capitalist society, and the nature of the real forces at work within it which made possible the attainment of a socialist society. Marx's ideas have assumed in later Marxist thought many different guises: a philosophical anthropology, a critical philosophy, a universal science or world view, a party dogma, a science of society. It is the last of these, i.e. Marxist sociology (conceived not in any narrow professional sense, but as encompassing, or taking the form of, anthropology, social history, political economy, and that kind of reflection upon methodology which engages the philosophy of science, as well as more conventional 'sociological' inquiries) which can, I contend, most fruitfully extend Marx's own studies.

Any such extension may involve, and in my estimation has already produced, substantial revisions of Marx's theoretical scheme, more particularly in its application to the development of forms of society in the twentieth century. More broadly, it affects all attempts to construct any kind of 'radical' sociology oriented to socialist values. Not only is it a matter of controversy, as I have already indicated and as I discuss more fully in some of the following essays, whether Marx's paradigm is adequate for understanding the recent development of classes, the role of the state, or the nature of crises, in present–day capitalist societies, but a host of new questions have emerged into prominence which were largely or wholly ignored in that scheme of thought. Among these questions is one which simply did not confront Marx, Engels and the first generation of Marxists, and was then for a long time obscured by the murky clouds of Bolshevik doctrine— namely, the structure of 'actually existing' socialist societies. It has been glaringly obvious for the past three decades at least that a Marxist sociology which makes any claim to being a science cannot confine itself to discussing socialism as a possible future 'society of associated producers', but must analyze (with the aid, if necessary, of new concepts) the socialist societies which have come into existence in the USSR and Eastern Europe, in China, and elsewhere. Such analyses, which have only recently begun to take a more substantial form, have to deal with problems of the emergence of a new class structure,[13] the nature of the state and the phenomenon of bureaucratic power,[14] the relation between centralized economic planning, or on the other hand decentralized self-management, and political democracy.[15]

But many other important and difficult problems face Marxist sociologists of the present generation. One is that of the limits to economic growth, or more broadly the whole relation of human beings to their natural environment as this affects the aims of the socialist movement, which were often formulated in the past too exclusively in terms of the expansion of material production and the unlimited satisfaction of material needs; another is the situation created by the rapid advance of the natural sciences which has brought not only, as Marx foresaw, an immense growth of productive forces, but along with that, a massive increase in the powers of destruction, so that the very existence of the human species is now in jeopardy. The main question may be not whether the tendency of social development is towards a socialist form of society, but whether there will be any human society at all in the future. The issues which this raises are closely linked with a phenomenon which, it is generally agreed, has been seriously neglected in the Marxist theory of society, beginning with Marx himself; namely, the significance, for the development of the modern world, of nation states and nationalism, and their relation to the socialist movement.[16]

From this perspective, sociology (including its Marxist form) and socialism are quite sharply separated. Not only the prospects of the socialist movement in present–day capitalist societies, but alternative projects for the institutional arrangements of a socialist society, and above all the nature and functioning of 'actually existing' socialism, are necessary objects of a realistic, objective sociological analysis from a socialist perspective. But is there not still a sense in which sociology and socialism have a close affinity, as I suggested that they had at their origins? This might be argued in two ways. First, it may be said that sociology, as an objective body of knowledge, a component of 'objective culture', regardless of the specific value orientations of particular sociologists, necessarily promotes a critical view of social arrangements, by its disclosure of inequalities, forms of domination, ideological misrepresentations and their sources. Some support for this view is to be found in the historical record; authoritarian regimes of whatever kind generally suppress or severely restrict the scope of sociological thought and research, and right–wing governments tend to look upon it with marked disfavour (in Britain this usually takes the form of arguing that sociology does not produce useable, 'practical' results). But this argument, so far as it is valid, connects sociology with a liberal or democratic type of society, not specifically with socialism.

Second, however, it may be argued, along the lines that I indicated at the beginning of this essay, that sociology necessarily embodies the idea of a conscious, rational regulation of society, and that this comes very close to the idea of socialism, as expressed notably by Marx in his conception of a 'society of associated producers' who would organize both their interchange with nature (the production process) and their social relationships rationally (though Marx also introduces a moral criterion when he refers to conditions which are 'proper and worthy for human beings'). This argument too, although it has a certain force, still does not establish a necessary affinity between sociology and socialism. Not only does sociological thought (in the work of Weber and Durkheim, for example) embrace many ideas besides that of rational regulation,[17] which was perhaps most prominent in the Enlightenment origins of sociology, but the specific content of socialism—namely, the idea of a classless, egalitarian *self*–regulating society—is by no means the only form in which a 'rational' organization of society can be conceived.

I conclude, then, that despite the links—historical and intellectual—between sociology and socialism they belong to quite distinct spheres. Socialism, as thought and action, arises from political interests and values; sociology, as a form of knowledge, from scientific values. Yet sociology, like other sciences (and especially the social sciences) is necessarily carried on in a milieu impregnated with political values, and it may quite legitimately be guided by a socialist outlook which plays some part in defining its underlying image of human nature and society, and its principal themes of inquiry. In an open, democratic socialist society, just as in capitalist society, sociology would have an important role (and in all probability a more important one) as an instrument of critical investigation of real social relations and their development. Its most appropriate motto, as a scientific discipline, would be that favourite one of Marx: *De omnibus dubitandum.*

NOTES

1. Nisbet, Robert, 'Conservatism', in Bottomore, Tom, and Nisbet, Robert (eds.), *A History of Sociological Analysis* (New York: Basic Books, 1978); see also Nisbet, *The Sociological Tradition* (New York: Basic Books, 1967), chaps. 1 and 2.

2. Marcuse, Herbert, *Reason and Revolution: Hegel and the Rise of Social Theory* (New York: Oxford University Press, 1941).

3. Korsch, Karl, *Karl Marx* (1938. Revised German edn, Frankfurt am Main: Europäische Verlagsanstalt, 1967).

4. The question is further complicated by the variety of meanings attached to the term 'positivism'; on this, see Keat, Russell, *The Politics of Social Theory* (Oxford: Basil Blackwell, 1981), chap. 1; and Halfpenny, Peter, *Positivism and Sociology* (London: Allen & Unwin, 1982).

5. Hirst, Paul Q., *Durkheim, Bernard and Epistemology* (London: Routledge & Kegan Paul, 1975). Durkheim himself (in *The Rules of Sociological Method*) described his method as 'scientific rationalism' and rejected the 'positivist metaphysics' of Comte and Spenser.

6. Stuart, Hughes H., *Consciousness and Society* (London: MacGibbon & Kee, 1959), chap. 8.

7. See the discussion in Outhwaite, William, *Understanding Social Life: The Method Called 'Verstehen'* (London: Allen & Unwin, 1975), and also Dawe, Alan, 'Theories of Social Action', in Bottomore and Nisbet (eds.), op. cit.

8. See especially Wellmer, Albrecht, *Critical Theory of Society* (New York: Herder & Herder, 1971), chap. 2, 'The latent positivism of Marx's philosophy of history'.

9. See also Bottomore, Tom, (ed.), *Modern Interpretations of Marx* (Oxford: Basil Blackwell, 1981).

10. Löwith, Karl, *Max Weber and Karl Marx* (1932. English trans. London: Allen & Unwin, 1982).

11. e.g. by Lucien Goldmann, in his conception of 'genetic structuralism'; see *Marxisme et sciences humaines* (Paris: Gallimard, 1970), 'Genèse et structure'. See also the essay below (pp. 74–87) on 'Structure and History', and Bottomore (ed.), op. cit., Introduction.

12. See Hilferding, Rudolf, *Finance Capital* (1910) (English trans. London: Routledge & Kegan Paul, 1981), Preface.

13. See Konrád, George, and Szelényi, Ivan, *The Intellectuals on the Road to Class Power* (Brighton: Harvester Press. 1979).

14. See Hegedüs, András, *Socialism and Bureaucracy* (London: Allison & Busby, 1976).

15. See Brus, Wlodzimierz, *The Economics and Politics of Socialism* (London: Routledge & Kegan Paul, 1973), and *Socialist Ownership and Political Systems* (Routledge & Kegan Paul, 1975).

16. The only substantial Marxist work on the subject remains that of Otto Bauer, first published almost eighty years ago, *Die Nationalitätenfrage und die Sozialdemokratie* (Vienna: Wiener Volksbuchhandlung, 1907, 2nd enlarged edn, 1924). A new sociological analysis both of nationalism and of the doctrines and institutional forms of socialist internationalism should have high priority in any Marxist research programme.

17. 'Rationality' itself is a complex and contested concept and there are also major empirical disagreements about the significance of rational and non-rational elements in social life. On the first aspect see especially Hollis, Martin and Lukes, Steven, (eds.), *Rationality and Relativism* (Oxford: Basil Blackwell, 1982); Brubaker, R., *The Limits of Rationality: An Essay on the Social and Moral Thought of Max Weber* (London: Allen & Unwin, 1984); and Habermas, Jürgen, *Toward a Rational Society* (Boston: Beacon Press; London: Heinemann, 1970).

2 Competing Paradigms in Sociology

During the past decade there has been a remarkable proliferation of new approaches and paradigms in sociology, to such an extent indeed that some writers have referred to a 'crisis' affecting the whole discipline, which they may judge either favourably, as a condition of intellectual ferment and renewal, or unfavourably, as a state of affairs in which sociological thought seems to have lost any rational coherence; and many others are uneasy about the exuberant growth of new sociological 'schools' and 'sects'. But it would be wrong to exaggerate the significance of these recent trends. Sociology (and this applies also to other social and human sciences) has always been what one writer has called a multi–paradigm science, that is to say, a science in which there are 'too many paradigms' (Masterman, 1970). And it was not unknown, at earlier times, for discussions about a 'crisis' in sociological thought to occur. One such occasion was in the last decade of the nineteenth century when the 'revisionist' controversy developed within Marxism, and in the wider field of social thought there was a general assault upon positivism (Hughes, 1958); and another was in the late 1920s and early 1930s, when a writer in the journal of the Austro-Marxists, *Der Kampf*, for example, expressed his satisfaction at finding a coherent exposition of sociological theory in the book he was reviewing at a time when confusion and a sense of crisis seemed to prevail everywhere (Lauterbach, 1933). Very often, in fact, a crisis in sociology seems to be associated with, and perhaps reflect, a sense of intellectual crisis in the wider sphere of cultural and political life; and this may well have been the case during the 1960s.

It is clear, at all events, that sociological thought has developed quite new orientations in the course of the past decade. Some indication of the extent of these changes can be found by looking at a collection of articles from the learned journals of the 1950s (Lipset and Smelser 1961), which was intended to portray the main trends in sociology at that time. The section devoted to theory was somewhat limited in outlook, and more or less confined to a consideration of functionalism; it contained no reference to such theoretical approaches as Marxism, phenomenology, ethnomethodology and structuralism, which are well known, and in varying degrees influential, in the sociological thinking of a decade later. Social stratification was discussed in the 1950s, it seems, without reference to social classes and property, and there was little attempt to analyze the structure of whole societies, or to deal comprehensively with social change. The editors of the collection singled out as being perhaps, its most significant general feature the complete triumph of 'scientific sociology', in contrast with the policy–oriented, more social–philosophical kind of sociology, though they recognized that some controversial issues remained, arising mainly from the criticisms of functionalism as an unhistorical, politically conservative theory which neglected, in particular, the elements of change and conflict in social life.

In the space of a few years all this has changed.[1] Functionalism no longer occupies such a prominent place as a sociological paradigm, and it is not now the main centre of theoretical controversies, even though some of the alternative paradigms may have developed, in part, from criticisms of the functionalist approach. It should also be noted that the influence of functionalism was always strongest in the USA. In Western Europe, where evolutionist theories, Marxism, a historical sociology inspired by Max Weber, and a more philosophical form of sociology (especially in Germany) were still active, the impact of functionalism was much less evident; while in the USSR and Eastern Europe, until the mid-1950s, sociology was regarded with disfavour, and a somewhat crude and dogmatic version of 'historical materialism' was established as the officially–approved science of society. One of the most significant features of the changes during the 1960s is that these geographical boundaries have, to a considerable extent, disappeared; and there is now a more clearly international body of theoretical sociology, and controversy about it. An important turning point in this process of change was the emergence, after 1956, of a New Left movement, both intellectual and political, which revitalized and diversified Marxist thought, emphasized more strongly the sociological aspects of Marx's theory, and by its vigorous criticism of what it saw as 'establishment sociology', opened the way for attempts to develop a 'radical' or 'critical' sociology, which is now one of the main currents of thought in the controversies about sociological theory.

The variety of theoretical and methodological conceptions, and the relatively frequent changes in the main orientations of sociological thought in recent years (reflected in the appearance of many new journals, each of which apparently expresses the outlook of a particular 'school'), make it difficult to identify with any great certainty those trends that seem likely to have some lasting significance. Nevertheless, a number of fairly well articulated and established paradigms have emerged or have been reformulated during the past decade, and it is worth while to consider how they diverge from each other, what the principal controversies are, and how these controversies have developed.

Functionalism, or as it came to be called 'structural-functionalism' (because its aim was to analyze the functioning of institutions, or elements of social life, as parts of a definite social system or structure), has lost, as I noted earlier, much of the importance as a paradigm that it once had; but in modified forms it continues to direct a good deal of sociological inquiry. The modifications that were introduced, largely through the work of R.K. Merton (1957), were intended to meet some of the major criticisms brought against the functionalist approach; in particular, that it postulated an unreal degree of functional unity or integration in every society, that it assumed the functional character of all the cultural items in a given society, and that it asserted the indispensability of every existing institution or cultural form. Merton took account of these criticisms by recognizing that the degree of integration of a given society was an empirical question to be decided by investigation, that cultural items and social institutions might be dysfunctional as well as functional, and that there might be functional alternatives to any existing institutions or cultural practices. Having thus formulated a more flexible version of functionalism, and outlined a paradigm which had the virtue of presenting in a systematic way a large number of important theoretical and empiral questions, Merton went on to qualify and restrict still further the claims of functionalist analysis by treating it as only one possible approach, or one mode of sociological interpretation. This seems to be the sense in which structural-functionalism continues to guide some kinds of sociological inquiry at the present time, namely, by providing a framework within which it is possible to relate partial activities to a larger whole, and thus, in one sense, acquire a fuller understanding of them.

But functionalism was also criticized on other grounds, from the point of view of the logic of scientific explanation; and the question was raised whether functional analysis could ever provide more than a descriptive classification. Durkheim had distinguished clearly between discovering the function of a particular social fact and discovering its cause (Durkheim, 1938), but many later functionalists did not pay too much attention to these problems of sociological explanation and they were inclined to refer more vaguely to 'sociological analysis' or 'sociological interpretation' (as did Merton himself). One writer, however, specifically contrasted functional and causal analysis (Dore, 1961), and the question of the nature of functionalist 'explanation' was taken up in other discussions of the logic of the social sciences (Hempel, 1959; Peters, 1958). The criticisms along these lines, however, have now merged into a much wider debate about 'explanation' and 'interpretation' in sociology which I shall consider later on.[2]

One consequence of the adoption of a functionalist paradigm is a certain indifference to historical processes and historical explanations. As Merton noted, functionalists tend to concentrate upon the static aspects of society and upon social equilibrium; and his own formulation of a broader and more flexible functionalist approach was intended to remove this limitation, among others, by introducing the concept of 'dysfunction' 'which implies the concept of strain, stress and tension on the structural level, [and] provides an analytical approach to the study of dynamics and change' (Demerath and Peterson, 1967). Even with such modifications, however, the functionalist paradigm did not really encourage, or give any prominence to, historical conceptions of social life, and in recent years it has been abandoned, to a considerable extent, in favour of models that are based more directly upon the idea of historical change.

The revival of interest in a historical sociology has clearly been influenced not only by theoretical controversies about the adequacy of a method that largely excluded history, but also by more general social and cultural factors: by the accelerating progress of science and technology, the sustained post–war economic growth in the industrial countries and its ramifying consequences, the problems of 'underdevelopment' and 'development' in the Third World, and the re-emergence on a large scale, especially in the decade of the 1960s, of radical and revolutionary social movements. This renewed attempt to construct a historical model of society has taken a number of different forms. On one side there has been a distinct revival of evolutionist views, often starting out from nineteenth century theories that had once been regarded as thoroughly discredited. Thus, Herbert Spencer's sociological ideas have attracted attention again (Peel, 1971), and there have been some more general studies of evolutionist conceptions (Burrow, 1966). Talcott Parsons, who was at one time a principal architect of the structural-functionalist model, has turned his attention to problems of social evolution and has reintroduced one of Spencer's basic ideas, that the evolution of societies consists above all in a process of increasing internal differentiation (Parsons, 1966).

One of the principal characteristics of the evolutionist paradigm is the attempt to comprehend the whole historical development of societies from their earliest to their latest forms. But within this general framework there are quite diverse views. If social development is conceived mainly in terms of increasing differentiation, then the process may well be regarded as being continuous, gradual and cumulative, without any sharp breaks. An alternative view, however, sees social development as discontinuous, and is more concerned with distinguishing particular stages of evolution, and types of society corresponding with these stages. Hence it provokes a new interest in the analysis of types of social structure, and although this has not yet spread very widely it has given rise to studies of 'industrial society' (Aron, 1967) and of 'post-industrial society' (Touraine, 1971; Bell, 1973), while among Marxist thinkers it has led to a reconsideration of 'precapitalist economic formations' (Hobsbawm, 1964) and to some interesting attempts to define and classify systems of production (Godelier, 1971). The discontinuous conception of social development also poses other important questions, concerning particularly the nature and causes of the transition from one kind of society to another, and in particular brings out the contrast between evolutionary and revolutionary types of social change.

But evolutionist conceptions are not the only form of historical sociology that has begun to flourish again. Gellner has clearly depicted an alternative by contrasting what he calls 'evolutionist' and 'episodic' views of the historical development of societies, the latter being based upon the idea that man's social history is marked by a single, overwhelmingly important transformation, so that this history can be most usefully divided into two periods—before and after the transformation (Gellner, 1964). It is evident that many historical-sociological interpretations conform quite closely with this episodic scheme. Weber's analysis of the rise of capitalism treats this transformation as a uniquely significant event in western social history, and even Marx's theory, though it rests upon a broad evolutionary scheme, attributes a special historical importance to the emergence and development of capitalism. However, the episodic view has appeared most clearly in the extensive recent discussions of 'development', 'industrialization', and 'modernization', most of which make use of the notion of two contrasting forms of society (e.g. traditional/modern, underdeveloped/industrial), and concentrate their attention upon the 'great transformation' which occurs between one and the other.

This 'episodic' version of historical sociology can well be

criticized for its excessive simplification of history. It may lead
to a serious neglect of the different levels of development in
those societies that are classed together as 'pre-industrial' or
'traditional', and on the other side it does not allow for future
transformations. Thus, for example, it is already difficult to fit
into this scheme the notion of another profound change
occurring in the present age, which has been represented by
some recent writers as a movement toward a 'post–industrial'
or 'technological' society. Another type of criticism concerns
the criteria for selection of the great transformation itself. The
concepts of industrialization and modernization define a different kind of transition, and different forms of society at the
beginning and end of the process, from those that are represented in a conception of historical development that deals
with the transition from feudalism to capitalism, and then
perhaps to socialism. It becomes necessary, therefore, to look
more closely at the way in which the basic or crucial features of
a type of society are characterized in these different conceptions, in order to judge the usefulness of the rival schemes.
This does not mean, however, that there cannot also be some
fruitful combination of elements from different schemes of
historical interpretation. A study such as that by Barrington
Moore begins with the notion of modernization, but then goes
on to consider three main alternative 'routes to the modern
world', through bourgeois revolutions, revolutions from
above, and peasant revolutions, which are explained in terms
of the class relations within each society, in an analysis which
clearly derives from Marxist theory (Moore, 1967).

Barrington Moore's study illustrates well the reemergence
of Marxism as an important sociological theory. Undoubtedly, the general reawakening of interest in historical
interpretations of society, and in the particular problem of
social development in the second half of the twentieth century, has contributed greatly to this intellectual revival of
Marxism, though many other factors, including changes in the
world political situation, have also played a part. At the same
time, it has to be recognized that recent Marxist thought has
developed in very diverse ways. A good deal of it has involved
the rediscovery of earlier Marxist thinkers, among them
Lukács, Gramsci and Korsch, whose work had been some-

what neglected or was known only within a relatively narrow circle, or it has been concerned with the analysis and interpretation of the lesser known writings of Marx himself, especially the *Economic and Philosophical Manuscripts* and the *Grundrisse*. Nevertheless, these scholarly preoccupations have resulted in a very definite change in theoretical outlook; namely, to a view of Marxism which emphasizes much more strongly the role of cultural and intellectual factors—of 'consciousness'—in the reproduction and transformation of social life, and in that sense can be regarded as formulating a 'voluntaristic' theory of action rather than a theory of 'economic determinism'.

Besides this general, but far from universally accepted, modification of the Marxist paradigm, there have emerged two more definite versions of Marxist theory that may be regarded as forming distinctive schools of thought. One of these, associated with the work of Althusser, I shall refer to later in discussing modern structuralism. The other is that of the Frankfurt School, and it has become widely known under the name of 'critical theory'. This term was used much earlier by the Frankfurt Marxists, and notably by Max Horkheimer in a series of articles published in the 1930s and recently reprinted (Horkheimer, 1968), to distinguish their form of Marxist thought from the economic determinism and evolutionism of official Marxism, to emphasize the significance of cultural factors (and of theoretical criticism itself) in the development of society, and to mark their affinity with a philosophical, rather than a social–scientific (and more especially positivist) formulation of Marxism. The meaning of critical theory was, in fact, close to that of 'critical philosophy' in the sense of Hegel and the Young Hegelians (among them Marx himself), and it has been expounded in these terms by another member of the Frankfurt School, Herbert Marcuse (1941, 1964).

But whereas the Frankfurt thinkers in the 1930s still remained quite close to the main preoccupations of classical Marxism—the economic contradictions of capitalism, the conflict between classes, the crucial social role of the working class—those who formed the post–war generation of the School (and notably Habermas and Wellmer) have concerned themselves with such different questions, and have criticized so extensively Marx's theoretical system, that critical theory in the form in which it is now influential has to be regarded as an independent body of social thought. The 'critical theorists' concentrate their attention upon scientific–technological society rather than capitalism (Habermas, 1970), reject the idea of a process of social and political liberation based mainly upon the transformation of the economic system, and the pre–eminent role of the working class in that process (Wellmer, 1971), and are especially concerned to criticize the positivism of the social sciences, which they see as having a necessary connection with a technological system of domination. In its assault upon positivism, critical theory has some affinities with the modern philosophy of language and meaning, and with phenomenology; at the same time it revives methodological issues that were articulated very comprehensively in the nineteenth century by Dilthey and continued to be discussed in diverse controversies, about the method of *Verstehen* and the interpretation of cultural phenomena. The likely outcome of these renewed methodological debates is far from clear, but it is evident that critical theory occupies an important place in what is now a very widespread movement to give an entirely different meaning to the activity of the social sciences.

Aside from these methodological questions, is it possible to define more precisely the character of critical theory? Its principal content is the analysis of the modern industrial, technological societies, and in this sense its concerns are close to those of other present–day sociological theories that seek to interpret the structure and development of industrial or post-industrial societies. In another way, too, there are similarities, for critical theory also assigns to knowledge and the production of knowledge a pre–eminent influence in the formation and transformation of modern societies, and tends to regard the principal conflicts within them as cultural and intellectual struggles rather than as clashes of economic interest or class conflicts. But critical theory also inherits from Marxism, and especially from Marx's earlier ideas, a concern with a long term process of human liberation, and in this sense it aims to construct a new philosophy of history as a general framework for empirical investigations.

This feature of critical theory associates it closely with the various attempts in recent years to develop a 'radical sociology'. But the latter does not yet exist in a coherent, integrated form as a new paradigm directing sociological thought; it is rather a collection of loosely related ideas drawn from Marxism (and more broadly from a variety of socialist and anarchist doctrines), from the work of the later Frankfurt School, from the radical thought of C. Wright Mills, and to some extent from the social movements of the 1960s. One formulation of the desire for such a sociology (Gouldner, 1970) mainly potrays the present intellectual uncertainties, but also reveals two general features in the move toward a new paradigm: (1) the concern that sociology, and other social sciences, should resume their task of examining *critically* the institutions and processes in present-day societies (whatever their regimes), instead of serving largely to facilitate their perpetuation; and (2) a commitment to a methodological view which asserts the significance, and relative freedom, of human action, as against any conception of social determinism that would imply either the immutability of a given social order, or some inescapable future state of society. These themes have also been examined, with reference to particular social theorists and schools, in two other recent books (Clecak, 1973; Gombin, 1971).

Although, as I have argued, one important movement in recent sociological thought has been the revival, in one form or another, of historical conceptions of society, this is by no means the only trend, and two other attempts to give a new orientation to sociology are profoundly unhistorical, if not antihistorical, in their general outlook. The first of these is structuralism. In a broad sense structuralism may be regarded as a long–established approach in the social sciences (Piaget, 1970), but the new structuralism, which has been much more influential in social anthropology than in sociology up to the present time, has some particular characteristics that justify treating it as a distinctive paradigm. In the first place it has a close association with linguistics. The structural anthropology of Lévi–Strauss had its principal source in structural linguistics (Lévi–Strauss, 1967), and a great deal of the work of structuralists, chiefly in social anthropology, consists in the analysis of cultural phenomena on the model of an analysis of language (Culler, 1973). This is the case particularly with Lévi-Strauss's own studies of myth, with a study such as that by Mary Douglas on pollution (Douglas, 1966), and with Michel Foucault's work on the history of science in which he attempts to establish the 'fundamental codes of a culture' (Foucault, 1970). In all these cases the aim is to disclose a structure of meaning, similar to the structure of a language. It is evident that these preoccupations also relate structuralism in certain ways to modern linguistic philosophy, so that it can be said that there is a convergence of work in a number of different fields in the development of the structuralist paradigm.

Another important feature of structuralism, again inspired by structural linguistics, is the preoccupation with what is called 'deep structure'. A distinction is made between the immediately observable surface aspects of social and cultural phenomena, and a more profound inner structure which has to be disclosed (or constructed) by analysis—a distinction between 'code' and 'message'—and it is often suggested, though I think erroneously, that while the new structuralists investigate this deep structure the conceptions of structure held by earlier social scientists remained at the surface level. In Lévi-Strauss's work this concern with deep structure seems to lead from the social or cultural to the psychological sphere, in the aim to relate cultural phenomena to the fundamental structure of the human mind, and the possibility is held out of a further reduction to physiological or physical structures.

It is in this sense, especially, that structuralism is unhistorical; what it attempts to establish is the universal character of cultural codes, over the whole range of human societies and historical periods. And in Lévi-Strauss's writing it takes on occasionally an anti–historical significance, as in the discussion of analytical and dialectical reason in the final chapter of *The Savage Mind* (Lévi-Strauss, 1966). As I have noted, structuralism has not yet established itself as a major influence in sociological theory, and seems to be confined to a fairly small circle that has developed around the work of H.C.

White, which began with an attempt to construct mathematical models of kinship structures, starting out from Lévi-Strauss's analysis of kinship (White, 1963). Nevertheless, structuralism has affinities with other work in sociology, notably with mathematical model-building, and with what is called 'network' analysis (Mitchell, 1969; Barnes, 1971), so that there is a diffuse kind of influence. More broadly, structuralism has affected Marxist thought, through the work of Althusser and his followers, and there has grown up a fairly clear opposition between a 'historical' and a 'structuralist' version of the Marxist theory of society. The structuralists assert that Marx's major scientific work consisted in an analysis of the 'deep structure' of modern capitalist society (notably in *Capital*), and that the focus of Marx's thought was this kind of structural analysis rather than the depiction and interpretation of a process of historical development.

The principal value of these ideas seems to be that they have concentrated attention on defining 'systems of production', and, more broadly, 'types of society', through structural analysis, and thus contribute to the efforts to resolve one of the most important theoretical problems in sociology. But this structuralist paradigm within Marxist thought has a certain ambiguity, and various weaknesses. It is not the intention of these thinkers, presumably, to establish, in the manner of Lévi-Strauss, fundamental and timeless structures of society. As Marxists, they are concerned with historical social structures, of which modern capitalism is one instance; and one direction for renewed investigation, that has already begun to be followed, would be the structural study of 'pre-capitalist economic formations'. This still leaves open a major question; that of the transformation of one structure into another, and in this sphere the contribution of the Marxist structuralists has not been impressive. The problem involves some conception of a historical process, and may well require the reintroduction of notions taken from a historical version of the Marxist theory, in which the development of social movements, changes in consciousness, and purposive human action are seen as crucial elements.

The second major development in sociological theory that has a markedly unhistorical character can be referred to

broadly as phenomenological sociology. Its principal source
has been the work of Alfred Schutz, especially since this
became available in English translations from the early 1960s
(Schutz, 1962, 1964, 1966, 1967); and Schutz's own conceptions resulted from an application of some of Husserl's ideas
to the social world, together with the adoption of the method
of *Verstehen*, or 'understanding social action', outlined by
Max Weber. But the phenomenological sociologists,
although they borrow very heavily from Schutz, have also
been influenced by other thinkers, notably Merleau–Ponty
(1962), and some of their views, especially their opposition to
positivism, have affinities with the more general themes of
both existentialism and linguistic philosophy. The chief point
of resemblance is to be found in their concentration upon the
understanding of 'meaning' as the only valid approach in the
study of social life. This coincides precisely, for example, with
the conception of social science formulated by a philosophical
follower of Wittgenstein (Winch, 1963). It may appear also
that phenomenological sociology has some affinity with structuralism in its primary concern with meanings, but in this case
there is a clear dividing line between the structuralist interest
in the formal structure of relations between meanings which
are largely taken for granted, and the phenomenological
interest in the interpretation of meanings themselves.

The general influence of philosophical phenomenology
upon the social sciences may be quite varied, as we can see by
contrasting Schutz's use of its ideas with the social theory
elaborated by Sartre in an amalgam of existentialism and
Marxism, in which the notion of historical development has a
crucial place (Sartre, 1963). What seems to be common to
most phenomenological social theory is a particular conception of the proper method of studying social and cultural
phenomena; and a good deal of the work of the phenomenological school consists in methodological clarification and
argument, rather than in working out a general theory.

There is, however, one recent school of mainly sociological
thought, derived very largely from phenomenology, which is
quite clearly attempting to construct a new paradigm—
namely, ethnomethodology. The main characteristic of this
school is its concentration upon the study of 'everyday life' or

'commonsense experience', or in the case of Garfinkel (who may be regarded as the founder of the school), more especially upon 'everyday rationality' (Garfinkel, 1967). At first sight this may not appear a very remarkable new departure. Most sociologists would agree that the depiction and interpretation of men's activities in the ordinary affairs of life constitutes an important sphere of research. The distinctiveness of ethnomethodology lies rather in the particular way that it conceives such studies; first, that what is being observed and recorded is conscious 'rule-following' activity, not any kind of casual process or outcome of structural arrangements, and second, that in understanding the rationality of everyday life, we already comprehend a theory (or theories) of society, without any need to superimpose upon it a 'sociological' theory that we construct ourselves.

The first of these views, in so far as it governs the general orientation of ethnomethodologoical research, presents a sharp contrast with a structuralist approach, for it could be said that ethnomethodology concentrates precisely upon the surface phenomena of social life that structuralism considers to be relatively unimportant and even misleading for scientific inquiry. The second view has a strong resemblance to the doctrine of linguistic philosophy in its heyday, for just as these philosophers took as their subject matter 'ordinary language' and did not conceive the business of philosophical discourse as being to reform or go beyond such language, so the ethnomethodologists take everyday life or commonsense experience (and, by implication, ordinary language) as their subject of investigation, and do not propose to correct or supplant the theories of society that already guide everyday life with a superior sociological theory. In this sense we might say that the 'Narodniks of north Oxford', as Gellner (1959) once described the linguistic philosophers, have found a new lease of life as the 'Narodniks of Southern California'.

The paradigms that I have discussed represent some of the principal trends in sociological theory at the present time, but they are far from comprehending all the different tendencies that now exist. There are very diverse conceptions of the main subject–matter and problems of sociological theory even within the various schools of thought that I have mentioned, as well as disagreements about the research strategies implied by these conceptions, and about the relation of sociological theory to policy making and to political commitment or action. Nevertheless, I think it is possible, even in the face of this diversity, to distinguish some broad lines of agreement and of contestation.

First, it may be noted that all the paradigms considered here conceive sociological theory in a very broad way, as a general social theory which draws, as the case may be, upon historical studies, philosophical ideas, and the work of economists and social anthropologists, as well as paying attention to those thinkers who have been primarily concerned with elaborating political doctrines (and becoming involved in political struggles), rather than confining themselves to a sphere of 'pure' theoretical sociology. The notion of sociological theory as a highly specific and specialized branch of thought seems now to be distinctly out of fashion, and on the other hand, the wider social theory that is sought has come to be regarded, by many sociologists, as closely bound up with practical social and political conflicts. In some respects, therefore, it could be said that sociological thought is realizing an earlier ambition to provide a comprehensive framework within which all the general 'problems of the age' are formulated and discussed; though, of course, it does this very imperfectly insofar as it offers so many more or less incompatible and competing schemes of interpretation.

A second general feature of recent paradigms is that they are all elaborated in the context of a broader concern with the logic of the social sciences. The theoretical controversies in sociology over the past decade or so have revived, while introducing some new elements, the *Methodenstreit* of the end of the nineteenth and the early twentieth centuries. As in those earlier methodological disputes, two of the principal features are an attack on positivism, and controversy about the place of value judgements in social science, especially those value judgements that are an important ingredient in political doctrines. The main tendency of recent sociological thought has certainly been anti–positivist, and there has been a renewal of interest in what can be called broadly a 'hermeneutic' method which goes back at least to Dilthey.[3]

The main difficulty with this hermeneutic approach is that it does not seem able to establish any definite criteria for deciding among the various subjective interpretations of social events, processes, or forms of life. If this approach can be characterized, in the words of Isaiah Berlin (1969), as producing the kind of knowledge that is involved 'when a work of the imagination or of social diagnosis, or a work of criticism or scholarship or history is described not as correct or incorrect, skilful or inept, a success or a failure, but as profound or shallow, realistic or unrealistic, perceptive or stupid, alive or dead', then it seems to depend much more upon the creative powers, or the quality of mind, of the individual interpreter of social life than upon any accumulated body of sociological theory or rules concerning the testing of propositions by reference to some kind of empirical reality. Its achievements appear in the form of works of art rather than contributions to a systematic social science, and there may emerge (perhaps has emerged) a variety of interpretations among which it is impossible to choose according to any general criteria of validity or truth.

Very often, indeed, the preference for an interpretation seems to be influenced predominantly by a commitment to values of a general cultural, or more narrowly political, kind; and it is not surprising, therefore, that the debate about social science and value judgements has also been resumed very vigorously in recent theoretical writings. Many of the competing paradigms in sociological theory (and this is particularly true of critical theory and of the various forms of radical sociology) include as an important element some formulation of the relation between theoretical models and research on one side, and political action and policy making on the other. It can hardly be said that this debate has yet advanced much beyond the earlier discussions; for the most part, it still revolves uneasily around the themes of Max Weber's essay on 'objectivity' and of Marxist conceptions of 'ideology', without finding any significant new expression in a form as substantial as Weber's essay. At least, however, the issue has been clearly defined again, and it seems likely that no paradigm will prove generally acceptable or persuasive that does not include among its basic statements or suppositions some reference to

the specific nature of the involvement of sociological theory—
and of all social theory—with the historical process of social
life from which the thinker cannot, any more than other men,
extricate himself.

NOTES

1. The change is itself an important socio–cultural phenomenon that poses
questions about the adequacy of some sociological theories. Thus, for
example, we have learned in recent years to think in terms of 'scientific
revolutions', rather than (or at least alongside) more gradual processes of
the advancement of knowledge, and this notion obviously has a wider
bearing.
2. There is a useful collection of essays expounding and criticizing functionalism from various aspects in Demerath and Peterson, 1967.
3. For some general discussion of these issues see Louch, 1966; Wellmer,
1971; Giddens, 1974; Outhwaite, 1974.

BIBLIOGRAPHY

Aron, R., *18 Lectures on Industrial Society*. (London: Weidenfeld & Nicol-
son) 1967.
Barnes, J.A., *Three Styles in the Study of Kinship*. (London: Tavistock)
1971.
Bell, D., *The Coming of Post-Industrial Society*. (New York: Basic) 1973.
Berlin, I., 'A note on Vico's concept of knowledge'. *New York Review of
Books* 12(8) 1969.
Burrow, J.W., *Evolution and Society: A Study in Victorian Social Theory*.
(Cambridge: Cambridge Univ. Press) 1966.
Clecak, P., *Radical Paradoxes*. (New York: Harper & Row) 1973.
Culler, J., 'The linguistic basis of structuralism', in *Structuralism: An Intro-
duction*, D, Robey, (ed.), 20–36 (Oxford: Clarendon) 1973.
Demerath, N.J., Peterson, R.A., *System, Change and Conflict: A Reader
on Contemporary Sociological Theory and the Debate over Functionalism*.
(New York: Free Press) 1967.
Dore, R.P., 'Function and cause'. *Am. Sociol. Rev.* 26(6): 843–53 1961.
Douglas, M., *Purity and Danger*. (London: Routledge & Kegan Paul) 1966.
Durkheim, E., *The Rules of Sociological Method*. (Glencoe: Free Press)
1938.
Foucault, M. *The Order of Things*. (London: Tavistock) 1970.
Garfinkel, H. *Studies in Ethnomethodology*. (Englewood Cliffs, NJ: Pren-
tice-Hall) 1967.
Gellner, E., *Words and Things*. (London: Victor Gollancz) 1959.
Gellner, E., *Thought and Change*. (London: Weidenfeld & Nicolson) 1964.
Giddens, A., (ed.), *Positivism and Sociology*. (London: Heinemann) 1974.

Godelier, M., *Rationality and Irrationality in Economics*. (London: New Left) 1972.

Gombin, R., *Les Origines du gauchisme*. (Paris: Editions du Seuil) 1971.

Gouldner, A.W., *The Coming Crisis of Western Sociology*. (New York: Basic) 1970.

Habermas, J., *Toward a Rational Society*. (Boston: Becon) 1970.

Hempel, C.J., 'The logic of functional analysis', in *Symposium on Sociological Theory*, L. Gross, (ed.) 271–303. (Evanston, Ill: Row, Peterson) 1959.

Hobsbawm, E.J., Introduction to Karl Marx, *Pre–Capitalist Economic Formations*, 9–65. (London: Lawrence & Wishart) 1964.

Horkheimer, M., *Kritische Theorie*. (Frankfurt: S, Fischer) 2 vols. 1968.

Hughes, H.S., *Consciousness and Society*. (New York: Oxford Univ. Press) 1958.

Lauterbach, A., Review in *Der Kampf* 26(12) 1933.

Lévi-Strauss, C., 1966. *The Savage Mind*. (Chicago: Univ. Press) 1966.

Lévi-Strauss, C., *Structural Anthropology*. (Garden City, NY: Doubleday) 1967.

Lipset, S.M., Smelser, N.J., *Sociology: The Progress of a Decade*. (Engle wood Cliffs, NJ: Prentice-Hall) 1961.

Louch, A.R., *Explanation and Human Action*. (Oxford: Basil Blackwell) 1966.

Marcuse, H., *Reason and Revolution: Hegal and the Rise of Social Theory*. (New York: Oxford Univ. Press) 1941.

Marcuse, H., *One-Dimensional Man*. (Boston: Beacon) 1964.

Masterman, M., 'The nature of a paradigm', in *Criticism and the Growth of Knowledge*, I. Lakatos, A. Musgrave, (eds.), 58–89. (Cambridge: Cambridge Univ. Press) 1970.

Merleau-Ponty, M., *Phenomenology of Perception*. (New York: Humanities Press) 1962.

Merton, R.K., *Social Theory and Social Structure*. (Glencoe: Free Press) 2nd rev. edn. 1957.

Mitchell, J.C., *Social Networks in Urban Situations*. (Manchester: Manchester Univ. Press) 1969.

Moore, B., *Social Origins of Dictatorship and Democracy*. (Boston: Beacon) 1967.

Outhwaite, R.W., *Understanding Social Life: The Method Called Verstehen*. (London: Allen & Unwin) 1974.

Parsons, T., *Societies: Evolutionary and Comparative Perspectives*.(Englewood Cliffs, NJ: Prentice-Hall) 1966.

Peel, J.D.Y., *Herbert Spencer: The Evolution of a Sociologist*. (London: Heinemann) 1971.

Peters, R.S., *The Concept of Motivation*. (London: Routledge & Kegan Paul) 1958.

Piaget, J., *Structuralism*. (New York: Basic) 1970.

Sartre, J.P., *Search for a Method*. (New York: Knopf) 1963.

Schutz, A., *Collected Papers*. (The Hague: Martinus Nijhoff) 3 vols. 1962, 1964, 1966.

Schutz, A., *The Phenomenology of the Social World.* (Evanston, Ill: North-western Univ. Press) 1967.

Touraine, A., *The Post–Industrial Society.* (New York: Random House) 1971.

Wellmer, A., *Critical Theory of Society.* (New York: Herder & Herder) 1971.

White, H,C., *An Anatomy of Kinship: Mathematical Models for Structures of Cumulated Roles.* (Englewood Cliffs, NJ: Prentice–Hall) 1963.

Winch, P., *The Idea of a Social Science.* (London: Routledge & Kegan Paul) 1963.

3 Marxism and Sociology

THE FORMATION OF MARX'S THOUGHT

For more than a century there has been a close, uneasy, contentious relationship between Marxism and sociology. The closeness is due to the fact that Marx's theory was intended, like sociology, to be a general science of society, and that it was similarly directed, in particular, towards gaining an understanding of the changes in society resulting from the development of industrial capitalism and from the political revolutions of the eighteenth century. Its scope and ambitions were quite evidently the same as those expressed in the sociological systems of Comte and Spencer, and to some extent it drew upon the same intellectual sources, among them the histories of civilization, the theories of progress Saint–Simon's analysis of industrial society, and the new political economy. On the other side, the unease and contention arise, as will be discussed more fully later, from the ways in which sociology and Marxism developed historically in largely separate spheres, from the direct conflict of theoretical views, and from the underlying, persistent uncertainty and controversy about whether Marxism is to be conceived as *one* sociological theory among others or as a unique body of thought, a complete intellectual world of its own, which constitutes a radical alternative to any kind of sociology as a means of understanding, and orienting action in, human society.

In the present essay I shall not concern myself directly with this last question, which I have discussed elsewhere,[1] but shall assume that Marxist theory deals with a specific and circumscribed set of problems which also constitutes the subject–matter of various sociological theories, regardless of the diversity of their conceptual schemes and methodological principles. From this point of view the differences between Marxism and sociology may appear no greater than those which exist between rival theories within what is commonly accepted as the field of sociological analysis. Moreover, as will be shown in due course, there are many connections and agreements, as well as mutual influences, between some versions of Marxist theory and some theoretical positions in sociology. In what follows, therefore, my intention is to set out the principal elements of Marx's own theory,[2] regarded as one of the principal types of sociological analysis, and then to follow its later development, the reinterpretations or creative innovations that have occurred, and the ways in which Marxist thinkers have responded both to critical attacks and to the new problems posed by changing historical circumstances.

Marx's theory is, in the first place, a remarkable synthesis of ideas derived from the philosophy, the historical studies, and the social sciences of his time, the formation of which can best be followed in the *Economic and Philosophical Manuscripts* of 1844.[3] Here Marx begins to define the most fundamental concept in his theory, that of 'human labour', which he will later develop in an array of related concepts. 'The outstanding achievement of Hegel's *Phenomenology*', Marx says, 'is, first, that Hegel grasps the self–creation of man as a process . . . that he therefore grasps the nature of *labour*.'[4] In these manuscripts we can see how Marx transforms Hegel's conception of 'spiritual labour' by introducing the quite different notion of labour to be found in the works of the political economists—labour in the process of material production, labour as the source of wealth. It is not that Marx here, or in his later writings, restricts the idea of labour simply to material production as has sometimes been suggested, for he always retains the broader notion of labour as human activity, in which material and intellectual production go on together. Man does not only produce the means for his physical existence, he creates at the same time, in a single process, a whole form of society. It is true, none the less, that the distinctiveness of Marx's concept consists in his emphasizing the importance of labour in the economic sense (the developing interchange between man and nature) as the foundation of all social life. Hence it may be argued, as it was by Karl Korsch, that Marxism should be regarded as political economy rather than sociology;[5] and it is certainly the case that Marx's theory is distinguished from many other sociological theories by the fact that it situates human society firmly in a natural world and analyzes all social phenomena in the context of the (historically changing) relation between society and nature.

There is a second transformation of Hegel's thought that Marx undertakes in the *Economic and Philosophical Manuscripts*; namely, the conversion of the idea of alienation into an economic and social concept by an analysis of the 'alienation of labour' as it can be grasped in the writings of the political economists. Like labour itself, the alienation of labour is for Marx a process which takes place, not exclusively in the intellectual or spiritual realm, but in the world of man's physical existence and material production. 'Alienated labour' is work which is imposed upon some men by others, 'forced labour' as opposed to free creative activity; and it is furthermore a kind of labour in which what is produced by the worker is appropriated by others, the 'masters of the system of production'.

From these two concepts, most fully elaborated in the manuscripts of 1844, but also expressed in other writings of Marx during that period, we can derive the main elements of his whole theory of society. To begin with, labour, in its principal form as the interchange between man and nature, is conceived as a historically developing process in which man changes himself and his society in the course of changing nature. This conception then leads naturally to the idea of stages in the development of labour and production, characterized by the prevalence, in different historical periods, of specific modes of production and corresponding forms of society. Moreover, this historical process has a progressive character; humanity moves from a condition of almost complete dependence upon given natural forces and resources through successive phases of increasing control over nature, so that it is possible for Marx to refer, in later discussions of

the social history of mankind (in the *Grundrisse*)⁶ to 'progressive epochs in the economic formation of society' and to
'higher forms' of society. This development of social labour,
however, does not occur in the form of a co–operative, communal effort to improve the productive forces and so to dominate nature more effectively. The conception of 'alienated
labour' already introduces the idea of the division of society
into two major groups, the relation between which determines the general character of economic and political life.
Later (in *Capital*, vol. III)⁷, Marx expresses this view in the
following way:

'It is always the direct relation between the masters of the conditions of
production and the direct producers which reveals the innermost secret, the
hidden foundation of the entire social edifice, and therefore also of the
political form of the relation between sovereignty and dependence, in short,
of the particular form of the state. The form of this relation between masters
and producers always necessarily corresponds to a definite stage in the
development of the methods of work and consequently of the social productivity of labour.'

In the *Economic and Philosophical Manuscripts*, therefore,
we find—whatever else may be derived from them in the way
of a 'humanist' social philosophy—the broad outlines of
Marx's sociological theory, in which the basic concepts of
labour, private property, mode of production, forms of
society, stages of development, social classes and class conflict
are either directly expressed, or at least intimated, in an
exposition, however fragmentary, which reveals the actual
development of Marx's thought, through an encounter
between Hegelian philosophy and political economy, in the
process of converting and reconstructing philosophical ideas
into the concepts of a theory of society which was described by
Marx himself in the preface as 'the fruit of an entirely
empirical analysis'. These manuscripts, of course, have their
place in a larger body of work produced during the seminal
years of 1843—5, and Marx's concept of social class, for
example, was elaborated in writings which owe much to the
studies of the modern proletariat by the French socialist
thinkers. By 1845 Marx had reached a point in the development of his ideas at which he could formulate in precise terms
the main principles of his theory:

This conception of history, therefore, rests on the exposition of the real process of production, starting out from the simple material production of life, and on the comprehension of the form of intercourse connected with and created by this mode of production, i.e. of civil society in its various stages as the basis of all history, and also in its action as the state . . . It does not explain practice from the idea but explains the formation of ideas from material practice, and accordingly comes to the conclusion that all the forms and products of consciousness can be dissolved, not by intellectual criticism . . . but only by the practical overthrow of the actual social relations which gave rise to this idealist humbug; that not criticism but revolution is the driving force of history . . . It shows . . . that at each stage of history there is found a material result, a sum of productive forces, a historically created relation of individuals to nature and to one another, which is handed down to each generation from its predecessors, a mass of productive forces, capital, and circumstances, which is indeed modified by the new generation but which also prescribes for it its conditions of life and gives it a definite development, a special character. It shows that circumstances make men just as much as men make circumstances. (*The German Ideology*, 1845—46)[8]

The formation of this theoretical scheme is explicitly assigned by Marx to the period 1843—5, and is described as the 'guiding thread' in his subsequent studies in a much later text, where there occurs a famous passage expressing in the same terms his general conception:

In the social production which men carry on they enter into definite relations that are indispensable and independent of their will; these relations of production correspond to a definite stage of developmnet of their material powers of production. The totality of these relations of production constitutes the economic structure of society—the real foundation, on which legal and political superstructures arise and to which definite forms of social consciousness correspond. The mode of production of material life determines the general character of the social, political and spiritual processes of life . . . At a certain stage of their development, the material forces of production in society come into conflict with the existing relations of production, or—what is but a legal expression for the same thing—with the property relations within which they had been at work before . . . Then occurs a period of social revolution. (Preface to *A Contribution to the Critique of Political Economy*, 1859)[9]

After the mid–1840s it is clear that the direction of Marx's intellectual interests changed considerably, but this reorientation can be understood in different ways. Louis Althusser has argued that in about 1845 there occurred an 'epistemological break', which separates the young Marx, the propounder of a 'humanist' and 'historicist' ideology still profoundly marked by the ideas of Hegel and Feuerbach, from the mature Marx, the creator of an original and rigorous science of society.[10] But this view (even if we ignore the fact that, in spite of the frequent references to 'scientificity' in Althusser's work, the distinction between science and ideology is never clearly and convincingly established) is difficult to sustain when the content and arguments of Marx's later writings, especially the *Grundrisse*, are compared closely with the earlier texts. It is more plausible, I think, to state that Marx, after having sketched the general outline of his theory, then turned to a more detailed and thorough analysis of the capitalist mode of production which was intended to be only the starting–point for a study of capitalist society as a whole in the context of an overall process of social development.

In fact, Marx sets out, in the introduction to the *Grundrisse*, a vast programme of studies which confirms this view. Here he restates firmly his conception of the historical development of production, while noting that 'all epochs of production have certain common characteristics'; analyzes the relation between production, distribution, exchange and consumption; examines the method of political economy, and sets out the elements of his own method. Finally he presents, in the form of notes, some of the major issues that would have to be confronted in any attempt to demonstrate in a detailed manner the connection between modes of production, forms of society and the state, and cultural phenomena, or to interpret the historical development of societies in relation to the concept of progress. Moreover, the *Grundrisse* contains a long section on pre-capitalist economic formations which is Marx's most extensive and systematic attempt to discuss the problems of historical development.[11]

It is evident that Marx was unable to complete his ambitious project and that his major works from the late 1850s until his death were largely devoted to an economic analysis, which itself remained incomplete, of capitalism as a specific mode of production. Nevertheless, he never entirely abandoned his studies of the diverse historical forms of society, and, especially in his last years (between 1880—2), he wrote extensive commentaries on the writings of scholars who were investigating in diverse ways the social and cultural history of mankind, among them L.H. Morgan, J.B. Phear, H.S. Maine and John Lubbock.[12] Hence Marx's studies in his mature years have two aspects: one, the refinement of his theoretical analysis of modes of production through an intensive study of modern capitalist production and a critical examination of the theories of his predecessors and contemporaries in political economy; the other, a continuing effort to locate the capitalist mode of production and capitalist society in a historical scheme of social development, which he outlined in his early work but also tried to elaborate and improve in sections of the *Grundrisse* and in his notes on Morgan and others.

The advances which Marx made in his economic analysis have been ably discussed by Martin Nicolaus in an essay devoted to the *Grundrisse*, 'The unknown Marx'.[13] The *Grundrisse* shows the development of Marx's thought on three principal questions. First, he elaborates the analysis of money and exchange which he began in the *Economic and Philosophical Manuscripts* and formulates a conception of money as a 'social bond' which expresses the historically–produced social relationships of capitalist society; but he now makes this account of market relationships subordinate to an analysis of capitalist production and the process of capital accumulation, or the self–expansion of capital. Second, in analyzing production he makes use of the new concept of 'labour power' (in place of the term 'labour' in his earlier writings) to describe the commodity which the worker sells in return for his wages, and he brings to light the unique quality of this commodity, namely, that it is capable of creating values where they did not exist, or of creating greater values than are needed to sustain it—which is to say that it creates surplus value, the source of capitalist profit. And finally, Marx discusses more fully in the *Grundrisse* than in his other writings the conditions under which capitalism will break down. Here, it seems to me, two kinds of factors are invoked, one negative, the other positive. In the first place, Marx argues that 'capitalism contains a specific barrier to production—which contradicts its general tendency to break all barriers of production—[namely] *over–production*, the fundamental contradiction of developed capitalism.' Marx goes on to characterize this over–production in various terms, but his view can largely be summed up in the statement that it involves the 'restriction of the production of use–value by exchange–value'; that is to say, the limitation of production occurs because the products (commodities) cannot be exchanged, and hence the surplus value which they contain cannot be realized. Or as Marx expresses it in *Capital*, vol. III: 'The ultimate cause of all real crises is always the poverty and restricted consumption of the masses, in contrast with the tendency of capitalist production to develop the productive forces in such a way that only the absolute power of consumption of society would be their limit.' This analysis provides the main content of Marx's general proposition that the transition to a new form of society begins when a contradiction or conflict develops in the existing society between the forces of production and the relations of production (which in the case of capitalism are constituted by money and exchange; in short, by the market). But the second, positive factor in the breakdown of capitalism is the creation, by the development of capitalism itself, of economic conditions in which a collective, or communal, direction of the process of social labour is already partly attained. In some remarkable passages at the end of the *Grundrisse* Marx expresses this idea:

To the extent that large–scale industry develops, the creation of real wealth comes to depend less upon labour time and the quantity of labour expended than upon the power of the instruments which are set in motion during labour time, whose powerful effectiveness is likewise unrelated to the labour time directly involved in their production, but depends rather upon the general state of science and the progress of technology, or the application of this science to production . . . With this transformation, what appears as the mainstay of production and wealth is neither the labour which man directly expends, nor the time he spends at work, but his appropriation of his own general productive powers, his understanding and mastery of nature; in short, the development of the social individual . . . The development of fixed capital indicates the extent to which general social knowledge has become a *direct productive force*, and thus the extent to which the conditions of the social life process have themselves been brought under the control of the general intellect and reconstructed in accordance with it.

The breakdown of capitalism and the transition to a new form of society are seen by Marx, in the *Grundrisse*, as a complex and protracted process in which economic crises and political struggles, but also the growth within capitalism of an alternative economic system and the awakening of 'all the powers of science and nature, of social organization and intercourse', all play a part.

How, then, does Marx's analysis of capitalism, and especially of the capitalist mode of production, which constitutes by far the greater part of his life's work, fit into the general theory of society which he outlined in his youth? As I have already indicated, there was no period in which Marx was not concerned in some way with the question of the historical development of society, conceived as a succession of distinct modes of production and social formations, and he returned to the study of such historical issues in his general discussion of precapitalist economic formations, particularly in the *Grundrisse*, in his writings on the 'Asiatic mode of production', and in his observations on early tribal and peasant societies based upon his reading of the work of Morgan, Maine and other scholars dealing with the early history of institutions. The conclusions of these studies are by no means as clear as those resulting from his infinitely more thorough analysis of capitalism, and they have been interpreted in a variety of ways by later writers. Thus, for example, Eric Hobsbawm, in his introduction to *Pre-Capitalist Economic Formations*, suggests that 'the general theory of historical materialism requires only that there should be a succession of modes of production, though not necessarily any particular modes, and perhaps not in any particular predetermined order'; and in considering this particular text he argues that Marx is not dealing with chronological succession or with the evolution of one system out of its predecessor, but rather with analytical stages in the general development of societies after the break–up of primitive communal society.[14]

These general difficulties concerning the precise scheme of social development that Marx was attempting to formulate are enhanced by the fact that he did quite evidently want to emphasize the uniqueness of the capitalist mode of production and capitalist society in relation to all previous modes of production and social formations. This contrast is expressed in various ways. For example, Marx's analysis suggests that whereas in a capitalist society the appropriation of surplus value takes place by more or less purely economic means (and therefore has to be revealed by penetrating the secret of commodity production), in all earlier societies it required some kind of non–economic coercion.[15] Again, if in capitalist society the fundamental contradiction is between the forces of production and the social relations of production constituted by exchange and money, a problem arises concerning the nature of the contradictions in previous forms of society and the manner in which a transition from one to another occurs. This question is also connected with the problem of social classes. In a broad sense Marx's theory postulates a universal division of society into classes (after the epoch of primitive communal society) in terms of the 'masters of the system of production' and the 'direct producers'; but in another sense classes are regarded as a distinctive feature of capitalist society, and Marx himself observed, in *The German Ideology*, that 'The distinction between the personal and the class individual . . . appears only with the emergence of class, which itself is a product of the *bourgeoisie*'. At all events, it can be argued that in Marx's terms the role of social classes is exceptionally important in capitalist societies, where class relations are the principal expression of the contradiction between forces and relations of production; whereas in earlier societies the dominant social relations may be those of kinship, religion or politics, may not express contradictions; and may presumably constitute societies which do not undergo any development.

This exposition of Marx's theory suggests a variety of problems, not only in the analysis of the main tendencies of development in capitalist societies, but still more in the construction of a general theory of social development or 'science of history'. Increasingly, the latter question seems to be approached by Marxist thinkers in terms of a three–stage model: an original, small–scale form of communal society; followed by the development of diverse social formations which are so many different 'exits' from this communal form, some successful and others less so (in the sense of making possible a further development), and finally the emergence, in one region of the world, of capitalism as a very distinctive type of society embodying hitherto undreamed of potentialities for development.[16] But, as will be seen later, the study of these problems has given rise, in recent years, to a wide variety of reformulations and extensions of Marxist theory.

THE DEVELOPMENT OF MARXISM, 1883–1917

During his own lifetime Marx's social theory received little attention from other scholars. The greatest interest was shown in Russia, where the first translation of *Capital*, vol. I appeared in 1872 and was followed later in the year by a substantial and generally favourable review in the St Petersburg journal *Vestnik Evropy*, which Marx himself commented on in the preface to the second German edition of *Capital* in 1873. In Germany, as Marx noted bitterly, his work was largely ignored except by socialist writers, most notably Joseph Dietzgen, who published a series of articles on it in the *Volkstaat* (1868); but in 1879 Marx's economic theory was more extensively discussed in the second edition of a textbook of political economy by Adolph Wagner, *Allgemeine oder theoretische Volkswirthschaftslehre, Erster Theil, Grundlegung* (General or Theoretical Political Economy, Part I, Foundations), on which Marx made a series of 'marginal notes' in 1879–80 with a view to publishing a critical essay on it.[17] From this time on Marx's theory attracted increasing attention,[18] and soon after his death it began to exert a growing influence, both intellectual and political, in two different ways which have continued to mark its development up to the present time, in the labour movement and in the academic social sciences.

Thus 'Marxism' became, as Marx intended in some sense that his work should become, the pre–eminent social theory or doctrine of the working–class movement. It established itself most strongly in this form in the German Social Democratic Party, whose leaders, as a result of the rapid growth of the socialist movement, and also through their close association with Engels, became the principal intellectual and political heirs of Marx and largely dominated the international labour movement up until 1914. But the SDP, because of the particular political conditions in Germany, took on, as Peter

Nettl has noted,[19] the character of 'a state within a state', and as such it developed on a large scale its own independent cultural and educational institutions, party schools, publishing houses and journals. Though not isolated to the same extent, socialist movements and parties in other countries also developed their ideas largely outside the official academic world; and the exposition and discussion of the Marxist theory took place mainly in books and journals published by socialist parties and groups.[20]

The first major debate within Marxism—the 'revisionist controversy'—arose in the German Social Democratic Party, and quickly spread to other socialist parties after the publication of Eduard Bernstein's *Die Voraussetzungen des Sozialismus und die Aufgaben der Sozialdemokratie* (1899).[21] Bernstein presented two main arguments in his book, both concerned with the claim of Marxism to be a social science. First, he insisted that if Marxism is a science, its results must ultimately be testable by empirical evidence, and that, regarded in this way, some parts of the Marxist theory needed to be revised because the trends of development in the western capitalist societies were diverging from those foreseen by Marx; in particular, the structure of capitalist society was not being simplified into a relation between two main classes but was becoming more complex; the middle classes were not disappearing; a polarization of classes was not taking place; misery was not increasing but diminishing; and economic crises were becoming less rather than more severe. Second, he argued that Marxism as a positive science needs to be supplemented by an ethical theory, but he discussed this question only briefly, and did little more than assert the existence and importance of an 'ideal' element in the socialist movement.[22]

Bernstein's book especially animated a controversy about the Marxist theory of crisis and the breakdown of capitalism, but it also helped to set in motion a broader reassessment of Marx's theory in relation to the economic and social changes that were taking place in the European societies, and to the new movements of thought in philosophy and the social sciences. On the question of crisis Kautsky replied to Bernstein by reasserting the orthodox Marxist view of the 'inevitable' economic breakdown of capitalism, and by turning the issue into one of defending the revolutionary core of Marxism (conceived in this deterministic manner) against reformism; but the problems were later analyzed in a more profound way in Rudolf Hilferding's *Finance Capital* and Rosa Luxemburg's *The Accumulation of Capital.*[23] These two works both attempted to develop Marx's analysis of capitalism in the light of changes which had occurred since his death and, in particular, sought to explain the continued expansion of capitalism by the phenomenon of imperialism. But whereas Luxemburg concluded that capitalism would ultimately suffer an inevitable economic collapse when it had finally absorbed all the pre–capitalist economies and the pre–capitalist enclaves within capitalism, Hilferding argued that capitalism, in its more organised form as finance capital, had the ability to overcome or moderate economic crises, and that it would be overthrown and replaced by socialism, not as a consequence of economic collapse, but as the result of the political struggle of the working class.

The wider debate about Marx's theory took place in many different forms—for example, in the writings of Sorel during the 1890s, in which he attempted to set out the principles of a 'materialist theory of sociology',[24] and in the essays Croce wrote in the same period on historical materialism[25]—but the most systematic effort to present Marx's ideas in a new form, to investigate new problems, and to discuss critically the recent developments in philosophy and the social sciences, is undoubtedly to be found in the writings of the Austro–Marxists. Their intellectual orientation was described in the following terms by Otto Bauer:

'What united them was not a specific political orientation, but the particular character of their intellectual work. They had all grown up in a period when men such as Stammler, Windelband and Rickert were attacking Marxism with philosophical arguments; hence they were obliged to engage in controversy with the representatives of modern philosophical trends. If Marx and Engels began from Hegel, and the later Marxists from materialism, the more recent 'Austro–Marxists' had as their point of departure Kant and Mach. On the other side these "Austro–Marxists" had to engage in controversy with the so–called Austrian school of political economy, and this debate too influenced the method and structure of their thought. Finally, they all had to learn, in the old Austria rent by national struggles, how to apply the Marxist conception of history to very complicated phenomena which defied analysis by any superficial or schematic use of the Marxist method.'[26]

Their principal works—Otto Bauer's study of nationalities and nationalism, Max Adler's sustained inquiry into the methodological foundations of Marxism as a science of society, Renner's analysis of legal institutions, and Hilferding's investigation of the recent development of capitalism—were so many attempts to establish Marxism as a system of sociology by formulating precisely its basic concepts and method and carrying out, in the framework of this paradigm which guided all their research, studies of the most important empirical realities of their time.[27]

During the first decade of the twentieth century, therefore, diverse schools of thought emerged within the socialist movement as a result of controversies about the interpretation of Marx's theory, attempts to revise or elaborate it in response to criticisms and to the appearance of new phenomena, and the development of empirical studies in the field of sociology and social history. Broadly speaking, three main tendencies can be distinguished: the orthodox Marxism of the German Social Democratic Party, repesented above all by Kautsky, which expressed a somewhat mechanical conception of the development of the capitalist economy toward an inevitable breakdown, a development reflected more or less automatically in the class struggle and the final victory of the working class; the revisionist view of Bernstein, which largely rejected the ideas of economic breakdown and of increasingly bitter class struggle and saw the advent of socialism as the culmination of a process of gradual permeation of capitalist society by socialist institutions and ideals; and Austro–Marxism, which developed a much more sophisticated sociological theory, took account of the growing complexity of capitalist society and the changing conditions of the class struggle, but maintained, though in a qualified way, a revolutionary outlook and emphasized the importance of the active intervention of a mass working–class movement, politically conscious and organized, in order to attain socialism. Also in this decade, however, there emerged another body of Marxist thought—that of Lenin and the Bolsheviks—which subsequently had an immense influence upon the whole character of Marxism. This will be examined in the next section.

In the period following Marx's death his theory, although it spread most rapidly in the socialist movement, also began to have an impact upon the academic social sciences, especially economics and sociology. Tönnies, in the preface to *Gemeinschaft und Gesellschaft* (Community and Association) (1887), acknowledged his indebtedness to Marx, whom he described as a 'most remarkable and most profound social philosopher', as the discoverer of the capitalist mode of production and a thinker who had attempted to give expression to the same idea that Tönnies himself was trying to express in new concepts.[28] At the first international congress of sociology in 1894 scholars from several countries (including Tönnies) contributed papers which discussed Marx's theory; and it was during the 1890s that Marxism began to be taught in a number of universities (notably by Carl Grünberg[29] at the University of Vienna and by Antonio Labriola[30] at the University of Rome), began to inspire new kinds of research, and began to be discussed more seriously in academic publications. The first substantial critical studies appeared at this time, one of the earliest being Stammler's attempt to turn Marx's theory on its head by showing that legal norms constitute the indispensable foundation of the system of production, and by substituting for the materialist conception of history a social teleology based upon Kantian ethics.[31] Another important work of criticism was Böhm–Bawerk's *Zum Abschluss des Marxschen Systems* (The Conclusion of the Marxian System) (1896), written from the standpoint of the Austrian marginalist school of economics, which raised objections to the labour theory of value as the foundation of Marx's analysis of capitalism, but was in turn criticized by Rudolf Hilferding in a monograph, *Böhm—Bawerks Marx—Kritik* (1904), where the 'subjectivist' approach of the marginalist school was rejected.[32] In France, Durkheim discussed the Marxist theory in a review of the French edition of Labriola's book on the materialist conception of history in the *Revue philosophique* (1897) and in subsequent reviews of various Marxist studies which he published in the early issues of the *Année sociologique*. Among many other studies that appeared during this

period mention should be made of the major analysis of
Marx's sociological method and hypotheses by T.G.
Masaryk, professor of philosophy in the Czech University of
Prague, *Die philosophischen und soziologischen Grundlagen
des Marxismus* (The Philosophical and Sociological Founda-
tions of Marxism) (1899), and the short critical exposition of
Marx's theory by E.R.A. Seligman, *The Economic Interpre-
tation of History* (1902; rev. edn, 1907).[33]

By the first decade of this century Marxism was firmly
established as an important social theory which was widely
debated in the socialist movement and in the academic world,
and it began to inspire much new social research.[34] Perhaps
the most important characteristic of the Marxist theory as it
appeared at this time was its very broad scope, illustrated by
the fact that the various expositions and criticisms of it were
undertaken by scholars working in such diverse disciplines
as economics, anthropology, history, and jurisprudence.
Labriola emphasized this feature when he wrote that 'The
various analytic disciplines which illustrate historical facts
have ended by bringing forth the need for a general social
science, which will unify the different historical processes.
The materialist theory is the culminating point of this unification'.[35] From this vantage point it is not difficult to understand
why Marxism should have had such a profound influence on
the establishment of sociology itself—which aims at the same
kind of unification—as an academic discipline and more
generally as a new intellectual framework for comprehending
the social world. Nowhere was this influence more apparent
than in German–speaking Europe. Austro–Marxism developed specifically in the form of a sociological theory,[36] and it
indeed constituted the major part of Austrian sociology in the
first three decades of this century.[37] In Germany, Marxism
was an important influence upon Tönnies' thought, as I have
indicated, and upon Simmel, most evident in his major study
of the social relationships which develop with the transition
from a natural economy to a money economy;[38] its subsequent influence in the writings of Korsch, Lukács, Mannheim and the thinkers of the Frankfurt Institute of Social
Research will be examined in later sections of this essay. But
the strongest impact of Marxist thought at the time when

sociology was being formed as an academic discipline is undoubtedly to be seen in Max Weber's writings. It is not simply
that Weber, in his best–known study, *The Protestant Ethic
and the Spirit of Capitalism* (1904), set out to show the limitations of the Marxist account of the origins of capitalism, and
that more generally, in his sociology of religion, he undertook
what he called 'a positive critique of the materialist conception of history', but that in all his work, from his early study of
Roman agrarian history to the diverse analyses incorporated
in *Economy and Society* (1922), and the outline of a general
economic history written at the end of his life, he frequently
took as his starting point problems or conclusions which had
been formulated by Marx. Indeed, it might be argued that the
greater part of Weber's sociology can be read more properly
as a prolonged and varied commentary upon the Marxist
theory—dealing with the origins and prospects of capitalism,
social classes, the state and politics, and problems of
method—though written from the standpoint of a very different world view,[39] than as an original, systematic theory of
society.

Thus, in the three decades since his death Marx's theory
had undergone a notable development, being extended, and
in some respects revised, to take account of the changes in
capitalism; creating whole new fields of research; and enter-
ing profoundly—in the continental European countries,
though not in the English–speaking world,[40]—into the construction of sociology as a general science of society. This
process was interrupted by the first world war; and although
some of the earlier styles of thought persisted after the war,
they did so in vastly changed circumstances, which gave rise to
quite new directions in Marxist theory.

THE BOLSHEVIK HEGEMONY, 1917–56

The Russian Revolution of 1917 and the establishment of the
first 'workers' state', and, on the other side, the failure of the
German revolutionary movement in 1918–19, opened a new
era in the development of Marxism. The centre of gravity of
Marxist studies now moved to Eastern Europe, the institu-

tionalization of Marxism as the ideology of a political regime began, and this official Marxism gradually acquired a preponderant influence in the development of Marxist thought. Soviet Marxism[41] began from the ideas of Lenin; and Lenin's interpretation of Marxism, which has to be seen in the context of political circumstances in the period from the beginning of the century to 1917, involved above all a new reassertion of the practical, revolutionary, significance of Marxism against the growth of revisionism and reformism in the European socialist movement.

The principal elements in Lenin's version of Marxism— concerning the role of the party, the peasantry as an ally of the proletariat, and the conditions of working–class political struggle in the imperialist stage of capitalism—reveal clearly this practical intent. Lenin did not set out to reexamine in any systematic way the Marxist theoretical system, but instead adopted a conception of Marxism as 'the theory of the proletarian revolution', and devoted his efforts to working out, and embodying in an effective organization, its implications for political strategy. Thus, in his analysis of imperialism[42] he drew largely upon the studies made by J.A. Hobson and Rudolf Hilferding, and his general characterization of imperialism did not differ greatly from Hilferding's, except that he drew more revolutionary conclusions, namely, that capitalism had entered a 'moribund' phase, creating more favourable conditions for its overthrow, but also that it had produced a division in the working–class movement between a reformist and revolutionary tendency which demanded an intensified effort to strengthen revolutionary parties and to combat reformism. Again, in his discussion of the peasantry, first in the case of Russia and later in relation to the colonial countries,[43] Lenin was not primarily concerned with elaborating a Marxist theory of the peasantry as a social class or of the stages of social development, but with analyzing the revolutionary potential of the peasantry in backward countries and the means by which some sections of the peasantry could be brought into a political alliance with the working class, or rather, with the revolutionary party of the working class. Lenin's most distinctive contribution to Marxism, indeed, was his conception of the party, based upon a distinction between the working class, which in his view could never attain spontaneously anything more than a 'trade–union consciousness' (i.e. a preoccupation with economic demands), and the revolutionary vanguard of fully class–conscious workers and intellectuals, which brought socialist ideas to the working–class movement of the oppressed (both workers and peasants) by virtue of its total commitment to revolutionary Marxism and its organization as a centralized and disciplined political party.

Leninism, as a doctrine and political movement to which others besides Lenin (notably Trotsky)[44] also contributed, brought into existence a new type of political system and a new kind of party which have had immense consequences for political life and for the development of Marxist thought in the twentieth century. In the first decade after the revolution there was considerable development of Marxist scholarship, in diverse forms, just as there was a burst of creativity in literature and the arts. David Riazanov, the founder of the Marx—Engels Institute in Moscow, began his remarkable collection of the published writings, manuscripts and letters of Marx and Engels in preparation for the monumental critical edition of their works, *Karl Marx/Friedrich Engels: Historisch – Kritische Gesamtausgabe*, (Historical–Critical Edition of the Complete Works of Karl Marx and Friedrich Engels) the first volume of which appeared in 1927, but which remained incomplete as a result of Riazanov's arrest and disappearance in 1931. Also during these years Nicolai Bukharin made important contributions to the theoretical controversies that were taking place in the social sciences and published in 1921 his *Historical Materialism: A System of Sociology* which, although it was intended mainly as a textbook, also introduced 'innovations' to meet criticism of Marxist theory by other social thinkers.[45] Indeed, some of the most interesting sections of the book are those in which Bukharin examines and criticizes the ideas of Max Weber, Michels and Stammler, or comments on recent studies influenced by Marxism. But, by the later 1920s, the growing ascendancy of Stalin put an end to these theoretical debates and the possibility of any serious advances in Marxist social science. Thereafter, Soviet Marxism became an increasingly rigid and dogmatic ideology, not in the sense of an entirely

arbitrary justification of the regime, but as a doctrine which
reflected the actual development of Soviet society—the process of achieving 'socialism in one country', or more simply,
rapid industrialization—at the same time as it helped to
sustain the Stalinist regime.[46] Its intellectual consequences
were to inhibit, throughout a large part of the international
socialist movement, any creative and original Marxist
thought, and in particular to obstruct any development of a
Marxist sociology, whether in the form of theoretical analysis
or empirical research.

The first world war, and the revolutionary situation in
Europe in the immediate post–war years, produced other
significant changes in Marxist thought, resembling those
which became embodied in Leninism, but having a more
profound theoretical character. Their most distinctive feature
was the stronger emphasis upon class consciousness and political activism, rather than the economic development of capitalism, as the principal factors in the transition to socialism.
Two books, published in 1923, examplified and contributed to
this intellectual reorientation: Korsch's *Marxism and Philosophy* and Lukács's *History and Class Consciousness.*[47] In
both works the idea of Marxism as a positive science of
society—as sociology—was rejected; instead, it was conceived as a 'critical philosophy' which expressed the world
view of the revolutionary proletariat just as, according to
Korsch, German idealist philosophy had been the theoretical
expression of the revolutionary bourgeoisie. Lukács, in the
opening pages of his book, defines Marxist theory as 'essentially nothing more than the expression in thought of the
revolutionary process itself', and he then goes on to argue, in
a way which provides a theoretical–philosophical foundation
for Lenin's conception of the party, that Marxism is the 'correct class consciousness of the proletariat' which has as 'its
organizational form, the communist party'.[48]

A similar view of Marxism was formulated by Antonio
Gramsci, though it became widely known only at a later time
when his writings in prison were published after the second
world war.[49] Gramsci also rejected any conception of
Marxism as a science of society or a sociological theory;
Marxism—the 'philosophy of praxis'—' "is sufficient unto

itself" . . . contains in itself all the fundamental elements needed to construct a total and integral conception of the world, a total philosophy and theory of natural science, and not only that but everything that is needed to give life to an integral civilization.'[50] In this case, too, Marxism was presented as a philosophical world view which guides the proletariat in its political struggle to create a new society and a new civilization.

These developments in Marxist thought, although they were largely influenced, as I have indicated, by the political conditions in Europe after the first world war, also occurred within a more general movement of thought, beginning in the 1890s, which has been described as a 'revolt against positivism'.[51] Croce's discussion of Marxism as a method of historical interpretation, closely related to Hegel's philosophy of history,[52] and Sorel's rejection of the idea of historical inevitability and his insistence upon the character of socialist thought, including Marxism, as a moral doctrine which primarily brought to the world 'a new manner of judging all human acts',[53] are important elements in this movement. There also emerged, soon after Korsch and Lukács had published their reinterpretations of Marxist theory, a group of thinkers associated with the Frankfurt Institute of Social Research, who in due course worked out in a much more elaborate fashion the conception of Marxism as a 'critical philosophy' which they opposed to sociological 'positivism'.[54] In the early years of the Institute's existence, under its first director Carl Grünberg, its work spanned empirical and theoretical studies, and it could be regarded as having embarked upon a course similar to that taken by the Austro–Marxists (with whom Grünberg was closely associated); namely, to reexamine the foundations of Marxist theory, to discuss critically new ideas and doctrines in philosophy and the social sciences, and to use a Marxist method in the investigation of new or hitherto neglected phenomena. But this is not what happened when a distinctive 'Frankfurt School' began to take shape in the late 1920s and early 1930s. Its leading thinkers, Adorno and Horkheimer, became preoccupied with methodological questions, and in particular with the opposition between Marxism as a critical philosophy deriving from Hegel and the positivism of the social sciences, which they increasingly identified with the whole development of science and technology since the Enlightenment. This opposition as a central object of theoretical concern is expounded in Marcuse's *Reason and Revolution* (1941), which provides in many respects the best statement of the ideas of the Frankfurt School as they had developed in the 1930s. Marcuse here formulates very sharply the contrast between critical reason, 'which had been intrinsically connected with the idea of freedom', and positivist sociology, which was to be 'a science seeking social laws' and hence eliminating the possibility of changing the social system.[55]

Although the thinkers associated with the Frankfurt Institute developed their ideas in the same intellectual context as did Korsch and Lukács and, to a large extent, Gramsci—that is to say, in a criticism of positivism and a reinterpretation of Marxism as the heir to classical German philosophy—these ideas came to maturity in conditions which were very different from those of the immediate post–war years. By the late 1920s left–wing intellectuals in Germany were confronted, in the political sphere, by a choice between Soviet Marxism, which had already entered its dogmatic, Stalinist phase, and the reformism of the Social Democratic Party. Most of the members of the Frankfurt School rejected both options and chose the path of keeping alive the critical spirit of Marxism, as they conceived it, outside the sphere of party politics. Increasingly, therefore, Marxism became for them a criticism of ideology, or a general criticism of bourgeois culture, addressed to an audience of intellectuals and students. Another circumstance also impelled them along this path— namely, the apparent weakness of the working class in the face of the rise of fascist movements—which led them to argue that the struggle for socialism could not be carried on successfully unless the working class developed a 'conscious will' for a liberated and rational society;[56] and it was evidently the responsibility of intellectuals to provide the criticism and the liberating ideas which might eventually shape this will.

In some respects Korsch and Lukács had to face similar problems. Both were in opposition to some aspects at least of Bolshevik orthodoxy, and their books were condemned as 'revisionist' and 'idealist' at the fifth Congress of the Communist International in 1924. Lukács repudiated his work and remained a member of the Communist Party, but in spite of his concessions to Stalinism it seems unlikely that he changed his fundamental views, and after 1956 he expounded them again in a manner which encouraged a more critical attitude in the political regimes of Eastern Europe.

Korsch, on the other hand, was expelled from the German Communist Party in 1926; he then participated in various left–wing movements until his exile in the United States after 1933, when he ceased to be active in politics. During these years his conception of Marxism gradually changed, and he ceased to regard it as the philosophy of the working–class movement, emphasizing instead its achievements as a social science. In his book on Marx as a sociologist, published in 1938, he gave a clear indication of how his own ideas had changed when he wrote:

In the subsequent development of Marxism, the critical materialist principle that Marx had worked out empirically . . . was elaborated into a general social philosophy . . . From this distortion of the strongly empirical and critical sense of the materialistic principle it was only a step to the idea that the historical and economic science of Marx must be based on the broader foundation not only of a social philosophy, but even of a comprehensive materialist philosophy embracing both nature and society, or a general philosophical interpretation of the universe;

and he summed up his own view by saying: 'The main tendency of historical materialism is no longer "philosophical", but is that of an empirical scientific method.'[57]

The writings of Korsch, Lukács, Gramsci, and the members of the Frankfurt Institute do not, of course, exhaust the work of Marxist thinkers outside, or partially outside, the orbit of Soviet Marxism during this period. The Austro–Marxists continued to develop Marxism as a social science in close association with political action until 1934, when Austrian Social Democracy was destroyed by fascism. In Germany, Marxism was one major influence on the work of Karl Mannheim, and we can see in his writings, as in those of Max Weber earlier, an attempt to define the contribution of Marxism to sociology— and more specifically to the sociology of knowledge and culture[58]—without accepting it as a world view.

Yet in spite of all these reexaminations and reinterpretations of Marxist thought, especially in the decade of the 1920s, I do not think it can be said that during this period from 1917 to 1956 the influence of Marxism upon sociology, or the development of the Marxist theory of society, was as vigorous or extensive as in the preceding and succeeding periods. One reason for this was the political dominance of Soviet Marxism, which pushed other versions of Marxism into a marginal position (or suppressed them altogether, as in the case of Lukács's *History and Class Consciousness*), with the result that they were, generally speaking, little known and largely ignored. But another major factor was the triumph of fascism in Europe. In Italy Gramsci propounded his ideas in conditions which precluded any extensive discussion or development of them (many of his most fundamental notions are formulated in notes and essays written in prison); in Austria the Austro–Marxist School was dispersed; and in Germany every kind of Marxist study and debate came to an end in 1933. It was another twenty years before the Marxist theory could again be adequately expounded and critically examined.

THE RENEWAL OF MARXIST THOUGHT

During the past two decades there has been a notable revival of Marxist thinking in the social sciences. The reasons for such a development are diverse. Most important, perhaps, is that the Bolshevik dominance over Marxism came to an end with the revelations about the Stalinist regime, the political and intellectual revolts in Eastern Europe, and the emergence of a less monolithic, more critical, view of Marxist theory, encouraged further by the rise of alternative centres of Marxist political practice, especially in China. Largely as a result of these changes a transformation of Marxist thought has also occurred in Western Europe, partly through the rediscovery and renewed discussion of earlier thinkers—among them Trotsky, Korsch, Lukács, Gramsci and the Frankfurt School—whose work had been neglected or consigned to oblivion during the period of Stalin's rule, partly through the formulation of new Marxist conceptions influenced both by fresh ideas in the social sciences and philosophy and by the changing character and problems of societies in the second half of the twentieth century. This Marxist revival has been stimulated too by the publication, translation and wider diffusion of important manuscripts of Marx which had previously been little known, especially the *Economic and Philosophical Manuscripts* (1844) and the *Grundrisse* (1857–8).[59]

The political and intellectual movements of the past twenty years have produced, therefore, a great burgeoning of Marxist scholarship, as well as many new attempts to rethink the whole Marxist theory of society, particularly in relation to the general development and results of the modern social sciences, with respect both to their substantive achievements and to their methodological orientations. Marxism no longer has the appearance, within the social sciences, of a body of thought which has long since been surpassed, or which can be set aside as a social doctrine expressing mainly value judgements and political aspirations. Marxism is not, as Durkheim once characterized socialism, simply a 'cry of pain'.[60] What is perhaps most striking in the recent development of the social sciences is that Marxist ideas have regained an important influence everywhere; in economics, where Marxism is now recognized as a major theory of economic growth[61] which has contributed much, in particular, to the study of the 'developing' countries; and in anthropology, where, as Raymond Firth has noted, contact with Marx's ideas was long avoided;[62] as well as in sociology, political science and history. In sociology especially, Marxist theory has emerged, though in diverse forms, as a major paradigm capable of accomplishing the aim which Labriola described as the establishment of a general social science which would 'unify the different historical processes' and bring together in a systematic form the results of the more specialized social sciences.[63]

In this recent development two principal orientations of Marxist thought have emerged which I shall refer to as 'structuralist Marxism' and 'critical theory'. The former owes its distinctive character to the work of Louis Althusser[64] on one side and to modern structuralist anthropology, itself strongly influenced by structural linguistics,[65] on the other. Althusser's own concerns are primarily epistemological; he sets out to establish a theory of knowledge in opposition to empiricism, to make apparent the 'immense theoretical revolution' that Marx accomplished, and to show the 'scientificity' of Marx's mature theory in contrast with 'ideological' thought.[66] However, in the course of this philosophical analysis he brings into prominence especially that aspect of Marx's theory which lays stress upon structural analysis: according to Althusser, Marx's theory

reveals the existence of *two problems* . . . Marx regards contemporary society (and every other past form of society) both as a *result* and as a *society*. The theory of the mechanism of transformation from one mode of production into another, i.e. the theory of the forms of transition from one mode of production to the succeeding one, has to pose and solve the problem of the *result*, i.e. of the historical production of a given mode of production, of a given social formation. But contemporary society is not only a result, a product; it is *this* particular result, *this* particular *product*, which functions as a *society*, unlike other results and other products which function quite differently. This second problem is answered by the theory of the structure of a mode of production, the theory of *Capital*.[67]

The structuralist version of Marxist theory has been expounded with great clarity, and its uses exemplified from anthropological studies, by Maurice Godelier.[68] In *Perspectives in Marxist Anthropology*[69] he distinguishes between functionalist, structuralist (i.e. the structuralism of Lévi–Strauss) and Marxist approaches and presents Marxism as a particular form of structuralism, characterized by two main principles: first, that 'the starting point in science is not to be found in appearances', but in the inner logic of a structure which exists behind the visible relations between men:[70] and second, that

'a materialistic approach which takes Marx as its point of departure, cannot consist merely of a lengthy enquiry into the networks of structural causality without eventually seeking to evaluate the particular and unequal effect that these different structures may have on the functioning—i.e. particularly the conditions of *reproduction*—of an economic and social formation. In analyzing the hierarchy of causes which determine the reproduction of an economic and social formation, materialism takes seriously Marx's fundamental hypothesis on the determining causality "in the final analysis" for the reproduction of this formation, of the mode or modes of production which comprise the material and social infrastructure of this formation.[71]

This general approach, therefore, takes as its principal

object of study—a 'theoretically constructed' object—the mode of production of material life and the corresponding social formation, which is conceived as a hierarchy of structures. From this point of view the analysis of structure has priority over historical analysis; in Godelier's words

whatever the internal or external causes or circumstances . . . which bring about contradictions and structural changes within a determined mode of production and society, these contradictions and changes always have their basis in internal properties, immanent in social structures, and they express unintentional requirements, the reasons and laws for which remain to be discovered . . . History, therefore, does not explain: it has to be explained. Marx's general hypothesis concerning the existence of a relation of order between infrastructure and superstructure which, in the final analysis, determines the functioning and evolution of societies, does not mean that we may determine in advance the specific laws of functioning and evolution in the different economic and social formations which have appeared or will appear in history. This is because no general history exists and because we can never predict what structures will function as infrastructure within these different economic and social formations.[72]

The structuralist approach, with some variations and differences of emphasis, has inspired much recent Marxist inquiry. Thus, besides the work of Godelier, mention should be made in particular of the studies of political power and social classes by Nicos Poulantzas,[73] which define the fundamental concepts of 'mode of production' and 'social formation' and distinguish different structures or 'levels'—economic, political, ideological and theoretical—that are combined and articulated in a specific way in each historically–determined social formation; of the analysis of pre–capitalist modes of production, and of the relation between mode of production and social formation, by Hindess and Hirst,[74] who formulate a particularly strong antihistoricist view, rejecting entirely the conception of Marxism as a 'science of history';[75] and of the investigations by Pierre Bourdieu and his colleagues of ideological structures and their relations with economic and political structures in the process of reproduction of a particular social formation.[76] These works, and others of a similar kind, have brought a new theoretical and methodological sophistication to Marxist studies, have emphasized (and in many cases sought to exemplify) the predominantly scientific character of Marxist thought, and in light of this, have adopted a more flexible and tentative approach to the problem of the relation between infrastructure and superstructure. The Marxist structuralists insist that the different structures which constitute any given social formation all have a certain autonomy, and that while the economic structure (the mode of production) has to be conceived as ultimately determinant, other structures may nevertheless be *dominant* in constituting and reproducing a particular form of society; furthermore, it is the development of contradictions both within and between the different structures, not simply the effects, conceived in a mechanical way, of purely economic contradictions, which lead eventually to the breakdown of an existing social formation and the emergence of a new one. Hence, it is argued, the state and the 'ideological apparatus' (through which a dominant cultural outlook is reproduced) undergo a partially—and even largely—independent development and have a major influence upon the evolution, the persistence or decline, of a particular social formation. The Marxist notion of 'crisis' has been reinterpreted in accordance with these views, and Althusser has introduced the term 'overdetermination' to express the idea of a confluence of separate lines of development, and a conjunction of crises occurring more or less independently in different spheres of society, which result in a revolutionary transformation.

It may be objected that some of the more abstract recent writings on infrastructure and superstructure do not advance much, if at all, beyond Engels' very general observations on the 'relative autonomy' of the superstructure;[77] although in the works of Godelier there is a more empirical, and illuminating, analysis of ideology, especially myth, in relation to the economic structure of primitive societies.[78] Nevertheless, there remains a large unresolved general problem concerning the exact degree of autonomy that is to be attributed to the various spheres of society, and the precise meaning of the claim that the functioning and development of a society as a whole are determined 'in the final analysis' by the economic structure. It will be useful, in this context, to consider the ideas of some of the thinkers associated with the other broad tendency in present–day Marxist thought, namely, 'critical theory'; for in spite of the very different character of their basic conceptions they agree largely with the structuralist Marxists in distinguishing three principal, quasi–independent spheres of social life—economic, political, and ideological—among which there is a complex interaction, rather than a simple unilinear determination by the economic structure. Thus, Jürgen Habermas in his *Legitimation Crisis* (1977), examines the manifestations of economic, political and ideological crises in late capitalist societies, as well as diverse interpretations of such crises, and argues that since the economic system has surrendered part of its autonomy to the state, an economic crisis cannot, in these conditions, directly provoke a crisis of the whole social system. The responsibility for dealing with the crisis is assumed by the state, and a crisis of the whole system could only develop if there were a political crisis and an ideological crisis in which the cultural system became incapable of providing the necessary motivations for the maintenance and reproduction of the existing society. In Habermas's view, therefore, the fundamental, increasingly difficult problem of late capitalist society is that of providing an adequate, persuasive *legitimation* of the social order.[79] Similarly, Claus Offe, in his studies of the state, and of one pervasive ideology which he calls the 'achievement principle',[80] gives pre–eminent importance, 'in an era of comprehensive state intervention'—when it is no longer possible to speak reasonably of ' "spheres free of state interference" that constitute the "material base" of the "political superstructure" '—to the ideological justifications of the social system: 'The late capitalist welfare state bases its legitimacy on the postulate of a universal participation in consensus formation and on the unbiased possibility for all classes to utilize the state's services and to benefit from its regulatory acts of intervention.'[81]

In the studies by Habermas and Offe, it will be seen , there is a move away from the idea of determination by the economic structure, even 'in the final analysis', while the state and ideology seem to be treated as the main determining forces; although it might still be argued—employing Godelier's distinction—that their *dominance* is the consequence of a particular mode of production—namely, that of advanced capitalism, which in this sense remains *determinant.* At all events, the concentration in these studies upon the critical analysis of ideology shows their affiliation with the Marxism of the Frankfurt School, but there is also a more marked divergence from Marx's own theory and a more direct criticism of certain aspects of it. This appears very clearly in Wellmer's exposition of critical theory, where he develops an argument against the 'objectivism' and the 'latent positivism' of Marx's theory of history, which are held to result from the undue emphasis that Marx placed upon the process of labour and material production as opposed to social interaction (or in Habermas's terminology upon 'instrumental' as opposed to 'communicative' behaviour), and from the epistemological implications of this view—namely, that the fundamental processes constituting, or transforming, particular forms of society can be analyzed with the precision of natural science and formulated as laws.[82] According to Wellmer, this conception—strongly though not exclusively present in Marx's thought—furnishes the starting–point for a technocratic interpretation of Marxism, to which he opposes a conception of Marxism as a theory of the development of a critical consciousness which aims at emancipation. His view is summed up in a discussion of the necessary conditions for a transition from capitalism to socialism; after observing that 'history itself has thoroughly discredited all hopes of an economically grounded "mechanism" of emancipation', he goes on to argue that it is necessary 'to take into account entirely new constellations of "bases" and "superstructures",' that 'the criticism and alteration of the "superstructure" have a new and decisive importance for the movements of liberation', and that 'to reformulate Marx's supposition about the prerequisites for a successful revolution in the case of the capitalist countries, it would be necessary to include socialist democracy, socialist justice, socialist ethics and a "socialist consciousness" among the components of a socialist society to be 'incubated' within the womb of a capitalist order.'[83]

Although there are considerable differences among individual thinkers, some of the general conceptions which characterize criticial theory are evident. In the first place, there is an emphasis upon consciousness and intentional activity as a major element in constituting, reproducing or changing a particular form of society. For critical theory it is not the case that 'being determines consciousness', particularly in the sense that consciousness is only a determined reflection of the conditions of material production. Consciousness is not simply an outcome of the human interaction with nature, but it is a distinct and independent capacity to use language, to communicate with others, to create symbols and engage in symbolic thought. From this aspect critical theory has to be seen as one of the schools of 'interpretative sociology', analyzing the social world by the interpretation of 'meanings', not by the investigation of causal relations, and hence rejecting not only Marx's 'latent positivism', but also the notion of 'structural causality' which is central to the thought of the Marxist structuralists. It is evident, furthermore, that the sources of critical theory include, besides Marxism, German philosophical idealism and especially phenomenology,[84] as may be seen in the work of Jürgen Habermas,[85] and in Sartre's attempted conjunction of existentialism and Marxism in order to comprehend the relation between the intentional actions of individuals (human 'projects') and the unintended, in some way determined, consequences of the behaviour of groups and classes.[86]

This commitment to an interpretative method is a major element in the preoccupation of critical theorists with cultural criticism or 'ideology–critique'; for in so far as the social world is conceived as a tissue of 'meanings', the reproduction or transformation of any particular social world becomes a matter of sustaining or modifying, in the consciousness of individuals, the dominant mode of representation of that world—the established interpretation of its reality and legitimacy—which is expressed in a system of cultural values and in ideologies (social, philosophical, and religious doctrines, legal systems, educational practices). From these concerns have emerged such analyses of late capitalist society as Habermas's study of science and technology as ideology, or of the problems of legitimation,[87] and Marcuse's account of the domination of these societies by neo–positivist philosophy and technological rationality.[88] This emphasis in critical theory upon the shaping power of ideologies and, in a more general way, upon the character of social struggles as a conflict of ideas, a contest among different interpretations of the social world, has itself attracted criticism from both Marxist and non–Marxist social scientists, who point to the existence of a quasi–causal relationship between men and the physical world (upon which Marx himself insisted) and to the neglect, by critical theorists, of the elements of power (in the last resort, physical coercion) and material interests in social life which are held to be connected with this human dependence upon, and interaction with, the natural environment.[89] Here, the idea of material causality, formulated by the structuralist Marxists, offers a clear alternative mode of analysis.

A third distinctive feature of critical theory, again setting it in opposition to structuralist Marxism, is its conception of social theory as being primarily concerned with historical interpretation. Social life is seen as a historical process—and progress—in which reason, in its critical form, is able to recognize and seize upon the opportunities for liberation which exist in any given condition of society; or as Marcuse argues, to form historical projects which can advance rationality and freedom beyond the level so far reached.[90] This teleological view, which posits a more or less determinate and intelligible historical process in which the human species, as the historical subject, advances towards the end after which it has always striven—namely, emancipation and the comprehensive organization of social life in accordance with universal reason—has its roots in Hegel's philosophy; and as I showed earlier in discussing the work of Lukács, Korsch and the Frankfurt School in the 1920s, it has long inspired one major version of Marxism, critical theory being only its most recent expression. From the standpoint of those who consider Marxism a science this teleological conception is quite unacceptable, and their criticisms may be summed up in Godelier's observation, quoted earlier, that history does not explain, but has to be explained; that is to say, accounted for in terms of efficient causes.

It will be apparent from the foregoing review that much recent Marxist scholarship has been devoted especially to problems of method, and this is very similar to the situation which prevails in sociology as a whole. Indeed, it is evident that the debates within Marxism and within sociology cover much of the same ground, being preoccupied with questions about the nature of a general social science, its scientific standing, and its relation to philosophy; and they also draw upon many of the same sources, among them phenomenological criticisms of the idea of a social science, theories of language, and structuralist doctrines. Hence it may be said that there is now a closer relation between Marxism and sociology, and even a merging of ideas, in their concern with problems in the philosophy of science. To a great extent this concern revives, though in different terms, the preoccupations that dominated the *Methodenstreit* in Germany in the nineteenth century, and especially a critique of positivist views such as was formulated by Dilthey and subsequently examined by Max Weber.[91] And just as Lichtheim remarks in an essay on the intellectual return 'from Marx to Hegel' that 'if then we find that contemporary thinking reproduces the problematic of an earlier historical situation—namely that out of which Marxism arose—we are entitled to suppose that it does so because the relationship of theory to practice has once more become the sort of problem it was for Hegel's followers in the 1840s',[92] so we might say that the methodological preoccupations of recent sociology arise in large measure from a situation of cultural and political uncertainty which has some resemblance to that of the period from the 1880s to the first world war.[93]

However, it would be wrong to leave the impression that Marxist scholarship in the past two decades has been more or less exclusively concerned with the reinterpretation of Marx's own texts and with methodological issues set in the context of wider discussions of the philosophy of the social sciences. As I have already indicated, there have been important substantive investigations: in anthropology, especially by Godelier, and in such studies of the state and of social classes as those by Offe and Poulantzas. There has also been an attempt, notably in the studies by Perry Anderson,[94] to investigate large–scale historical problems with the aid of new theoretical conceptions. Perhaps the most impressive contribution by Marxists is to be found, however, in that large and growing area of study which has come to be known as the 'sociology of development'. It is not too much to say that in this field both the theoretical framework and research strategies have been radically transformed by Marxist criticism of the predominant model of the 1950s, which was expressed particularly in the notion of 'modernization', and by the elaboration of new Marxist concepts.

Three important ideas have been formulated in the course of Marxist discussions of development, which themselves are quite diversified and have not produced anything like an 'orthodox' Marxist view. First, it is insisted that the economic and social development of non–industrial countries cannot be adequately comprehended solely in terms of factors internal to those countries, but have to be analyzed in the context of a world economy which is predominantly capitalist. Second, from this standpoint a distinction is made between metropolis/satellite, or centre/periphery, and it is argued that the peripheral countries are either actively 'underdeveloped' by the capitalist centres or are subjected to a process of 'dependent' and distorted development. Analyses of this kind are presented in Paul Baran, *The Political Economy of Growth* (1962); in A. Gunder Frank, *Capitalism and Underdevelopment in Latin America* (2nd edn, 1969);[95] and, particularly with reference to the theory of 'dependent development', in the writings of a number of Latin American economists and sociologists.[96] The debate about underdevelopment and dependency has also revived discussion of the Marxist theory of imperialism and has led to various attempts to revise and reformulate the theory to take account of post–war phenomena such as the dissolution of the colonial empires and, on the other side, the rapid growth of multinational corporations.[97] Finally, in the same context, Marxists have given much attention to the concept of a 'post–colonial mode of production' as a framework for analyzing, within the world economy, the social structure and especially the character and actions of social classes in those non–industrial countries which have emerged from colonial rule.[98]

There has been, of course, much recent work in other areas of social life—for example, studies of the family influenced both by the concern with 'cultural reproduction' and by feminist criticisms of Marxist theory, and studies in the field of criminology—but it is primarily in the analyses of 'late capitalism' and of 'development' that the concepts of a new Marxist sociology, or 'political economy', are being worked out, though as I have shown in quite varied forms. In concluding this brief historical account it will perhaps be useful to reconsider, in light of this diversity and effervescence of present–day Marxist thought, the distinctive character of Marxism which I sketched at the outset—namely, its dual existence as a theory of society embedded in the intellectual and scientific life and institutions of modern societies, and as the doctrine of a social movement. Obviously, this connection between theory and political practice remains (and I would argue indeed that a similar, though often less obvious and less systematic, relation to practical life exists in the case of all social–science theories), but some important changes have occurred. The development of Marxism as a theory is now accorded a greater independence from direct political concerns and is more clearly located in the context of a general development of sociological theory, as is evident from the relations that I have shown to exist between recent Marxism and other movements of thought in the social sciences and in the philosophy of science. There is now no 'orthodox' Marxism which can claim to generate infallibly a 'correct' political (or party) view of aims and strategies in practical life. On the contrary, the diversity of theoretical stances, the acknowledgement of unresolved theoretical problems, and the recognition of the complex and partly indeterminate character of historical development have begun to produce a more tentative attitude to political action, in which many different considerations, not necessarily encompassed by the theory itself, have to find a place. Thus the idea of a large degree of autonomy in both scientific work and political action is now widely accepted. But still it may be said that this process of liberation of Marxist thought from dogmatism has itself to be seen in its social context; and from the standpoint of one type of Marxist theory it might well be regarded as an element in that general movement of human emancipation which Marx himself defined in such original and dramatic terms.

NOTES

1. Bottomore, Tom, *Marxist Sociology* (London: Macmillan, 1975).
2. In speaking of Marx's theory, I do not mean to deny the importance of Engles' contribution to the general development of Marxist thought. But the fundamental and distinctive elements of this intellectual system were, as is universally acknowledged, the creation of Marx himself, and Engels' collaboration—except at the very beginning of their association, when he was largely responsible for directing Marx's attention to the writings of the political economists and economic historians, partly through his essay 'Outline of a Critique of Political Economy', which was published in the *Deutsch–Französische Jahrbücher* (1844)—involved for the most part the application of these theoretical ideas to particular problems concerning the history of societies, or the development of the labour movement, and the exposition in more popular terms of the Marxist theory. After Marx's death Engels became, as we shall see, not only the editor of Marx's manuscripts, but also the first of many interpreters and systematizers of his ideas.
3. These manuscripts were first published in 1932, and several English translations are now available. In the text I shall quote from my own translation in Bottomore, T.B., *Karl Marx: Early Writings* (London: Watts, 1963).
4. Bottomore, *Early Writings* p. 202.
5. Korsch, Karl, *Karl Marx* (London: Chapman & Hall, 1938).
6. The manuscript now known as the *Grundrisse* was written by Marx in 1857–8 and first published as a whole in 1939–41. The English translation, by Martin Nicolaus, was published in 1973. (Harmondsworth: Penguin, 1973).
7. *Capital*, vol. III was published by Engles from Marx's manuscripts in 1894. There are several English translations; the passage cited here is taken from Bottomore, T.B. and Rubel, Maximilien (eds.), *Karl Marx: Selected Writings in Sociology and Social Philosophy* (London: Watts 1956) pp. 112–13.
8. The manuscript of *The German Ideology*, written by Marx and Engles in 1845–6, was first published in 1932. The English trans. cited here is taken from Bottomore and Rubel, *Karl Marx: Selected Writings*, pp. 70–1.
9. The passage cited here is taken from Bottomore and Rubel, *Karl Marx: Selected Writings*, pp. 67–8.
10. Althusser, Louis, *For Marx* (London: Allen Lane, 1969).
11. This section of the manuscript has been published separately in an English translation, with a very useful introduction by Eric Hobsbawm, under the title *Pre–Capitalist Economic Formations* (London: Lawrence & Wishart, 1964).
12. Marx's excerpts and critical comments have now been transcribed and edited, with an introduction, by Krader, Lawrence, *The Ethnological Notebooks of Karl Marx* (Assen: VanGorcum & Co., 1972).

13. Reprinted in Blackburn, Robin (ed.), *Ideology in Social Science* (London: Fontana/Collins, 1972) pp. 306–33.
14. Hobsbawm, *Pre–Capitalist Economic Formations*, pp. 19–20, 36–7.
15. Cf. Anderson, Perry, *Lineages of the Absolutist State* (London: New Left Books, 1974) p. 403: '*All* modes of production in class societies prior to capitalism extract surplus labour from the immediate producers by means of extra–economic coercion. Capitalism is the first mode of production in history in which the means whereby the surplus is pumped out of the direct producer is 'purely' economic in form—the wage contract: the equal exchange between free agents which reproduces, hourly and daily, inequality and oppression. All other previous modes of exploitation operate through *extra–economic* sanctions—kin, customary, religious, legal or political.'
16. This last conception is by no means irreconcilable with some elements in Max Weber's account of the origins and development of capitalism; or to put the matter in another way, Weber's thesis can be partly assimilated into, and partly complements, Marx's analysis.
17. An English translation of these 'marginal notes', which throw additional light on Marx's methodological views, together with a useful commentary, is to be found in Carver, Terrell, *Karl Marx: Texts on Method* (Oxford: Basil Blackwell, 1975).
18. See, for example, the laudatory essay by Bax, E. Belfort, 'Karl Marx', in *Modern Thought*, December 1881.
19. Nettl, Peter, 'The German Social Democratic Party 1890–1914 as a Political Model', *Past and Present*, April 1965, pp. 65–95.
20. For example, in Karl Kautsky's journal *Neue Zeit*, in the *Marx–Studien* and *Der Kampf* of the Austro–Marxists, and in Sorel's *Le Devenir social* to which most of the leading European Marxists contributed during its brief existence from 1895–98.
21. An English translation, under the title *Evolutionary Socialism*, was published in 1909 (reprinted New York: Schocken Books, 1961).
22. I shall not attempt to discuss here the problems of Marxist ethics. There is a good account of the context of Bernstein's ideas—of his 'positivism' and his views on ethics, both influenced by neo–Kantianism—in Gay, Peter, *The Dilemma of Democratic Socialism* (New York: Columbia University Press, 1952). An excellent study of Marxist ethics is Stojanovic, S. *Between Ideals and Reality* (New York: Oxford University Press, 1973).
23. Hilferding, Rudolf, *Das Finanzkapital* (1910, English trans, London: Routledge & Kegan Paul, 1981) Luxemburg, Rosa, *The Accumulation of Capital* (1913; English trans., London: Routledge & Kegan Paul, 1951).
24. See especially Sorel's essays on Durkheim, 'Les théories de M. Durkheim', in *Le Devenir social*, April and May 1895.
25. See the English translation of some of these essays collected in Croce, Benedetto, *Historical Materialism and the Economics of Karl Marx*, with an introduction by A.D. Lindsay (London: Howard Latimer, 1913).
26. Bauer's essay, 'What is Austro–Marxism?' published in 1927, is translated in full in Bottomore, Tom, and Goode, Patrick, *Austro–Marxism* (Oxford: Oxford University Press, 1978), which contains a selection from the principal writings of the Austro–Marxists, together with an introductory essay on the formation and the principal ideas of the Austro–Marxist

school.

27. The works referred to are Bauer, Otto, *Die Nationalitätenfrage und die Sozialdemokratie* (1907); Adler, Max, *Der soziologische Sinn der Lehre von Karl Marx* (1914), *Soziologie des Marxismus* (2 vols., 1930–32; enlarged edn. with a third volume, 1964), and many other works; Renner, Karl, *Die soziale Funktion der Rechsinstitute* (1904; rev. edn., 1928); Hilferding, Rudolf, *Das Finanzkapital* (1910). Only Karl Renner's book has so far been translated into English, under the title *The Institutions of Private Law and Their Social Functions* (London: Routledge & Kegan Paul, 1949), but selections from the others are published in Bottomore and Goode, *Austro–Marxism*.

28. English trans., *Community and Association* (London: Routledge & Kegan Paul, 1955). Much later, in 1921, Tönnies published a study of Marx [English trans., *Karl Marx: His Life and Teachings* (East Lansing: Michigan State University Press, 1974)] in which he reiterated the importance of Marx's influence and in the second part of the book examined some of the economic and sociological problems that arise in Marx's theory.

29. Carl Grünberg, who has been called 'the father of Austro–Marxism', taught economic history and the history of the labour movement at the University of Vienna from 1894 to 1924, when he became the first director of the Frankfurt Institute for Social Research. He is now chiefly remembered for the periodical *Archiv für die Geschichte des Sozialismus und der Arbeiterbewegung*, which he founded (in 1910) and edited, to which many distinguished Marxist scholars contributed.

30. Antonio Labriola taught philosophy at the University of Rome from 1874 to 1904, published the first Italian translation of *The Communist Manifesto* in 1890 and a collection of essays, *The Materialist Conception of History*, in 1896.

31. Stammler, Rudolph, *Wirtschaft und Recht nach der materialistischen Geschichtsauffassung*. Stammler's book was itself criticized at length by Croce, in one of the essays collected in *Historical Materialism and the Economics of Karl Marx*; by Max Weber, in an essay published in 1907, 'R. Stammlers "Ueberwindung" der materialistischen Geschichtsauffassung', reprinted in *Gesammelte Aufsätze zur Wissenschaftslehre* (1922); and by Max Adler, in 'R. Stammlers Kritik der materialistischen Geschichtsauffassung', reprinted in *Marxistische Probleme* (1913).

32. English translations of Böhm–Bawerk's book and Hilferding's rejoinder have been published together in a volume edited by Paul Sweezy (New York: Augustus M. Kelley, 1949).

33. For a more detailed account of the reception and discussion of Marxism as a sociological theory, see T.B. Bottomore and M. Rubel (eds.), *Karl Marx: Selected Writings in Sociology and Social Philosophy* (1956), Introduction, part II.

34. Besides the studies already mentioned that were undertaken by the Austro–Marxists, there were such works as Tugan–Baranovsky, M., *Geschichte der Russischen Fabrik* (in Russian 1898; rev. German trans., 1900) and Grosse, E., *Die Formen der Familie und die Formen der Wirtschaft* (1897), as well as the publications of Carl Grünberg in the field of agrarian history and labour history, where the influence of Marxism was

obviously very great. Some idea of the extent of Marxist research, especially in the general field of social history, can be gained from Grünberg's *Archiv* from 1910 onward.

35. Labriola, A., *Essays on the Materialistic Conception of History* (English trans., Chicago: Charles H. Kerr, 1908) p. 149.

36. In addition to the writings of Max Adler, see those of Otto Neurath, who formed a link between Austro–Marxism and the Vienna Circle, especially his monograph *Empirical Sociology* (1931; English trans. in Neurath, O., *Empiricism and Sociology*, Dordrecht: D. Reidel Publishing Co., 1973).

37. See the illuminating essay by Torrance, John, 'The Emergence of Sociology in Austria 1885–1935', in *European Journal of Sociology*, XVII, 2 (1976), pp. 185–219.

38. Simmel, Georg, *Philosophie des Geldes* (1900; English trans. London: Routledge & Kegan Paul, 1978). See also the discussion of Simmel's relation to Marx by Salomon, Albert, 'German Sociology', in Gurvitch, Georges, and Moore, Wilbert E. (eds.), *Twentieth Century Sociology* (New York: 1945).

39. This is well brought out in Löwith, Karl, 'Max Weber und Karl Marx' (1932), part of which is translated in Wrong, Dennis, (ed.), *Max Weber* (Englewood Cliffs, NJ: Prentice–Hall, 1970).

40. Marxism played only a small part in the development of American sociology, either at its beginnings or later, while in Britain, where sociology itself scarcely began to develop until after the second world war, Marxism had only a modest intellectual (or political) influence at any time. It is only since the 1960s that this situation has begun to change.

41. The most systematic theoretical study of Soviet Marxism is Marcuse, Herbert, *Soviet Marxism* (London: Routledge & Kegan Paul, 1958). See especially chap. 2, 'Soviet Marxism: The Basic Self–Interpretation'.

42. Lenin, V.I., *Imperialism, the Highest Stage of Capitalism* (1916) in *Collected Works* vol. XIX (London: Lawrence & Wishart, 1942).

43. For Lenin's views and later developments, see Carrère d'Encausse, Hélène, and Schram, Stuart R., *Marxism and Asia* (1965, English trans., London: Allen Lane, 1969).

44. Trotsky, like Lenin, was primarily concerned with asserting the possibility of a socialist revolution in a backward country. He developed this idea in his theory of the 'permanent revolution' (first formulated after the revolution of 1905 and expounded again in the introduction to *Permanent Revolution*, 1920) which also introduced the idea that 'for backward countries the road to democracy passed through the dictatorship of the proletariat'.

45. This English translation of the book appeared in 1925. On Bukharin's contribution to Marxist theory, see Cohen, Stephen F., *Bukharin and the Bolshevik Revolution* (London: Wildwood House, 1974), especially chap. 4, 'Marxist Theory and Bolshevik Policy: Bukharin's *Historical Materialism*'.

46. See the discussion in Marcuse, *Soviet Marxism*.

47. Korsch, Karl, *Marxismus und Philosophie* (1923; English trans., London: New Left Books, 1970); Lukács, Georg, *Geschichte und Klassenbewusstsein* (1923; English trans. London: Merlin Press, 1971). For

further critical discussion of the ideas of Korsch and Lukács, see Botto-more, *Marxist Sociology*, chap. 3, and *Sociology as Social Criticism*, (London: George Allen & Unwin, 1975) chap. 7; and Lichtheim, George, *Lukács* (London: Fontana/Collins, 1970).
48. Lukács, *History and Class Consciousness*, p. 75. Lukács's argument is based upon a distinction between what he calls 'psychological' class consciousness (the actual consciousness which workers have in particular historical situations) and an 'imputed' or 'possible' rational consciousness (i.e. Marxism). Much later, in the preface which he wrote in 1967 for the new edition of the book, Lukács again insisted strongly upon the importance of this distinction, which he now associated explicitly with Lenin's distinction between 'trade–union consciousness' and 'socialist consciousness'.
49. See Gramsci, Antonio, *Selections from the Prison Notebooks*, ed., trans. and with an introduction by Quintin Hoare and Geoffrey Nowell Smith (London: Lawrence & Wishart, 1971).
50. From Gramsci's critical notes on Bukharin's *Historical Materialism*, in *Selections from the Prison Notebooks*, p. 462. Lukács also criticized Bukharin in much the same terms in a review published in 1925 (English trans. 'Technology and Social Relations', in *New Left Review*, 1966) in which he argued that the dialectic can do without sociology as an independent science.
51. See Hughes, H. Stuart, *Consciousness and Society* (London: MacGibbon & Kee, 1958), especially chap. 2.
52. Benedetto Croce, *Historical Materialism and the Economics of Karl Marx*.
53. In his preface to Merlino, Saverio, *Formes et essence du socialisme* (Paris, 1898).
54. The Institute was created in 1923, as the outcome of a 'Marxist Work Week', held in 1922, at which one of the principal subjects of discussion was the conception of Marxism expounded in Korsch's forthcoming book *Marxism and Philosophy*. On the history of the Frankfurt Institute, see the very comprehensive study by Martin Jay, *The Dialectical Imagination* (Boston: Little, Brown, 1973).
55. Marcuse, Herbert, *Reason and Revolution: Hegel and the Rise of Social Theory* (New York: Oxford University Press, 1941) p. 343.
56. This view was expressed particularly by Horkheimer, in a series of articles published in the mid–1930s and reprinted in *Kritische Theorie* (2 vols. 1968).
57. Korsch, *Karl Marx*. The quotations are translated from the revised German edition of the book (1967) pp. 145, 203.
58. See, in particular, Mannheim, Karl, *Ideology and Utopia* (1929; English trans., New York: Harcourt, Brace, 1936).
59. See notes 3 and 7 above.
60. Durkheim, Emile, *Socialism* (New York: The Antioch Press, 1958).
61. See the discussions in Horowitz, David, (ed.), *Marx and Modern Economics* (1968).
62. Firth, Raymond, 'The Sceptical Anthropologist? Social Anthropology and Marxist Views on Society', in *Proceedings of the British Academy*,

LVIII (London: Oxford University Press, 1972).

63. See p. 46 above.

64. See especially Althusser, Louis, and Balibar, Étienne, *Reading Capital* (London: New Left Books, 1970).

65. In particular, the work of C. Lévi–Strauss. See his *Structural Anthropology* (London: Allen Lane, 1968), the short study of his ideas by Leach, Edmund, *Lévi–Strauss* (London: Fontana/Collins, 1970), and for a more general view, Robey, David, (ed.), *Structuralism: An Introduction* (Oxford: Oxford University Press, 1973).

66. With what success is a matter of dispute. My own judgement is that Althusser fails completely to establish two of the main points of his argument—namely, the existence of a total 'epistemological break' between the 'young Marx' and the 'mature Marx', and the precise criterion for distinguishing between science and ideology—and that his general discussion of problems in the philosophy of science is obscure, muddled and unfruitful. See the criticisms along these lines of Leszek Kolakowski, 'Althusser's Marx', in *The Socialist Register* (1971). pp. 111–28.

67. Althusser and Balibar, *Reading Capital*, p. 65.

68. Godelier, Maurice, *Rationality and Irrationality in Economics* (London: New Left Books, 1974) and *Perspectives in Marxist Anthropology* (Cambridge University Press, 1977). Although much of Godelier's work is in the field of social anthropology as traditionally conceived, his methodological writings and many of his substantive analyses belong equally to the domain of sociological thought.

69. See especially the introduction and his first essay, 'Anthropology and Economics'.

70. Godelier, *Perspectives in Marxist Anthropology*, p. 24. 'A mode of production is a reality which "does not reveal itself" directly in any spontaneous and intimate experience of those agents who reproduce it by their activity ('indigenous' practices and representations), nor in any enquiries in the field or the knowledgeable external observations of professional anthropologists. A mode of production is a reality which requires to be reconstructed, to be reproduced in thought, in the very process of scientific knowledge. A reality exists as 'scientific fact' only when it is reconstructed within the field of scientific theory and its corresponding application.'

71. Ibid., p. 4.

72. Ibid., p.6.

73. Poulantzas, Nicos, *Political Power and Social Classes* (London: New Left Books, 1973) and *Classes in Contemporary Capitalism* (London: New Left Books, 1975).

74. Hindess, Barry and Hirst, Paul Q., *Pre–Capitalist Modes of Production* (London: Routledge & Kegan Paul, 1975) and *Mode of Production and Social Formation* (London: Macmillan, 1977).

75. In the concluding section of *Pre–Capitalist Modes of Production*, p. 321, Hindess and Hirst write: 'It is not supposed that more developed modes (in our sense of the term) succeed less developed ones, or that there are *any* necessary relations of succession between modes of production . . . The concepts of the modes of production developed here do not form a history in thought, mirroring in their succession the evolution of the real . . . We

72   *Sociology and Socialism*

reject the notion of history as a coherent and worthwhile object of study.'
76. See especially Bourdieu, Pierre and Passeron, Jean–Claude, *Reproduction* (London: Sage Publications, 1977).
77. See, for example, Kolakowski's comment in 'Althusser's Marx' that 'the whole theory of "overdetermination" is nothing but a repetition of traditional banalities which remain exactly on the same level of vagueness as before.'
78. See especially Godelier's *Perspectives in Marxist Anthropology*, part IV.
79. Habermas, Jürgen, *Legitimation Crisis* (London: Heinemann, 1976).
80. Offe, Claus, 'Political Authority and Class Structures: An Analysis of Late Capitalist Societies', *International Journal of Sociology*, II:1 (1972) pp. 73–105; and *Industry and Inequality* (London: Edward Arnold, 1976).
81. Offe, 'Political Authority and Class Structures'.
82. Wellmer, Albrecht, *Critical Theory of Society* (New York: Herder & Herder, 1971).
83. Wellmer, *Critical Theory of Society*, pp. 121–2.
84. See the discussion in Outhwaite, William, *Understanding Social Life* (London: George Allen & Unwin, 1975), particularly chap. 5, where the relation between Marxism and the 'interpretative' tradition in the social sciences is examined.
85. Especially *Zur Logik der Sozialwissenschaften* (Frankfurt: Suhrkamp Verlag, 1967) and *Knowledge and Human Interests* (London: Heinemann, 1972).
86. Sartre, Jean-Paul, *Critique of Dialectical Reason* (1975), and *Search for a Method* (New York: Alfred A. Knopf, 1963). Originally published together as *Critique de la raison dialectique* (Paris: Gallimard, 1960).
87. Habermas, Jürgen, 'Science and Technology as Ideology', in *Toward a Rational Society* (Boston: Beacon Press, 1970); and *Legitimation Crisis*.
88. Herbert Marcuse, *One–Dimensional Man* (London: Routledge & Kegan Paul, 1964).
89. For a critical discussion of this question, see Brian Fay, *Social Theory and Political Practice* (London: George Allen & Unwin, 1975), pp. 83–91 and chap. 5.
90. Marcuse, *One–Dimensional Man*, chap. 8.
91. On this point, see further the discussion in Bottomore and Nisbet (eds.), *A History of Sociological Analysis*, chap. 7.
92. Lichtheim, George, *From Marx to Hegel and Other Essays* (London: Orbach & Chambers, 1971), p. 14.
93. Some characteristics of that period are examined in Hughes, *Consciousness and Society*.
94. Anderson, Perry, *Passages from Antiquity to Feudalism* (London: New Left Books, 1974) and *Lineages of the Absolutist State*.
95. Baran, Paul, *The Political Economy of Growth* (New York: Monthly Review Press, 1962); A. Gunder Frank, *Capitalism and Underdevelopment in Latin America* (New York: Monthly Review Press, 1969).
96. Among others, Cardoso, F. and Sunkel, O. For a general account, see Dos Santos, T. 'The Crisis of Development Theory and the Problem of Dependence in Latin America', in H. Bernstein, (ed.), *Underdevelopment*

and Development (Harmondsworth: Penguin 1973), pp. 57–80. The concept of 'dependency', although it originated in Latin America, can obviously be applied elsewhere, and its value in the analysis of problems in the development of Middle Eastern countries is examined in Turner, Bryan, *Marxism and the End of Orientalism.* (London: Allen & Unwin, 1978). See also Colin Leys, *Underdevelopment in Kenya* (London: Heinemann, 1975).

97. For a general view, see Rhodes, R., (ed.), *Imperialism and Underdevelopment* (New York: Monthly Review Press, 1970).

98. For a short account of the 'postcolonial mode of production', see Turner, op. cit.

4 Structure and History

In the mid–1960s I happened to be reading a book by Dwight Macdonald, somewhat curiously entitled *Memoirs of a Revolutionist*, and I was struck particularly by a passage in which he recollected his youthful political activities in the following terms (1957; p. 4.):

> I remember once walking in the street and suddenly really *seeing* the big heavy buildings in their obstinate actuality and realizing I simply couldn't imagine all this recalcitrant matter transformed by socialism. How would the street *look* when the workers took it over, how would, how could revolution transfigure the miles and miles of stubborn stone?

This perhaps expresses the feelings of many radicals, especially in periods of reaction, when they confront the massive apparatus of regulation and repression embodied in an existing form of society. At the same time it portrays in a dramatic way one important aspect of the opposition between structure and history—and between structural and historical modes of studying social life—namely, the contrast that can be drawn between society conceived as a fixed, stable and persisting structure, and society conceived as a process in which there is continual breakdown and renewal, development and decline, the disappearance of old forms and the creation of new ones.

But of course this image conveys a very simplified and partly misleading notion. Though men have talked about 'eternal empires', a 'thousand year Reich', or even 'stable democracies', it seems to be the case that social structures are far from possessing the rock–like solidity and indestructability that some writers have attributed to them. Just at the time when I was reading Macdonald's book we were in the midst of a great wave of radical movements which, for a few years at least, made more apparent the fragility of social structures, and in two instances—the mini–revolution in France and the humanist–socialist movement in Czechoslovakia—seemed to be on the verge of accomplishing profound changes in society. And in a broader perspective the whole of the twentieth century thus far can be seen as a particularly agitated historical period, in which wars, revolutions and counter-revolutions have created and destroyed, and are still creating and destroying, many different types of social structure.

Yet we should not go to the other extreme and regard social life as a ceaseless, formless flux of events. As sociologists we want to say that every distinct society has a particular relational structure, that it exhibits a certain order, a specific interconnectedness of the diverse elements or spheres of social life; and most of us would want to claim further that beyond or behind the unique structures of particular societies there are more general structural 'types'—that there are 'tribal', 'feudal', 'capitalist', 'socialist', 'industrial', and perhaps even 'post–industrial' forms of society. The real problem is to formulate a conception of social structure which does justice to these elements of regularity and order in social life, while not neglecting the flow of historical action by individuals and social groups which sustains, recreates, revises or disrupts this order.

A useful starting–point for such a formulation is to be found in the work, now somewhat neglected, that was done by the French sociologist Georges Gurvitch.[1] According to his view social structure is a 'permanent process', a 'perpetual movement of destructuration and restructuration'. This notion has the advantage that it gets us away from the idea of an abstract impersonal social structure which is fixed and given once for all, and makes a place for that aspect of social life which has been strongly emphasized in recent phenomenological sociology, namely, the production and reproduction of society by real human beings living and thinking in a particular milieu. Gurvitch recognized this feature explicitly when he observed, in the course of his analysis, that 'social structures are at the same time the producers and the products of cultural activities [*des oeuvres culturelles*].

But this conception of social structure as the outcome, at any given time and place, of processes of destrucuration and restructuration still leaves open a number of questions which need to be explored further. First, we can ask: What is the source of these processes themselves? Here Gurvitch offered indications of an answer by distinguishing social structure as only *one aspect* of a 'total social phenomenon', which also comprises other levels and forms of human sociability. This idea is summed up in the comprehensive definition of social structure which he provided at the end of his discussion, and which I shall quote at some length since it is not available in English:

Every social structure is a precarious equilibrium (which has to be constantly recreated by ever–renewed effort) between a multiplicity of hierarchies incorporated in a total social phenomenon . . . of which it provides only an approximate representation. It is an equilibrium between the specific hierarchies of the various levels of social life, of the manifestations of sociability, of social regulation, of different social times, of mental orientations, of the modes of division of labour and accumulation, and in some circumstances of functional groups, and of social classes and their organizations. This equilibrium is reinforced and consolidated by the models, signs, symbols, habitual social roles, values and ideas—in short, by the works of civilization—which are proper to each social structure (Gurvitch, 1962, p. 214).

This account allows for the influence of a variety of factors in the processes of destructuration and restructuration, and it may be useful at this point to consider some examples in order to illustrate this kind of historical movement. One obvious source of variation in the social structure is the continual circulation of the membership of a society. Older members die, and new members are born into it. Other changes in its composition may occur as a result of migration, conquest or other circumstances. It is difficult to conceive that such circulation leaves the social structure entirely untouched, for it seems doubtful, even in the light of our ordinary experience, that incoming members are ever socialized so thoroughly that they precisely re–enact the social life of their predecessors. A more plausible view is that which Karl Mannheim (1956) suggested in his essay on generations, when he wrote that belonging to the same generation or age–group endows the individuals concerned 'with a common location in the social and historical process', limits them 'to a specific range of potential experience, predisposing them for a certain characteristic mode of thought and experience, and a characteristic type of historically relevant action.' Mannheim thought that cultural creation in particular depended to a large extent upon this flow of new individuals who make a fresh contact with the accumulated heritage, which 'always means a changed relationship of distance from the object and a novel approach in assimilating, using, and developing the proffered material'. In this case, then, by the elaboration of new ideas and values, younger generations clearly play a part in the destructuring and restructuring of society; but they may also do so in other, related, ways, by interpreting roles differently and thus eventually bringing about a new organization of roles, by forming new groups which engage in different types of action, and so on. These consequences of the succession of generations have not been very fully studied as yet,[2] but their importance is evident.

Another historical process which may profoundly affect social structure is the growth (or for that matter, though it is a less familiar phenomenon, the decline) of knowledge. This is associated to some extent, as I have indicated, with the succession of generations, but it can also be treated as a partly independent process. Its consequences may be seen in the emergence of new social groups with new values and interests, in the refashioning of some institutions (for example, educational institutions), and in the decay of others (as is suggested by the decline of religion in relation to the progress of science). A good deal of recent sociology has been much concerned with the effects of knowledge upon social structure; on one side, for instance, Daniel Bell has argued that the growing importance of theoretical knowledge is bringing into existence a new form of society which he calls 'post–industrial', while from an entirely different perspective Habermas and Wellmer, elaborating one of the distinctive ideas of the Frankfurt School, assert that the pre–eminence in present–day culture of scientific and technological thought (or 'instrumental reason') is the principal factor which maintains a system of domination and obstructs human liberation. But this recognition of the independent significance of knowledge is to be found, of course, in much earlier sociological writing; it is tantalizingly present, for example, in parts of Marx's discussion in the *Grundrisse*, where the transition from a capitalist to a socialist society is occasionally, and rather vaguely, related to what Marx describes as the progress of the general intellect.

I would like to turn, finally, to a third example of a historical process that has important consequences for the social structure; namely, the development of the division of labour, and more broadly, of social differentiation. This process, which is associated with the growth of knowledge and with the increasing size and density of a society, including the growth of urban centres, produces a variety of effects. On one side, as Pirenne (1914) noted in his study of the social history of capitalism, it brings into existence new social groups which at different stages take a leading role in the economy, develop economic activity in new directions, and initiate modifications of the social structure. In a Marxist view of this process the various groups are seen as sections of a class which eventually establishes its dominance over the whole society and creates its own distinctive structure. On the other side, increasing social differentiation may be regarded as producing a much greater cultural diversity, a greater range of intersecting social circles, as Simmel (1950, pp. 409–24) suggested in his account of the metropolis and mental life; or it may be seen, in a related way (by Durkheim, for instance), as fostering a much greater, and perhaps excessive, individualism. In either case, the process of differentiation as a cultural phenomenon is likely to have an impact upon the social structure, modifying the ideas and values which sustain it, engendering new mental orientations, provoking redefinitions of established roles, and creating new interests.

These examples will have shown, I hope, that the idea of social structure as a changing reality produced by processes of destructuration and restructuration, which themselves may arise from non–structural sources in the totality of social life, can be fruitful in the analysis of actual social situations or courses of events. Nevertheless, some major theoretical problems remain. The process of destruction and recreation of social structure, as Gurvitch depicted it, is a continuous one; and this conception takes little account, and provides no analysis, of those breaks in historical continuity, in periods of social revolution, when there is a more comprehensive, fundamental, and abrupt transition from one form of society to another. Clearly we need to distinguish here between partial and total change, between a process of gradual modification and adjustment and a process of rapid transformation. How are we to make this distinction, and in what way can we relate one process to the other? First, it needs to be said that the distinction is not absolutely clear cut. A major historical movement to a new social structure and form of society is not something that occurs overnight, and in this sense it is perhaps more reasonable to speak of an 'age of revolution' rather than a revolution, and to recognize that the processes of gradual and rapid change may be closely interwoven and often difficult to disentangle. But this line of argument should not be carried so far as to obliterate the distinction altogether; most of us would want to recognize, in our different ways, the existence of distinct types of society—feudal/capitalist/socialist or non–industrial/industrial—and of determinate historical periods in which the transition from one to another took place.

Accepting such a position, what can we then say about the causes of, or reasons for, such major upheavals in social life in relation to the process of building up and breaking down a social structure that goes on all the time? One obvious answer would be to say that the accumulation of small and gradual modifications eventually reaches a critical point at which a fundamental change in the social order becomes unavoidable—and here we might think of the growth of towns, the geographical discoveries and the expansion of trade, the development of artisan and commercial groups within the European feudal societies, which brought into existence an alternative form of society (as Marx would say, in the womb of the old society); or again, we could think of the extension of factory production and the growth of the labour movement in nineteenth–century capitalist society, which gave rise to a new confrontation between capitalism and socialism as alternative societies. In both these cases the changes in the composition and distribution of the population, in the division of labour, in social roles, and so on were accompanied by cultural changes, the development of the natural sciences and their applications, the formulations of new social doctrines, and revisions of legal, moral, religious and artistic conceptions; and we could, therefore, regard these historical processes as resulting from what J.S. Mill called the 'intermixture of laws' or, as I would express it, from the intersection of separate and distinct quasi–causal chains and the accumulation of their effects during certain periods in the history of a society, which produce a dominant tendency toward a major change in the social structure.

But the examples I have given also permit another account of such major social changes. It may be argued that there are certain elements in the totality of social life which have a crucial importance in determining the general form of a society at any time and the occurrence of a transition from one form to another. Marxism obviously makes a claim of this kind, by attributing the main characteristics of a specific type of society to the dominance of a particular class and explaining the major historical transitions by the rise of new classes and their successful struggles to establish themselves as ruling classes. Equally obviously, in spite of its frequently discussed weaknesses and difficulties, more especially in the interpretation of the development of modern capitalism, the Marxist theory has the immense merit of defining with some precision major historical forms of society and of providing, at least in principle, a genuinely explanatory account of the transitions between them. The general Marxist framework of explanation, in terms of the relations between classes and their connections on one side with the system of material production and on the other side with cultural production, can be used in various ways; and it does not, in my view, commit us to a single philosophy of history or to a rigid conception of the total historical process. One interesting variant of the Marxist approach is to be found, for instance, in Barrington Moore's *Social Origins of Dictatorship and Democracy* (1966), which gives a central importance to the analysis of class relations but is set within a theoretical scheme which identifies the historical transition that is being explored as 'modernization', as the passage from pre–industrial to industrial types of society, in democratic and nondemocratic forms, not as the sequence from feudalism via capitalism to socialism.

A second set of problems concerns the extent to which a major transition from one form of society to another might be explained as the consequence of stresses or 'contradictions' within a particular social structure itself. Here again the Marxist theory has provided the principal model, although it has proved difficult to give it a general application or to demonstrate in a precise way the necessary effects of the postulated contradictions. On the first of these points I shall only remark briefly that while there are frequent references in the Marxist literature to the 'contradictions of capitalism', there are few references to the 'contradictions of feudalism' (or of other types of society), and the whole notion of 'structural contradiction', in its most general form, does not seem to have been very fully worked out.

So far as capitalist society is concerned it has generally been recognized that Marx referred to two main contradictions: that between the capitalist class and the working class and that between the productive forces (i.e. the development of the output of goods or use–values, influenced by technological progress and by the division and coordination of labour) and the relations of production (i.e. the market economy and exchange). The first of these should not perhaps be regarded as a structural contradiction at all since it involves rather the opposition and conflict between actual individuals and social groups (and obviously has analogues in other forms of society), though it is evidently related to structural characteristics of ownership, political authority, and so on.

On the other hand, the second contradiction is *structural* and might be conceived as producing, through its own development, a major change in the form of society. This is the line of argument advanced, for example, by Maurice Godelier (1967) in an essay on 'System, Structure and Contradiction in *Capital*', who suggests, first, that Marx saw this contradiction as manifesting itself in the form of periodic economic crises and, second, that it makes necessary the appearance of a socialist economic system:

the *structure* of socialist relations of production *corresponds* functionally with the conditions of rapid development of the new, gigantic, more and more socialized productive forces created by capitalism . . . This correspondence is totally *independent* of any a priori idea of happiness, of 'true liberty', of the essence of man, etc. Marx demonstrates the necessity and superiority of a new mode of production. . . . This value judgement is not a judgement of 'people', it does not demonstrate any progress in 'morality', any victory of 'ethical principles' in socialist society as against capitalist society. It is a judgement of the 'properties' of a structure.

But this argument involves considering, in the first place, Marx's theory of crisis, which is far from being unambiguously expounded or interpreted. It is not at all clear that Marx thought the periodic crises, even worsening crises, would actually bring about the 'break–down' of capitalism; on the contrary he seems to have regarded crises as enabling capitalism to resume, temporarily, its development of the productive forces. The theory of 'capitalist breakdown' and the inevitability of socialism has been a subject of intense controversy within Marxism since the end of the nineteenth century, and it has become increasingly difficult to accept as plausible the more deterministic, economistic versions of the theory, such as Godelier adopts.

In any case, it seems to me more accurate, in a comprehensive reading of Marx's analysis of the historical transition from capitalism to socialism, to assign a very much greater importance to the development of classes and class conflict. An interpretation such as Godelier's, in terms of a process determined wholly by structural contradictions without any intervention of human consciousness, distorts radically the sense of Marx's thought on the possibility of socialism, in which the growth of class consciousness and of working–class organizations—that is to say, a succession of conscious, historic actions—has a crucial place. We might say, therefore, that in Marx's theory structural contradictions establish only the preconditions, or potentiality, for large–scale social change and that this will be realized only in so far as other, non–structural processes occur, in the development and organization of new social groups, the formulation of new interests and values, and a general transformation of culture and consciousness.

Thus, there is embodied in this theory a recognition of the distinction between structural elements and historical forces which corresponds closely with the view that I have been putting forward here. Indeed, I have devoted my attention chiefly to the Marxist theory because it is the main source of such a view and presents in the most systematic manner the range of problems and possible ways of analyzing them which arise from the interrelations between social structures and historical movements which together constitute the total social phenomenon. I am not claiming, however, that Marxism provides the only possible model. Certainly, there is a dearth of alternatives, and we often find ourselves confronted by revisions of Marx which do not offer a different and equally comprehensive paradigm, or else by models and approaches which emphasize only one aspect and deal exclusively either with structural relations and the logic of structures or with the seamless and shapeless web of everyday social life. But it remains possible that a structural analysis different from that of Marx could be made, and that it could be related in different ways to historical movements which themselves would be differently evaluated. Only it has still to be done.

So far in this paper I have discussed social structure in what is doubtless a very familiar and traditional way, without reference (except obliquely in talking about Godelier) to the recently fashionable 'structuralist' doctrines which have spread from structural linguistics into the field of anthropology, mainly through the work of Lévi–Strauss, and have even taken possession of a small portion of Marxist territory. One reason for not devoting too much attention to this approach is that it has not yet had any considerable impact upon, or made a significant contribution to, sociological thought and inquiry. Nevertheless, it does raise some general questions which deserve to be mentioned briefly.

The first of these is really a minor issue, though it has been inflated by some writers. The new structuralists sometimes claim that the object of their investigation is something 'hidden', a 'deep structure' which has to be discovered by inference and rational analysis and which is to be distinguished from the 'surface structure' or directly observable social relations with which, it is suggested, the earlier theorists of social structure were largely concerned. But this is a great exaggeration. Every serious scholar or scientist is concerned with much more than the immediately visible appearance of things and looks for some inner principle or system, to which the fleeting empirical phenomena can be related, or in terms of which they can be explained; he constructs models and hypotheses representing this hidden structure. In sociology from the outset, attempts have been made to construct theoretical models of the different types of society, in which the particular features of a given society are related as 'messages' to a 'code' which may be conceived as 'feudalism', 'capitalism', 'industrialism', 'bureaucratic rationality', and so on. The examples are numerous and inescapable, from Saint–Simon's analysis of the 'industrial regime' to Marx's analysis of capitalist production, Max Weber's ideal types, and the theoretical models of Durkheim and Pareto. What the new structuralists have done is simply to write more explicitly and fully (sometimes obsessively) about the construction of models, largely under the influence of a general movement towards a more developed and sophisticated philosophy of the social sciences.

But the idea of a 'deep structure' may also be interpreted in another sense, as referring to a basic or universal structure, and this raises more substantial issues. In the work of Lévi–Strauss the intention is to reveal the fundamental properties of all human societies and to relate these to fundamental characteristics of the human mind, thus establishing psychological universals which would presumably constitute the ground for all sociological explanations. This attempt poses a number of problems. In the first place, it has been objected (Leach, 1970, pp. 19–20, 97–8) that in the two spheres of social life to which Lévi–Strauss has applied his method—kinship and myth—there are serious discrepancies between his interpretation and the ethnographic evidence. This kind of objection cannot be met by simply dismissing 'mere empiricism', for the distinction between code and message requires at least that the messages are consistent in some way with the code and that the code produces specific, identifiable kinds of message.

A second objection is that this method of structural analysis has not been applied seriously to any societies beyond the tribal level, and in particular to modern societies; that it is difficult at present to see how it could be successfully applied to phenomena other than those of kinship and myth; and hence that its claim to reveal universal characteristics of human societies rests as yet upon very slight foundations. Finally, it can be objected that even if the method succeeded eventually in demonstrating the existence of some universal properties of human societies, this would still not answer the greater part of the questions which are of interest to the sociologist; for there is manifestly a great diversity of forms of society and historical changes from one form to another, and it is these phenomena above all that the sociological theorist attempts to explain.

It is clear, in any case, that a Marxist thinker cannot be a 'pure' structuralist in the manner of Lévi–Strauss, for the Marxist theory has as its starting–point the idea of historically distinct social structures; and the most obvious feature of its method is that it aims to locate all social phenomena in a specific historical context. Marx, it is true, recognized that there might be 'abstract characteristics common to all forms of society', including characteristics of the system of production, but he attached much greater importance to the specific historical forms that these characteristics assumed and to the actual sequence of such forms. A Marxist structuralism, then, would have a more limited character; it would be concerned with the basic structure of each particular type of society, not with universal structural properties. And it would be qualified, as I have already indicated, by making actual historical events and processes depend not simply upon the unfolding, unconscious logic of a structure but also upon the conscious value preferences, choices and decisions of men, both individually and collectively, in the given historical situations that confront them.

The principal contribution of recent structuralist doctrines has been, I think, to reassert the importance of structural analysis and of the development of structural models in the social sciences. Its influence upon sociology, as I have already suggested, has not yet been very marked, but it may well lead us in the future to pay greater attention to the definition and classification of types of society and to the elucidation of the processes of change from one type to another, as well as helping to introduce a greater rigour into such analyses; although we could well have learned these lessons elsewhere. The impact upon Marxism seems to have been rather stronger, especially in the criticism of that Hegelian form of Marxism which relies heavily upon philosophical insights into the historical process and presents its conclusions in sweeping interpretations that largely ignore both structural relationships and the detail of historical events. Here the influence of structuralism may be to encourage Marxist social scientists to analyze in a more precise and thorough way the general structure of capitalist societies, and also of socialist or collectivist forms of society, in the late twentieth century; and to investigate more closely than they have yet done some of those partial structures—for example, the class structure or the political system—which exist within the global structure of a given society.

But if the influence of recent structuralism may be salutary in certain respects, its more extreme versions, especially those in which it is presented as a doctrine about reality rather than a method, do not seem likely to advance sociology along fruitful paths. The idea of a 'deep structure' may be developed into a conception of a 'basic', 'fundamental', or 'ultimate' structure, which would be quite misleading in its implication that there is some timeless, unalterable, constraining arrangement of social relations, perhaps psychologically or biologically grounded, which renders all historical inventiveness, experiment, innovation or retrogression irrelevant to the understanding of social life. In the first place, this view suggests a very sweeping claim to have discovered one, and only one, fundamental structure; and it ignores the point made by Piaget (1970) that advances in scientific understanding have often been made by negating a particular structural model. In any structural analysis we should remain aware of the possibility of other models, recognize the partly arbitrary character of each particular model (along the lines indicated by Max Weber's discussion of the 'ideal–type') and experiment with different models. Second, the more extreme structuralist view fails to consider one important feature, namely, the creation and destruction of structures, that I discussed earlier. Piaget also makes this point, though only from one aspect, when he refers to the need to take into account 'genetic construction' in the analysis of biological, psychological, and social phenomena. The models that we build can scarcely be adequate if this genetic or historical aspect is excluded.

But is it, then, simply a matter of saying that a structuralist method needs to be complemented by other methods—by historical inquiry, by the study of functions, and so on? Up to a point, this may be acceptable. There is a contrast between structural analysis and historical analysis, in their methods and in their formulation of problems; and they may well complement each other, without becoming merged in some more comprehensive approach. Nevertheless, I am reluctant to agree with those who argue, in the intellectual confusion of the present time, that each and every approach has some value in its own sphere and that we should simply accept their diverse results as parts of the vast unwieldy sum of sociological knowledge. Something more than this is needed: at the least, a more systematic conception of the relation between different methods and, if possible, a better integrated array of methods.

Marx's theory of society I regard as having been a sociological crystallization out of the philosophy of history, in which the analysis of social structure and the interpretation of broad historical movements went hand in hand (as the chapters of *Capital* themselves illustrate so strikingly). We cannot begin again today from Hegel's philosophy of history, any more than we can accept as a basis for our studies all of Marx's propositions about the character of modern societies and the main trends of their development; but I am inclined to think—and many of the new directions in sociological thought tend to support this view—that the working out of an acceptable general theory in sociology may depend more than anything else upon the formulation of a new theory of history. And this might well be an updated, more flexible version of the 'economic interpretation of history'.

NOTES

1. See especially the discussion in Part II, chap. IV, of his *Traité de sociologie* (1962).
2. Although they may be referred to in particular cases; for example, in *The Structure of Scientific Revolutions*, Kuhn (1962) notes that a paradigm change in a particular field of science may depend upon the disappearance of an older generation of scientists who are totally committed to the established paradigm.

5 Is There a Totalitarian View of Human Nature?

The word 'totalitarian' was first employed in the 1920s to describe the fascist regime in Italy.[1] Later, its use was extended to refer to National Socialism in Germany and to Soviet communism. But it was only in the 1950s, during the cold war period, that the term became firmly established in the vocabularies of political science and journalism, and it was then very widely and loosely applied in the description of social movements, parties, leaders and doctrines, as well as political systems.[2]

Nevertheless, the central idea remained that the expression 'totalitarian' characterized a specific type of political system, although this system might be regarded as depending upon the existence of a number of distinctive social factors. One of the best-known definitions, that of Carl Friedrich, runs as follows in its most recent formulation:

The features which distinguish [totalitarian] regimes from other and older autocracies, as well as from heterocracies,[3] are six in number. They are . . . (1) a totalist ideology; (2) a single party committed to this ideology and usually led by one man, the dictator; (3) a fully-developed secret police; and three kinds of monopoly or, more precisely, monopolistic control: namely that of (a) mass communications; (b) operational weapons; (c) all organizations, including economic ones, thus involving a centrally-planned economy.[4]

There are, however, many other definitions which display a considerable diversity;[5] they range from Hannah Arendt's characterization of 'total terror' as the essence of totalitarianism,[6] to those which emphasize the coordination of social activities in pursuit of a single goal,[7] or the aim of effecting a 'total social revolution'.[8]

In spite of this diversity there are some common themes, and there seems to be a tendency in recent writing to delimit the concept of totalitarianism by insisting upon the fact that it was developed in relation to three specific political systems which appeared only in the twentieth century. Following this line of thought the continued usefulness of the term may be questioned, since two of these political systems—Italian fascism and German National Socialism—have ceased to exist after fairly brief lives, while the third—Soviet communism— has changed considerably since the death of Stalin.[9] Even the term 'mass society', which some writers connected with totalitarianism,[10] is now less widely used, although the same idea has been expressed in other forms,[11] and it will be necessary to consider it again in relation to possible totalitarian conceptions of human nature. With the moderation of cold war attitudes in the later 1960s there went also a greater readiness, on the part of western political scientists, to distinguish between Nazi and fascist totalitarianism on one side and the totalitarianism of the Soviet Union on the other, the former being seen as inherent in the regime, the latter as a temporary phenomenon created mainly by Stalin's personal dictatorship.[12]

THE MARXIST CONCEPTION OF HUMAN NATURE

It will be apparent from the foregoing account that the term 'totalitarian' has been used essentially to describe a political system; and those who have discussed this phenomenon have not usually claimed that it involves a distinctive social theory, which might include a particular conception of human nature. In the Nazi and fascist regimes, it is difficult to discern any coherent doctrine at all, and as one commentator has put it: 'The Nazi regime, like the Italian, was little more than a preparation for war.'[13] But the situation is different with Soviet communism, and with communist regimes generally, since in these cases a systematic ideology, derived from Marxism, has an important role in shaping, or at least sanctioning, social aims and policies. Here, therefore, it might appear that a definite conception of human nature, and of ways of changing it, would be a significant feature of the regime as a whole. This aspect was emphasized by Brzezinski when he defined the purpose of totalitarianism as that of 'effecting a total social revolution, including the condition of man'.[14]

Such a view, however, presents many difficulties. In the first place, the political movements inspired by Marxism have given rise, in different social and political conditions, to quite diverse forms of communist society—for example, at different periods in the Soviet Union, in China and in Yugoslavia—and it is by no means evident that anyone would want to describe all these types of society as totalitarian.

More fundamental, though connected with the previous point, is the fact that the Marxist conception of human nature can be interpreted in a variety of ways, and may therefore contribute to articulating very different ideologies and political practices. On one side are those interpretations which discover in Marx's works a doctrine of emancipation, in which human reason is assigned a prominent place and a new stage of social development is envisaged in which men will succeed in establishing a rational control over nature and over their own social life—in other words, begin self–consciously to 'make their own history'. On the other side are the interpretations which emphasize the more or less total determination of human nature, in every historical period, by the existing form of society, and especially by the system of production; and which conceive historical development as the inexorable working out of social laws.

Both these interpretations can be supported, in some measure, from Marx's works. The first of them can draw upon the discussion of man as a 'species–being' in the *Economic and Philosophical Manuscripts*, but also upon many other references to 'human nature' in *Capital* and elsewhere.[15] The second can base itself upon several formulations of 'historical materialism'; for example, in the well–known preface to *A Contribution to the Critique of Political Economy*, or in Marx's approving citation of a Russian reviewer in the preface to the second German edition of *Capital*:

Marx regards the social movement as a natural sequence of historical phenomena, governed by laws which are not only independent of the will, the consciousness, and the purposes of men, but on the contrary, determine their volition, consciousness, and purposes.

The possibility of these two lines of interpretation is given by the unresolved opposition, within Marx's own conception of a *critical science*, between historical necessity and human liberty, between the elaboration of a science of society and the formulation of a revolutionary project, the end of alienation.[16] The actual occurrence of one or other kind of interpretation seems to depend very largely upon social and political conditions. In periods of rapid change, when the opportunity to break out from existing constraints appears, the doctrine of emancipation tends to be stressed—as in the debates which took place in Czechoslovakia between 1966 and 1968. The ideas of that time are well expressed in the work of Radovan Richta and his colleagues, *Civilization at the Crossroads.*[17] Richta notes, in particular, the contrast between a socialist society which is still engaged in an early phase of industrialization, in which the needs of individuals are subordinated to the demands of production and a socialist society (as yet only conceivable) based upon advanced science and technology, in which 'a sphere of consumption (education, knowledge, culture) is created which corresponds with the needs of the individual for self–development . . . ', and there emerges a 'pioneer of the new life' who is

responsible, self–reliant, liberated from the conventional wisdom, critical in his outlook, capable of deciding what is right, and with the courage to call things by their names—for a prejudice is a prejudice even if it is collective, and backwardness is backwardness even if it is displayed by a high official.[18]

On the other hand, the 'laws of social development' are likely to be more strongly asserted in periods of relative immobility, or, as in the Soviet Union during Stalin's rule, in a period of consolidation of a post–revolutionary regime which had to justify its actions in circumstances which had little to do with the construction of socialism. In this last case, however, the Marxist theory degenerated into a flexible ideology from which, in Kolakowski's words, 'the backbone of reason has been eliminated'. According to the scientific slogans, a new culture, a new human nature, the 'new Soviet man', should have developed by themselves as a consequence of the revolutionary transformation of the social system; but at the same time it was declared essential to *impose* the new culture and new human nature, and the ruling élite (aided by the secret police and the executioner) had to become, in Zhdanov's gruesome phrase, 'engineers of the human soul'.

SOCIETY AND THE INDIVIDUAL

The experience of Stalinism, along with that of National Socialism and fascism, shows that the three regimes which provide the main examples of totalitarianism, far from having a conception of human nature as infinitely malleable and easily adapted to the needs of the regime, were forced, by the resistance to the implementation of their policies, into intensive efforts to mould this recalcitrant human nature through propaganda, indoctrination, censorship, and other more violent means. In fact, the totalitarian regimes resembled other social systems in this respect, however different their means; as Herbert J. Spiro has remarked,[19] the goal of remaking mankind in the image of the totalitarian system is one of their least distinctive features, since other societies may well pursue similar aims. What is important in such efforts to form a particular type of human personality or character within the society, and sometimes over a much larger area in periods of imperial expansion,[20] is not that they rest upon a theory of the malleability of human nature, but that they are undertaken as a political necessity by the rulers of society, encounter very often a strong resistance, and are never wholly or permanently successful.

It is not the case, then, that totalitarian regimes somehow embody a distinctive totalitarian view of human nature. But is there such a totalitarian view at all? Let us consider, first, what it would involve. It would have to assert that the human nature—the ensemble of needs, sentiments, aspirations and so on—which can be observed in a particular collectivity at a particular time is *wholly* the product of social factors, and that changes in human nature, likewise, are the outcome of changing social conditions (the development of the economy, political upheavals, cultural transformations, etc.). This conception excludes two other ideas: first, that human nature is determined largely by biological factors; and second, that human nature is the product of the free activity of autonomous beings—the work of reason upon original nature, the outcome of choices and decisions.

I noted earlier that Marx, in some contexts, criticized the idea of the autonomous individual,[21] and occasionally went to the extreme of representing human nature as *merely* the manifestation in the individual of the social relations, or social institutions, of the age.[22] Max Adler, indeed, argued later that it was Marx's concept of man as a social being, or 'socialized humanity', which provided the basis for a general social science.[23] But it was not only Marx and the Marxists who formulated this idea; the development of the social sciences, and particularly of sociology, in the late nineteenth century occurred to a large extent in opposition to the 'abstract individualism' of previous social thought (the social contract theories, the rationalism of the Enlightenment, Utilitarianism).[24] It was in the work of Emile Durkheim that the predominance of the social over the individual was most strongly asserted, in those contexts where he emphasized the influence of education (as part of a more general process of 'socialization') not simply in forming, but in constituting, individuals with specific ways of 'seeing, feeling and acting'. But Durkheim's conception of the relation between individual and society was ambiguous. In part, he was making a methodological point, asserting the need to study 'social facts' as a distinct order of reality, and thus defining the sphere of inquiry of sociology. When he dealt with the substantive issue, he was inclined, for the most part, to assign a superior value to society as the source of rational and moral behaviour, and to devalue the individual as a merely organic being, driven by sensual, irrational passions. At the same time, however, he valued quite highly the autonomy, or individualism, of modern European man, while arguing that this was itself a social product and could be regarded as the potential source of a new moral unity.[25] Durkheim did not really confront the issue as to whether this newly autonomous individual, regardless of how he had developed, might stand in a different relation to the constraining power of society.

In any case, Durkheim's notion of the pre–eminence of society was far from being accepted universally as one of the fundamental ideas of sociology. Elsewhere, and particularly in Germany, the criticism of 'abstract individualism' took the form of propounding a reciprocal relation between the individual and society. This conception was well expressed by Simmel:

> The individual is contained in sociation and, at the same time, finds himself confronted by it. He is both a link in the organism of sociation and an autonomous organic whole; he exists both for society and for himself . . . His existence, if we analyze its contents, is not only partly social and partly individual, but also belongs to the fundamental, decisive, and irreducible category of a unity which we cannot designate other than as the synthesis or simultaneity of two logically contradictory characterizations of man—the characterization which is based on his function as a member, as a product and content of society; and the opposing characterization which is based on his functions as an autonomous being, and which views his life from its own center and for its own sake.[26]

A similar conception seems to prevail in Max Weber's thought, though it is formulated here principally in methodological terms, in the contrast—and the search for a relation—between the causal explanation of social phenomena and the interpretation of such phenomena from the standpoint of the individual's purposive actions.

In recent sociology, partly under the influence of phenomenological ideas, there has been a growing emphasis upon the autonomy and primacy of the individual; it is the individual who is seen as constructing society, rather than society as constructing the individual. There has been a related development in Marxist thought, again influenced by phenomenology, through existentialism; Sartre reproaches Soviet Marxism with having 'completely lost the sense of what it is to be a man', and seeks to reintroduce into the understanding of historical movements the actions, or 'projects', of individual men.[27]

At the same time, however, one minor current of thought within the social sciences—behaviourism—continues to affirm very strongly the *social conditioning* of man; and the behaviourist doctrine has recently been expounded in an extreme and provocative form by B.F. Skinner.[28] This is not the place for an extensive criticism of Skinner, which would require a more general examination of the behaviourist enterprise, and I shall confine my attention to a few salient points. The first thing to notice is that Skinner only *proclaims* the 'scientificity' of his theoretical scheme; nowhere in the book does he formulate any specific, testable propositions about human behaviour. In this sense, there is nothing to argue about; for he is not asserting anything precise which someone else might deny, and on which evidence might be sought.[29]

Nevertheless, there are aspects of his general prescription for a possible future science which are open to question. One of these is the idea of 'designing a culture', which contains several notions that appear to be incompatible with the tenets of Skinner's behaviourism. The very conception of 'designing' a culture seems to involve the kind of 'mentalism' against which Skinner fulminates, for what is the designer of a culture doing except thinking about alternatives, making choices, exercising his reason? It is important to note, further, that it is not simply any kind of culture that is to be designed; what the designer has to ensure, according to Skinner, is the survival of 'our'—North American—culture. But this is a value choice; many people would not place such a high value upon the survival of this particular cultural form, and some indeed are intent upon replacing it by a different culture. The representation of survival as the highest value is either an arbitrary assertion of preference or else a moral judgement open to rational argument; in either case I do not see how the formulation of such a value can be translated adequately into Skinner's behaviourist vocabulary.

But the most curious aspect of Skinner's doctrine is revealed when one asks the question how the book itself should be read. If we say that the reader should be concerned with the validity of its arguments and the truth of its propositions about the world (so far as it contains any), this introduces 'mentalist' notions—the exercise of reason, the intelligent activity which we call scientific inquiry—against which the thesis of the book is directed. The message of the book cannot be true or false; it merely has, as a (new) part of the environment, reinforcing or aversive consequences. In my own case, I am inclined to say that the consequences are highly aversive; but I am not altogether sure that I have understood what the behaviour is that the book is supposed to be reinforcing or inhibiting.

INDIVIDUALISM—THE UNCERTAIN FUTURE

Skinner's book illustrates very well a general point which emerges from the preceding discussion. There may be totalitarian views (that is, more or less speculative beliefs and reflections) about human nature, but there is not a *theory* of human nature which provides a systematic and genuinely explanatory account of the three elements in human behaviour: man's biological constitution; his nature as a self–conscious, language–using, project–forming, reasoning being; and his existence as a member of society and a participant in culture. Of the attempts that have been made so far to construct a theory, those which involve some kind of reductionism (explanations in terms of biological factors alone, or in terms of social and cultural determinants alone) seem to be the least plausible and least enlightening. What is more in accord with our experience, and with commonsense interpretations of experience, is the approach exemplified by some of the thinkers discussed earlier, which tries to elucidate and comprehend the interaction between the various elements of human behaviour—between biological inheritance and reflective action, between the autonomous, self–creating individual and the context established by social institutions and cultural norms.

In this framework of thought the problem is not that of deciding between rival conceptual schemes, asserting on one side the reality of completely autonomous individuals and on the other side the total determination of the individual by his social and cultural environment; but rather that of describing and analyzing the relationship between individual and society in definite social and historical conditions. As we saw earlier, Durkheim thought that the growth of individualism in modern society was itself an outcome of social changes; and

other nineteenth–century sociologists gave similar interpretations. Thus Simmel[30] related individualism to the development of a money economy; his analysis is in large part an
expansion, though from a different perspective, of Marx's
discussion of money as a social bond. Marx himself had
already noted the connection between the capitalist economy
and individualism.[31]

In the course of the twentieth century, however, many
sociologists have lost this conviction of the association
between the development of modern society and the growth
of individual autonomy, and they have come closer to Max
Weber's more pessimistic vision (already expressed in a qualified way by Simmel) of a society in which men are reduced to
the condition of cogs in a machine. The failure of western
societies to make the leap into socialism which Marx envisaged, and to end their dependence on *things*; the development of socialist societies characterized by extreme authoritarianism and repression of individuality; the great expansion
of large organizations and bureaucratic administration; the
increasingly dominant concern with technological efficiency—all these have played a part in bringing about the
reorientation of thought. At all events, the themes of the
decline of individual autonomy and of the massive growth in
the power of institutions, or 'the system', have become more
prominent in the social theory of the last few decades; in
Riesman's contrast between the 'inner–directed' and 'other–
directed' man, in Wright Mill's concern about the growth of
'mass society' and the decline of independent 'publics', in
Marcuse's analysis of the undermining of critical reason and
the more or less total dominance of established institutions in
the one–dimensional society.

But none of these interpretations rests upon a totalitarian
conception of human nature; on the contrary, they all appeal
to something in the individual—his critical reason or his moral
consciousness—which is capable of resisting the domination
by institutions, or any kind of extreme determination of his
thoughts and activity by his environment. During the last
decade there has been plenty of evidence of such resistance—
in the diverse movements of revolt which have emerged in all
modern societies (regardless of whether their regimes are

such as can be described crudely as capitalist or socialist) and also in the trends of thought, in Marxism and in sociology, which I have discussed above, that aim at reinstating the individual with his subjectively constituted purposes as the producer, critic, and rebuilder of social life.

However, the relationship between the individual and society in practical life, and between this practical life and its conceptualization in thought, is obviously very complex. Thus the observation of the growing domination of institutions and large–scale organizations over the individual, even disregarding the fact that it may be given a greater or lesser significance in the total view of social life, may lead either to the formulation of theories which represent this determination of the individual's life as an inescapable feature of the age, or to the expression of individualistic rebellion against this state of affairs. On the other hand, a totalitarian political system, as I have already argued, does not rest upon, and certainly does not arise from, a view of human nature as infinitely malleable. A regime of this kind develops out of particular social and political conditions, and may make use of various ideas and doctrines in its attempts to control the actions of individuals. Equally, those who hold a totalitarian view of human nature are not thereby committed to anything which could be called a totalitarian political outlook; they may believe, in some in-coherent way, that an environment can be designed which will necessarily produce a liberal society or even a utopian world.

NOTES

1. Schapiro, Leonard, *Totalitarianism* (London: Pall Mall Press, 1972), p. 13.
2. Barber, Benjamin R., 'Conceptual Foundations of Totalitarianism', in Friedrich, Carl J., Curtis, Michael and Barber, Benjamin R., (eds.), *Totalitarianism in Perspective: Three Views* (London: Pall Mall Press, 1969), pp. 6–7.
3. In his earlier version Friedrich referred here to 'western–type democracies'.
4. Friedrich, Carl J., 'The Evolving Theory and Practice of Totalitarian Regimes', in Friedrich, Curtis and Barber (eds.), *Totalitarianism in Perspective*, p. 126.
5. Numerous definitions are cited and examined in Barber, 'Conceptual

Foundations of Totalitarianism', pp. 8ff.
6. Arendt, Hannah, *The Origins of Totalitarianism* (Cleveland: Meridian Books, 1958), p. 466.
7. Moore, Barrington, Jr, *Political Power and Social Theory* (New York: Harper & Row, 1965), p. 54. This account of totalitarianism in terms of centralized political controls broadens considerably its historical range; according to Moore, totalitarianism 'arose prior to industrialism and independently of industrialism'.
8. Brzezinski, Z.K., *Ideology and Power in Soviet Politics* (New York: Frederick A. Praeger, 1967), pp. 46–7.
9. Spiro, Herbert J., 'Totalitarianism', in Sills, David L. (ed.), *International Encyclopedia of the Social Sciences* (New York: Macmillan Free Press, 1968), propounds this view.
10. C. Wright Mills, for example, in his discussion of mass society in *The Power Elite* (New York: Oxford University Press, 1956), observes that in the United States 'we realize that we have moved a considerable distance along the road to the mass society. At the end of that road there is totalitarianism, as in Nazi Germany or in Communist Russia.'
11. For example, by Marcuse, Herbert, *One–Dimensional Man* (Boston: Beacon Press, 1964).
12. See the discussion in Friedrich, Curtis and Barber (eds.), *Totalitarianism in Perspective*, pp. 80–2, 94–5, 105–16.
13. Ibid., p. 65.
14. Brzezinski, *Ideology and Power in Soviet Politics*, pp. 46–7.
15. See the discussion of Marx's concept of man in Petrović, Gajo, *Marx in the Mid–Twentieth Century* (New York: Doubleday Anchor Books, 1967), pp. 67–89.
16. But similar difficulties confront every attempt to construct a social science, as some other examples later in this essay will suggest.
17. Richta, Radovan, *et al.*, *Civilization at the Crossroads*, 3rd edn, (White Plains: International Arts and Sciences Press, 1969).
18. Quoted from the section on 'a new vision of the individual' in chap. 4.
19. Spiro, 'Totalitarianism'.
20. There are numerous examples; one delightfully candid expression of this aim is Macaulay's statement (in 1835) of the purpose of British educational policy in India: 'to form . . . a class of persons Indian in blood and colour, but English in tastes, in opinions, morals and intellect.'
21. For example, in his essay 'Contribution to the Critique of Hegel's Philosophy of Right': *man* is not an abstract being, squatting outside the world. Man is *the human world*, the state, society.'
22. For example, in the Sixth Thesis on Feuerbach: 'The real nature of man is the totality of social relations.'
23. Adler, Max, *Der soziologische Sinn der Lehre von Karl Marx* (Leipzig: C.L. Hirschfeld, 1914), especially pp. 13–15.
24. See Nisbet, Robert A., *The Sociological Tradition* (New York: Basic Books, 1966), for a discussion of the 'revolt against individualism' as a crucial element in the transformation of European thought which gave birth to sociology. See also the brief analysis of the criticisms of 'abstract indivi-

dualism' in Lukes, Steven, *Individualism* (Oxford: Basil Blackwell, 1973), pp. 73–8.
25. See especially his essay 'Individualism and the Intellectuals', *Political Studies*, XVII (March 1969), 19–30.
26. Quoted in Wolff, Kurt H., (ed.), *Georg Simmel, 1858–1918* (Columbus: Ohio State University Press, 1959), pp. 350–1. The essay quoted, 'How Is Society Possible?', is the second in Simmel's *Soziologie: Untersuchungen über die Formen der Vergesellschaftung* (Leipzig: Duncker und Humblot, 1908).
27. Sartre, Jean–Paul, *Critique de la raison dialectique* (Paris: Gallimard, 1960).
28. Skinner, B.K., *Beyond Freedom and Dignity* (New York: Alfred A. Knopf, 1971).
29. Skinner's general procedure is simply to translate easily intelligible conventional expressions into his own (rather less intelligible) language. This operation does not *explain* anything, and even makes understanding, in a broader and vaguer sense, more difficult. There is an excellent example on pp. 146–7.
30. Simmel, Georg, *Philosophie des Geldes* (Leipzig: Duncker & Humblot, 1900), chaps. 4–6. Some of the ideas in the later part of the book are expounded briefly in his essay 'The Metropolis and Mental Life' (1903), in Wolff, Kurt H., (ed.), *The Sociology of Georg Simmel* (Glencoe: The Free Press, 1950), pp. 409–24.
31. See especially the discussion in Marx's manuscripts of 1857–8, later published under the title *Grundrisse der Kritik der politischen Oekonomie* (Berlin: Dietz Verlag, 1953); for example (pp. 75–6), 'Relations of personal dependence (at first completely natural and spontaneous) are the first forms of society, in which human productivity develops only to a limited extent and at isolated points. Personal independence, based upon dependence on *things*, is the second great form, in which for the first time a system of general social exchange, universal relationships, universal needs, and universal capacities, is established. Free individuality, based upon the universal development of individuals, and the subordination of their communal, social productivity, as their own social powers, is the third stage. The second stage creates the conditions for the third.'

6 A Marxist Consideration of Durkheim

The relation between Durkheimian and Marxist social theory has been, for the most part, one of mutual disregard.[1] Durkheim himself, although he claimed to have been familiar with Marx's work from an early stage in his career,[2] paid scant attention to it, and was little influenced by Marxist thought.[3] He wrote reviews of two Marxist studies (1897, 1898), and under his direction *L'Année sociologique*, between 1898 and 1901, reviewed several other Marxist works as well as some French translations of Marx,[4] but the comment of P. Lapie that 'the materialist conception of history is in favour; every page of *L'Année sociologique* is an indication of this' is a considerable exaggeration. In his lectures on socialism, which he began to give at Bordeaux in 1895–6, Durkheim had intended to devote the third year to Marx and German socialism, but the course was abandoned after the first year, which was devoted largely to Saint–Simon.

It is clear, at all events, that Durkheim was a convinced opponent of Marxism, and of any kind of socialism which went beyond the idea of gradual social reform within the limits of a capitalist economy, even though he conceded some merit to Marx's theory as a major attempt to construct a social science, observing in his review of Labriola (1897) that he considered 'extremely fruitful this idea that social life should be explained, not by the notions of those who participate in it, but by more profound causes not perceived by consciousness [and also] that these causes are to be sought mainly in the manner according to which the associated individuals are grouped.' His principal objection to Marxism was that it attributed too much importance to economic factors and to class struggles, in its explanation of social development, and neglected what Durkheim considered the most significant element of all—especially in relation to contemporary political problems—namely, the moral role of the state.[5] Thus, in his review of Grosse (1898) he expressed the view that the inadequacy of the 'economic materialist' conception was most evident in the study of the family, and in the first of his lectures on socialism he argued that neither class struggle nor concern for the economic interests of workers formed an essential element of socialism, but that the socialist doctrine arose out of two movements, one from above and one from below (from the state and from the 'general interest' of society). In his conclusion to these lectures he claimed that the failure of Saint–Simon (and by inference, of Marx, since 'these practical theories . . . have not advanced much since the beginning of this century') was due to the fact that he and his followers 'wanted to get the most from the least, the superior from the inferior, moral rule from economic matter', and this is impossible; what is required is 'to discover through science the moral restraint which can regulate economic life.' Similarly, in his review of Labriola (1897), Durkheim asserted that 'the sad class conflict which we see today' was not the cause of the malaise in European societies, but a secondary phenomenon arising from the lack of (moral) regulation of the new kind of industrial society, and this, of course, summarized the view, set out at length in the third part of *The Division of Labour* (1893) on the 'abnormal forms of the division of labour', where he attributed class conflict to the fact that the distribution of social functions does not always correspond with the distribution of natural talents, and went on to argue that if there were a proper regulation of the division of labour the institutions of class or caste would produce social harmony rather than discord.

Those of Durkheim's followers who were active socialists—among them Halbwachs, Mauss and Simiand—do not seem, for all that, to have had any sustained interest in Marxism as a science of society, or to have modified in any radical way their essentially Durkheimian conception of sociology. At the most it might be said, in the words of one member of the group, that they came to 'consider economic phenomena to be the most important',[6] or in the case of Halbwachs that his studies of social classes, and especially the working class, 'brought him closer to Marxist sociology'.[7] Overall, however, the influence of the Durkheimian school is well summed up in Raymond Firth's comment (relating to social anthropology, where the influence was particularly marked) that: 'Insulated from Marx by the Durkheimian tradition . . . British social anthropology stressed solidarity rather than conflict as its primary field of study' (p. 11). But he goes on to observe that 'In the social and political upheavals of the post–war period, it is perhaps especially to French social anthropologists that Marx's propositions have often seemed more relevant than those of Durkheim'; and this is equally true for sociologists, not only in France.

From the side of Marxism there has been a similar indifference to Durkheimian sociology. The major critical examination from a rather idiosyncratic Marxist standpoint is still the long essay reviewing *The Rules of Sociological Method*, which was published by Sorel (1895). Sorel criticized Durkheim on several counts: for basing his methods on the study of 'things in themselves' rather than on the relations between things, as Marx had done; for ignoring the fundamental theoretical claim of the 'materialist theory of sociology' that 'the various systems, political, philosophical, religious, cannot be considered as independent, with their own particular foundation', but that there must necessarily be posited 'beneath this whole superstructure, the economic relationships'; and for neglecting, as a consequence of his hostility to socialism, the crucial factor of class conflict. After Sorel there is very little in the way of substantial Marxist criticism of Durkheim's sociology.[8] An essay on Durkheim and Marx by G. Kagan, while vaguely sympathetic to Marxism, is more concerned to demonstrate the existence of some common ground, as well as evident divergences, between the two theories; notably in the attempt of both thinkers to explain social phenomena in terms of economic relationships (the mode of production for Marx, the division of labour for Durkheim)[9] and more generally to establish sociology in the dual form of a theoretical science and the basis of a rational politics. Georges Friedmann, however, from a position more strongly influenced by Marxism, undertook a radical criticism of Durkheim's theory of the division of labour, pointing out that the division of labour gives rise to two different kinds of solidarity, one being the unity of an enterprise or firm as a whole, the other the solidarity of workers as a class, and concluding that the latter is generally stronger:

'it is not the interdependence of the operations imposed on them by the division of labour that leads to a feeling of moral solidarity, and creates a network of lasting relationships within this human group. It is not their technical status . . . but their social status that gives rise to this feeling, their daily awareness of their common situation in regard to their employer . . .and in general within the society of which they form a part' (1956, pp. 78–9).

While Durkheimians and Marxists—as the preceding account indicates—have shown an equal disregard for each other's work, the relation between them in another respect has been highly unequal. Durkheimian (like Weberian) sociology soon established for itself a secure, and prominent, position in academic social science, whereas Marxism, because of its revolutionary character, was for a long time either excluded altogether from the universities or allowed a very restricted place there. Only in the past two decades or so, particularly in the English–speaking countries, has Marxist sociology (as well as Marxist economics and anthropology) become more firmly established in the academy; and this no doubt accounts for the fact that there is now beginning to emerge a more systematic and rigorous confrontation between Marxist and other sociological theories.

II

Let us now consider the lines along which a Marxist criticism of Durkheimian sociology might be formulated. First, however, it is necessary to utter a warning. Marxism is no longer, if it ever was, a completely unified theory, the fundamental principles of which are everywhere expressed in exactly the

same form. As I have argued elsewhere (1975, and in Bottomore and Nisbet, 1978) Marxist sociology is now probably
best regarded as a very general paradigm within which there
exist strong family resemblances between different specific
theoretical formulations, which may also, however, have
significant connections with other, non-Marxist theories or
models. Hence, in embarking on a Marxist evaluation of
Durkheim I shall try to retain, and communicate, an awareness that Marxist criticism might well take a somewhat
different form, and lead to another kind of judgement on
Durkheim's sociology.

There are three principal directions which a Marxist criticism might follow. The first is that of a philosophical, mainly
epistemological, critique of Durkheim's basic conception of
sociology as a science. There is a good example of this
approach in Paul Hirst's study of Durkheim's 'attempt to
provide an epistemological foundation for a scientific sociology in *The Rules of Sociological Method*' (1975, p.1.). But I
shall not follow this course here, mainly because the issues
raised by this kind of critical examination do not so much
relate specifically to Durkheim as to the broad and widely
debated question of the proper philosophical foundations of
any sociology.[10]

A second path leads to a critical examination of the general
theoretical and political orientation of Durkheim's thought.
Here a number of familiar themes appear—the emphasis in
Durkheim's sociology on solidarity rather than conflict, order
rather than change, and the role of ideas (especially moral
ideas) rather than structural elements, in determining the
form of social life—which have been much discussed by others
besides Marxists, and indeed relatively little by the latter. But
a Marxist analysis, proceeding from an entirely different
paradigm, should be able to contribute a more systematic,
more incisive and more explicitly political kind of criticism
than that which is now prevalent, which confines itself to
pointing out, in an eclectic fashion, possible inadequacies in
the Durkheimian model, without proposing any radically different theory in its place. In fact, Sorel's essay, referred to
above, provides a good example of such Marxist criticism in its
attack on Durkheim's 'psychologism' (i.e. his choice of 'col-

lective consciousness' and 'collective representations' as fundamental concepts in his theory), his exclusion of the 'materialist' conception of a structural basis of social life constituted by economic relationships, and his neglect of the phenomena of class conflict; and it is an excellent starting–point for developing a more comprehensive critical evaluation of Durkheim's thought with respect to the three themes I have distinguished.

There can be no doubt about Durkheim's intense preoccupation with social solidarity, or about the political significance which this idea had for him. Throughout his work, from *The Division of Labour* to *The Elementary Forms of the Religious Life*, the theme of solidarity has a pre–eminent place, whether the source of the phenomenon is sought mainly in the interdependence of individuals created by the division of labour, in the moral regulation of society by the state and intermediate (occupational) associations, or in the binding force of a religion. The political bearing of Durkheim's primary sociological concerns is equally unmistakeable; as numerous commentators have observed he was wholeheartedly committed to strengthening (in part by introducing modest reforms) the institutions of the fragile Third Republic against the dangers which menaced them from the traditionalists in the Army and the Church, who never accepted the republican regime, and from the socialists, who were engaged in organizing the working class in its struggle against capitalism. His preoccupation with social solidarity was directly related to his concern for the unity of French society in the conditions resulting from the defeat of 1870, the Paris Commune and the increasing division between left and right in politics. As a Marxist critic, Paul Nizan, later wrote: 'In the name of [Durkheim's] science, teachers in the primary schools teach children to honour *la patrie française*, to justify class collaboration, to accept everything, to commune in the cult of the flag and bourgeois democracy.'[11]

The other side of this preoccupation was Durkheim's neglect or rejection of the significance of social conflict. In his review of Labriola, as I noted earlier, he argued that the 'sad class conflict' of the time was only an unimportant secondary phenomenon, and in the third part of *The Division of Labour*, on the 'abnormal forms' of the division of labour, he examined at greater length the conflict between labour and capitalism, which disrupts the solidarity generated by the interdependence of functions, but can be overcome through the integrating actions of the state and occupational associations. However, it is not only that Durkheim dismissed class conflict as a transitional and minor phenomenon, he also ignored almost entirely the conflicts among nation states, and hence contributed nothing of value to a sociological analysis of one of the most crucial events of the twentieth century, the first world war. His two pamphlets written during the war (1915, a,b) were admittedly propaganda exercises, published in the series of the Committee for the Publication of Studies and Documents on the War (of which Durkheim was the Secretary); the first of them (in collaboration with E. Denis) dealing only with the diplomatic exchanges preceding the outbreak of war, the second attributing responsibility for the war to the 'German mentality' as expressed in the nationalistic writings of Treitschke. Aside from these pamphlets I cannot find, in the whole body of Durkheim's work, any serious attempt to analyze the nationalism, imperialism and international conflict which has shaped the world of the late twentieth century. From this aspect Durkheim's sociology is, without question, vastly less useful for analyzing the condition of modern society and as a guide to political action than are the more realistic studies, not only of Marxist sociologists, but also of Max Weber.

What can be said in favour of Durkheim's emphasis on social solidarity is that it did give expression, in a particular context, to the growing nationalism of the European countries in the latter part of the nineteenth century, and thus recognized (while at the same time, unfortunately, helping to reinforce) a phenomenon which Marxists for their part were apt, both then and later, to minimize or ignore. On the other hand, Durkheim's ideas concerning the possibility of enhancing solidarity and eliminating (or greatly reducing) conflict in class–divided capitalist societies now seem largely unrealistic in the light of subsequent historical experience and of the present condition of these societies.

The second line of criticism of Durkheim, namely, that he

placed an exaggerated emphasis on social order at the expense of paying adequate attention to social change, can also, I think, be well sustained, and again particularly from a Marxist standpoint. For notwithstanding some attempts to show that there is present in Durkheim's thought a distinctive evolutionary scheme,[12] it must be said that his conception of a transition from 'mechanical' to 'organic' solidarity, or from 'traditional' to 'modern' societies, is very vaguely sketched, and has nothing like the precision and wealth of detail which is to be found in the historical sociology of Marx and Weber in their studies of social change in the ancient world, or more particularly, of the transition from feudalism to capitalism. Nor, I think, can it be claimed that Durkheim provided a very illuminating or convincing analysis of the processes of social change in the modern societies themselves. He rejected the Marxist view that radical social change would be brought about by class struggle, yet it is precisely by this means that both radical and more modest social changes have in fact occurred in the course of the twentieth century; and his alternative conception of change being accomplished by the moral action of the state makes the large and unrealistic assumption that the state, in a class society, is or can be a neutral representative or embodiment of the 'general interest'. It seems to me by no means a mere accident of intellectual history that Durkheim should have become, in effect, the anthropologists' sociologist, while either Marx or Weber became the sociologists' sociologist; for the former were engaged primarily in the study of what could be regarded as static and 'unhistorical' societies, about which the most significant questions seemed to be what kind of relationships and rituals maintained them in their given form,[13] whereas the latter dealt for the most part with societies which had experienced dramatic transformations, including political revolutions, in the transition from feudalism to capitalism, and were still undergoing a turbulent, conflict–ridden development.

The third opposition adduced in criticisms of Durkheim is that between an explanation of social phenomena in terms of moral and religious beliefs and the associated practices, and one in terms of underlying structural conditions. In this sphere, however, it is more difficult to unravel and evaluate

Durkheim's conceptions. For on one hand it is evident that he attached the greatest importance to the influence of belief systems in the shaping of social life, and that by far the larger part of his sociological work is devoted to the analysis of such systems. In *The Elementary Forms of the Religious Life* Durkheim, while referring to the 'social causes' of religion, explicitly rejected a total social explanation, saying that

> it is necessary to avoid seeing in this theory of religion a simple restatement of historical materialism: that would be misunderstanding our thought to an extreme degree. In showing that religion is something essentially social, we do not mean to say that it confines itself to translating into another language the material forms of society and its immediate vital necessities . . . collective consciousness is something more than a mere epiphenomenon of its morphological basis. (1912, pp. 423–4).

In effect, Durkheim treats religion as an 'emergent' property, which takes on a life of its own, and his theory is really more concerned with the social functions of religion than with its social causes. As he went on to argue 'there is something eternal in religion', and

> 'there can be no society which does not feel the need of upholding and reaffirming at regular intervals the collective sentiments and the collective ideas which make its unity and its personality. Now this moral remaking cannot be achieved except by the means of reunions, assemblies, and meetings where the individuals, being closely united to one another, re-affirm in common their common sentiments . . . If we find a little difficulty today in imagining what these feasts and ceremonies of the future could consist in, it is because we are going through a stage of transition and moral mediocrity . . . But this state of incertitude and confused agitation cannot last forever. A day will come when our societies will know again those hours of creative effervescence, in the course of which new ideas arise and new formulae are found which serve for a while as a guide to humanity' (ibid., pp. 427–8).[14]

Here Durkheim expressed in the clearest possible fashion his overriding concern with the creation, or recreation, of a moral community, necessarily inspired by religio–sacred beliefs; a concern which is evident through all his intellectual and practical undertakings, most strikingly in his preoccupation with moral education and with the moral role of the state.

On the other hand, with the recent development of a 'structuralist' approach in the social sciences, particularly through the work of Lévi–Strauss, more attention has been given to the structural aspect of Durkheim's sociology. [15] There is undoubtedly present in Durkheim's thought a conception of society as a structured whole, most clearly expressed perhaps in his thesis on Montesquieu (1892) where he wrote: 'If social science is really to exist, societies must be assumed to have a certain nature which results from the nature and arrangement of the elements composing them, and which is the source of social phenomena.' However, this not very precise notion of structure merged, for Durkheim, with the notion of function, as is apparent from his essay on the scientific domain of sociology (1900) where he wrote that, while 'undoubtedly, the phenomena that have to do with structure have something more stable about them than have functional phenomena. . . there are only differences of degree between these two orders of fact.' As a whole, Durkheim's sociology is functionalist rather than structuralist in orientation, and it is therefore exposed to the kind of Marxist criticism which Godelier has brought against functionalism generally, namely, that while it 'presupposes that the different surface social relationships within a society form a system, that is, that they have a functional interdependence which permits them to exist as an "integrated" whole, and which tends to reproduce itself as such—as a society', it has serious theoretical defects: first, 'that by confusing social structure with external social relations, functionalist analysis is condemned to remain a prisoner of appearances within the social system studied', and second, that it does not provide any explanation of 'why and under what conditions such and such a social factor assumes such and such a function' (pp. 34–5).

As we have seen, Durkheim explicitly rejected the idea of an underlying social structure constituted by economic relations, and this rejection is reasserted in the passage on religion cited above where he carefully distinguishes his theory of religion from historical materialism. Durkheim's sociology was centred on an analysis of the social functions of various factors—the division of labour, religion, the state as a moral agency—which he did not systematically relate to each other or to any fundamental structural principle; and in its later phases it was above all concerned with the moral influences on society, that is, with the effects of certain kinds of unexplained belief systems.

Marxist sociology, as the work of 'structuralist' Marxists has made particularly clear,[16] is based firmly on the idea of an underlying 'deep' social structure, constituted by the 'mode of production'; and I think it can be claimed that Marxist analysis (or for that matter Weber's study of modern capitalism which was profoundly influenced by Marxism) has provided a much more convincing account of the course of development of modern societies over the past century than have Durkheim's functionalist studies. Hence it has also been a superior guide to practical action. Nevertheless, in certain respects, Marxist thought has failed to engage with important problems which Durkheim raised, and this is particularly the case in the study of religion. There has been no substantial attempt to develop a Marxist theory of religion—nothing that is in any way comparable with Max Weber's extensive study of the world religions, which itself can be seen as contributing some of the elements required in a Marxist analysis through its examination of the relations between religion and economic life—although some recent work by Marxist anthropologists, influenced particularly by the structural analysis of myth, shows a more profound interest in primitive religions (see, e.g., Godelier).

More broadly, it may be said that Marxist studies of ideology have paid altogether too little attention to those beliefs and practices which create and sustain the unity of a society against the divisive forces of class consciousness and class conflict; and that in the specific conditions of the rise and consolidation of modern nation states in Europe in the nineteenth and twentieth centuries (and subsequently elsewhere in the world) Marxist sociologists have for the most part unrealistically neglected the immensely powerful forces of nationalism, which were recognized explicitly by Max Weber and in a less obvious way by Durkheim. But a Marxist analysis of nationalism, as the classic study by Otto Bauer shows, does not need to abandon a structural approach which looks for an explanation in the historically specific conditions of production, and replace it by an unhistorical account in terms of the collective consciousness—or more precisely, as Durkheim did in his war pamphlet of 1915, in terms of the 'German mentality'—although it may well be the case that Marxist theory, in this as in other fields, needs to pay greater attention (as some Marxist sociologists themselves have argued recently) to the ways in which an underlying 'structural causality' does or does not work itself out fully in conscious social action.[17]

Following this critical examination of the general orientation of Durkheim's thought I should now like to consider some more specific features of his sociology, and first, his conception of the state. It has been widely recognized that Durkheim, in the works which he published during his lifetime, devoted little attention to the construction of a sociological theory of the state; and in this respect his work stands in striking contrast not only with Marxism but also with Max Weber's sociology. Only in a course of lectures given during the 1890s and published posthumously (1950),[18] did he discuss the state in a systematic way and even there his treatment of the question is brief and selective. In three of the lectures Durkheim offered his own definition of the state: 'The state is a special organ responsible for elaborating certain representations which are valid for the collectivity. These representations are distinguished from other collective representations by their higher degree of consciousness and reflection . . . Strictly speaking, the state is the very organ of social thought' (p. 62) and then considered in general terms the relation between the individual and the state. Three further lectures were devoted to examining one particular form of the state— democracy—but Durkheim confined himself to a mainly philosophical analysis of the democratic idea and formulated, as Lukes has observed, 'a liberal political theory that was reminiscent both of T.H. Green and of Alexis de Tocqueville'.

There is no attempt in these lectures to establish a framework for, or to pursue, a sociological analysis of *actual* democratic political regimes, or to undertake any comparative study of different forms of the state which would relate these forms to other characteristics of social structure. As Melvin Richter has justly commented: 'Durkheim never investigated political institutions with anything like the attention and care he gave to his work on suicide and religion . . . In this part of his work, he disregarded the principles of method he had himself established, for he dealt with the state in a highly abstract way, producing little evidence for his conclusions' (p. 199). What is clear, however, is that Durkheim made use of this idea of the state—as a moral regulating agency—in all his published works, and notably in *The Division of Labour* and *The Elementary Forms of the Religious Life*, wherever he considered the functions of the state or the government in social life. His conception thus excluded entirely the idea of the state as a repressive organ, as the embodiment of power and violence, or as the representative of particular social interests; and on the other hand it assumed the existence of a fundamental harmony of interests in the collectivity, expressed in certain (assumed) collective representations. In short, it was totally unrealistic.

It is evident that Durkheim's conception of the independence and neutrality of the state as a moral regulator of social life is closely connected with his denial of the long–term significance of class divisions and class conflict. In the final part of *The Division of Labour*, the only place where he gave more than passing attention to social classes, Durkheim treated class conflict as an 'abnormal' and transient form, where the division of labour 'deviates from its natural course' which is the creation of organic solidarity. This abnormal situation had two main aspects: first, that the relations between social functions (and notably between capital and labour) were not adequately regulated by a body of rules, but existed in a condition of *anomie*; and second, that inequalities external to the division of labour itself (inequalities of wealth and family social position in particular) endangered social solidarity by imposing a 'forced division of labour' which involved a distribution of social functions and did not correspond with the distribution of natural talents, and an unequal exchange of values in the market. But as Lukes has noted, Durkheim's account of the ills of capitalism remained incomplete, since it did not proceed to an investigation of their causes, nor did it point clearly to the remedies, but rather assumed 'an identity between the "normal", the ideal and the about–to–happen' (p. 177). In both these respects a Marxist analysis of modern capitalism is unquestionably superior. It provides, on one side, an explanation of the lack of regulation of industrial relations, and the forced division of labour, in terms of the development of the capitalist mode of production in its early *laissez—faire* period; while on the other side it shows not only how these conditions can be changed, but how they have in fact been modified to some extent in a later phase of capitalist development through the political struggle of the working class, which has succeeded in establishing trade–union rights and industrial legislation, moderating unequal exchange, and reducing somewhat the discrepancy between social functions and natural aptitudes by increasing the opportunities for social mobility.

Finally, Durkheim's rejection of the idea that class conflict is an endemic phenomenon in modern capitalist societies was determined not only by his overriding concern with the creation of a new kind of social solidarity in the Third Republic, and more broadly with the problems posed by what he undoubtedly saw as a 'moral crisis', but also by the exclusion from his theoretical scheme of any systematic analysis of economic structure. It is quite mistaken, in my view, to regard even *The Division of Labour* as showing some intention on Durkheim's part to ground his sociology in a study of economic relationships, notwithstanding the suggestions to the contrary made by Barth and Kagan. For the 'division of labour' as Durkheim conceived it could be better described in a terminology which is not economic but sociological, as the 'differentiation of social functions'; and this conception was the basic element in an evolutionary scheme—strongly influenced by the ideas of Spencer—according to which increasing differentiation results from morphological factors (changes in the size and density of population), not from changes in the economic structure.[19] There is a manifest radical opposition between Durkheim's theory, which treats social development as a gradual process of social differentation which necessarily produces (with only temporary 'deviations') social solidarity, and Marx's theory which conceives development as a series of 'breaks' and rapid transformations, resulting from contradictions within the mode of production that are expressed historically as conflicts between classes. Not only did Durkheim explicitly reject 'historical materialism' (that is, the explanation of other social facts by their relation to the economic system); in his sole venture into a discussion of the economic sphere as such (at a meeting of the Société d'Économie Politique in 1908) he argued that economic facts themselves are dependent on collective representations, and that if any kind of primacy could be attributed to economic factors it was only in so far as they affected the distribution and density of population, and the form of human groups, thereby influencing the various states of opinion (see Aimard, pp. 5–8; Lukes, pp. 499–500).

From a Marxist standpoint Durkheim inverts the real relationships in society; he takes no account of the material basis—the mode of production—and explains social phenomena by the movement of ideas. This is the case even though in one passage of *The Rules of Sociological Method* (1895, p. 111) Durkheim seemed to propose some kind of material basis in claiming that 'the facts of social morphology [i.e. the volume (population) and density of society] . . . play a preponderant role in collective life',[20] for elsewhere in the same work (pp. 12–13) he argued that morphological phenomena had no such preeminence, but were of the same nature as other social facts, that the political divisions of society were essentially moral and that a society's organization was determined by public law (Lukes, pp. 228–9) and in his later studies it is evident that he came to attribute an ever greater importance to the role of moral ideas expressed in collective representations. For Durkheim it *is* 'the consciousness of men that determines their being', and not, as Marx argued, 'social being [that] determines their consciousness'.

III

By way of conclusion to this essay I should like to make a brief comparison between Durkheimian and Marxist sociology with respect to their present significance for understanding the condition of human societies in the late twentieth century. Such an aim corresponds very closely with their own intentions, for both Durkheim and Marx (and, of course, Max Weber) conceived their sociology as having a very direct practical bearing, providing knowledge, enlightenment and guidance in action for those political groups to which they gave their allegiance. By contrast, a great part of sociological theory at the present time (including some forms of Marxist theory) is largely denuded of political significance or value; and because it has no purchase on political reality, no clear relation to any major political movements, it has become increasingly narcissistic, obsessed with the epistemological status of the discipline itself, and—dare one say it?—futile.

No doubt the most effective way to break out of this circle would be simply to embark on the construction of new theoretical schemes which do relate to the major political issues of the age, and a few thinkers are doing so.[21] But their work is often a 'reconstruction', which necessarily draws on the ideas of the major thinkers of the past, and it is evident that the revival of Marxist thought over the last two decades has had a prominent role in this process. At the same time, the debate about Marxism has posed questions about many fundamental Marxist conceptions, which I have discussed elsewhere (Bottomore and Nisbet, 1978) and will only briefly mention here. What is the nature of capitalism in the late twentieth century? What is the political significance now of the major social classes which Marx distinguished in capitalist society? To what extent is the modern interventionist state a more autonomous force in social life? And in what ways does an analysis of the present day 'state socialist societies' make necessary a thoroughgoing revision of Marx's theory of history?

There has been no such debate on this scale about Durkheim's sociology, and I think this reflects the fact that there is indeed much less to be learned from his work. The development of French society between the wars did not correspond at all with Durkheim's expectations of a growth of social solidarity, for the Third Republic continued to be riven by class conflict until its collapse in 1940. And if there has been, in the post–war western capitalist societies, some abatement of class conflict this is due rather to the economic revival of capitalism and the reforms achieved by politically–powerful working–class movements than to the expression by a neutral and autonomous state of new collective representations. It is by no means certain, in any case, that the relative peace and consensus of the 1950s and 1960s will survive the economic crisis of the 1980s.

On the other hand, it is true that a more interventionist state, such as Durkheim anticipated and desired, has emerged in the western societies since the war. The question is whether this phenomenon can best be explained in Durkheimian terms as the manifestation of an underlying, necessary movement towards greater social solidarity, or in more Marxist terms as a new stage in the development of capitalism, characterized by the dominance of large corporations and a certain equilibrium between classes[22] which necessitates state provision of welfare and other infrastructural services on a large scale. In this case, too, I think an analysis broadly inspired by Maxism—in the sense, particularly, of starting from an examination of changes in the system of production—is more likely to be illuminating. Even the political importance of nationalism in the modern world, which as I noted earlier finds a clear expression in Durkheim's conception of social solidarity, is not wholly resistant to a Marxist explanation, such as was attempted by Bauer, though the idea of the relation between European nationalism and the rise of the bourgeoisie may provide only a partial explanation.

In sum, Durkheim's sociology seems to me not to embody any superior solutions, but to formulate a certain number of issues to which Marxist thinkers have to pay attention. Among them are those of the relation between 'nation' and 'class', and between material factors and social consciousness (or 'collective representations' at various levels) in the development of modern societies. In dealing with these issues, the Marxist theory of society will no doubt continue to be profoundly revised; so much so, perhaps, that it will make the leap into a new theory.

NOTES

1. A similar relation, as Tiryakian has shown, existed between Durkheim and Weber; but in later sociological theory there has been rather more in the way of comparison and confrontation between Durkheimians and Weberians.

2. In his review of Labriola's *Essays on the Materialist Conception of*

History (1897).

3. The difference in the relation between Weber and Marx on one side, and Durkheim and Marx on the other, is due in part no doubt to the very different intellectual contexts in which the thought of Weber and Durkheim developed (and in particular the influence of the philosophy of history and historical studies in Germany), but also to the fact that whereas in Germany there was already a powerful socialist movement, inspired by Marxism, in the closing decades of the nineteenth century, French Marxism at that time was still relatively weak and did not present a serious intellectual challenge to the academic social sciences. So far as Durkheim did feel obliged to comment more extensively on Marxism after the mid–1890s this was due to the wider diffusion of Marxist ideas in France (particularly through the writings of Sorel) and to the interest shown by some of his own most brilliant students in Marxist socialism. See Mauss, who noted that one of their 'Social Study' circles was devoted to a systematic reading and analysis of *Capital*; and also Lukes and Clark who give a fuller account of the socialist activities of the younger Durkheimians.

4. For an account of these reviews see Raymond Firth (p. 10).

5. The manner of this regulation was later worked out in greater detail in Durkheim's discussion of the role of the state on one side, and of occupational associations on the other. See especially his preface to the 2nd edn of *The Division of Labour*, and also *Professional Ethics and Civic Morals*.

6. H. Bourgin, cited in Lukes (p. 329).

7. Georges Friedmann (1955, pp. 17, 22). Friedmann refers not only to that work, but also particularly to Halbwachs (1933).

8. However, more thorough research in the future, emerging from the increasing interest in the history of sociology, and the greater attention paid to Marxist thought in that history, may well uncover some valuable critical studies, in Marxist journals and elsewhere, for example, in the journal of the Durkheimian socialists, *Notes critiques—sciences sociales*, to which Lukes refers (p. 328, n.34).

9. Kagan draws attention to the fact that Paul Barth in his survey of sociological theories, ranged Marx and Durkheim together in the category of proponents of an 'economic conception of history'.

10. Hirst himself makes this point at the outset when he says that his study is not concerned with Durkheim *per se*, but has as its object 'to question and to challenge the dominant conceptions of epistemology in sociology'; and indeed the ultimate aim of his work, inspired by Althusser's version of Marxism, is to demolish all non–Althusserian conceptions of 'scientificity'.

11. Paul Nizan (p. 97) cited in Lewis Coser (p. 169). There was an equally strong reaction from the Catholic right; Bouglé (p. 168) quotes the remark of a Catholic sociologist, Jean Izoulet, that 'the obligation to teach the sociology of M. Durkheim in the two hundred *écoles normales* of France is the most serious national peril which our country has known for a long time.'

12. See the qualified argument in this sense by Anthony Giddens (pp. 235–72).

13. As Firth recognizes. He then goes on to attribute the emergence of an

influential Marxist anthropology to the fact that anthropologists, in the post–war period of national independence movements and decolonization, have been 'confronted with societies in conditions of radical change' (p. 7).

14. A socialist—Sorel, for instance—would have said, with some justice, that this 'creative effervescence' and these 'new ideas' had already emerged in the form of the socialist movement.

15. Lévi–Strauss himself has recognized affiliation between his own conception of structure and that of Durkheim and the Durkheimians. (See Bottomore and Nisbet pp. 565–71.)

16. See the brief account of their work in Bottomore and Nisbet (pp. 136–8, 590–4).

17. It would be preferable, perhaps, to refer always to 'quasi–causality' or 'quasi–causal relations', in order to recognize adequately the intervention of consciousness in all social processes. Max Adler was one of the principal Marxist thinkers to examine carefully the notion of 'social causality' in this sense.

18. The lectures were given in Bordeaux from 1890–1900, and again in Paris in 1904 and 1912. The published text is taken from a manuscript written between 1898 and 1900.

19. See the brief discussion of the contrasting views of Durkheim and Marx on the division of labour in Aimard (pp. 218–29), and the more comprehensive study of theories of the division of labour in Bouglé (pp. 98–161).

20. Even if Durkheim had maintained consistently that a material basis of social life (the size and density of population) had some kind of explanatory priority, his view would still be open to the criticism which Marx, in the introduction to the *Grundrisse*, specifically levelled against the method of political economy when he wrote: 'It appears to be correct to begin with the real and concrete . . . , therefore, e.g., in political economy, with the population, which is the basis and the subject of the whole social act of production. Nevertheless this is shown, on closer consideration, to be false. Population is an abstraction, if I omit the classes, for example, of which it consists. Those classes are an empty word if I do not know the elements on which they are based . . . Therefore if I begin with population, then that would be a chaotic conception of the whole.'

21. I have in mind particularly the work of Jürgen Habermas and Alain Touraine.

22. In this context it does not matter whether the classes in question are conceived as bourgeoisie and proletariat (Marx) or as a technocratic–bureaucratic ruling group and various subordinate, dependent groups (a conception to be found in some recent discussions of 'post–industrial society').

BIBLIOGRAPHY

Adler, Max, *Marxistische Probleme. Beiträge zur Theorie der materialistischen Geschichtsauffassung und Dialektik* (Stuttgart: Dietz, 1913).
Aimard, Guy, *Durkheim et la science économique* (Paris: Presses Univer-

sitaires de France, 1962).

Barth, Paul, *Die Philosophie der Geschichte als Soziologie*, 2nd edn, (Leipzig: Reisland, 1922).

Bauer, Otto, *Die Nationalitätenfrage und die Sozialdemokratie*, 2nd edn, (Vienna: Wiener Volksbuchhandlung, 1924).

Bottomore, Tom, *Marxist Sociology*. (London: Macmillan, 1975).

Bottomore, Tom and Robert Nisbet, *A History of Sociological Analysis* (New York: Basic Books, 1978).

Bouglé, Célestin, 'Théories sur la division du travail'. Reprinted in *Qu'est-ce-que la sociologie?* (Paris: Félix Alcan, 1907).

Bouglé, Célestin, *Bilan de la sociologie française contemporaine* (Paris: Félix Alcan, 1935).

Clark, Terry N, 'The Structure and Functions of a Research Institute: *L'Année Sociologique*', *Archives Européennes de Sociologie* 1968, IX(1): 72–91.

Coser, Lewis, *Masters of Sociological Thought* (New York: Harcourt Brace Jovanovich, 1971).

Durkheim, Emile, *Quid Secundatus Politicae Scientiae Instituendae Contulerit* (1892), Latin thesis on Montesquieu (French trans. 1937 and 1953; English trans. in *Montesquieu and Rousseau: Forerunners of Sociology*. Ann Arbor: University of Michigan Press, 1960).

Durkheim, Emile, *The Division of Labour in Society*, (1893). (English trans. New York: Macmillan, 1933).

Durkheim, Émile, *The Rules of Sociological Method*, (1895) (English trans. Chicago: University of Chicago Press, 1938).

Durkheim, Émile, Review of Antonio Labriola, *Essais sur la conception matérialiste de l'histoire* in *Revue Philosophique*, (1897), XLIV: 645–51.

Durkheim, Émile, Review of Ernest Grosse, *Die Formen der Familie und die Formen der Wirtschaft* (1898) in *L'Année Sociologique* I:319–32.

Durkheim, Émile, *Sociology and its Scientific Field* (1900) (English trans. in Kurt Wolff (ed.), *Émile Durkheim, 1858–1917*. Columbus: Ohio State University Press, 1960).

Durkheim, Émile, *The Elementary Forms of the Religious Life*. (1912) (English trans. London: Allen & Unwin, 1915; 2nd edn, 1976).

Durkheim, Émile, (with E. Denis) *Who Wanted War? The Origin of the War according to Diplomatic Documents*. (1915) Published simultaneously in French and English (Paris: Armand Colin).

Durkheim, Émile, *'Germany Above All': German Mentality and the War*. (1915). Published simultaneously in French and English, (Paris: Armand Colin).

Durkheim, Émile, *Socialism*. (1928) (English trans. New York: Collier Books, 1962).

Durkheim, Émile, *Professional Ethics and Civic Morals*. (1950) (English trans. London: Routledge & Kegan Paul, 1957).

Firth, Raymond, *The Sceptical Anthropologist? Social Anthropology and Marxist Views on Society* (From the Proceedings of the British Academy) (London: Oxford University Press, 1972).

Friedmann, Georges, Biographical notice preceding Maurice Halbwachs,

Esquisse d'une psychologie des classes sociales (1955) (Paris: Marcel Rivière, 1955).

Friedmann, Georges, *The Anatomy of Work*, (1956). (English trans. London: Heinemann, 1961).

Giddens, Anthony, *Studies in Social and Political Theory* (London: Hutchinson, 1977).

Godelier, Maurice, *Perspectives in Marxist Anthropology* (Cambridge: Cambridge University Press. 1977).

Halbwachs, Maurice, *L'Évolution des besoins dans les classes ouvrières* (Paris: Félix Alcan, 1933).

Halbwachs, Maurice, *Esquisse d'une psychologie des classes sociales* (Paris: Marcel Rivière, 1955).

Hirst, Paul Q, *Durkheim, Bernard and Epistemology* (London: Routledge & Kegan Paul, 1975).

Kagan, Georges, 'Durkheim et Marx', *Revue d'Histoire économique et sociale*, 1938, XXIV: 233–44.

Lapie, Paul, Review of Antonio Labriola, *Essais sur la conception matérialiste de l'histoire.' L'Année Sociologique* 1898, I:270–77.

Lévi–Strauss, Claude, *The Scope of Anthropology* (London: Jonathan Cape 1967).

Lukes, Steven, *Emile Durkheim: His Life and Work* (London: Allen Lane, Penguin Press. 1973).

Marx, Karl, *Grundrisse der Kritik der politischen Ökonomie (Rohentwurf)* (English trans. Harmondsworth: Penguin Books, 1973).

Mauss, Marcel, Introduction to Durkheim, *Socialism.* 1958.

Nizan, Paul, *Les Chiens de garde* (Paris: Rieder, 1932).

Richter, Melvin, 'Durkheim's Politics and Political Theory' (1960). In Kurt H. Wolff (ed.), *Émile Durkheim, 1858–1917,* (Columbus: Ohio State University Press).

Sorel, Georges, 'Les théories de M. Durkheim.' *Le Devenir social* 1 and 2 (April/May 1895): 1–26, 148–80.

Sorel, Georges, Preface to Saverio Merlino, *Formes et essence du socialisme* (Paris, 1898).

Tiryakian, Edward A, 'A Problem for the Sociology of Knowledge: The Mutual Unawareness of Émile Durkheim and Max Weber.' *Archives Européennes de Sociologie* 1966 VII(2): 330–36.

7 Max Weber and the Capitalist State

What is important in Max Weber's political theory is not simply his analysis of the concept of power, which has been widely debated, but his specific model of the modern state. In the present essay I propose to examine the main component parts of that model—Weber's conceptions of the nation state, bureaucracy and democracy—and to consider the practical political orientations which are implicit in it, or explicitly derived from it.

Weber was, as Wolfgang Mommsen (1959, 1974) in particular has made clear, a passionate nationalist and imperialist who 'never envisaged any other world than his own, which was largely characterized by the rivalry of nation states' (Mommsen, 1974, p. 37). In his Inaugural Lecture at Freiburg in 1895 Weber formulated the basic principle of his political theory as being the 'absolute primacy of the interests of the nation state' which constitute an 'ultimate standard of value' in both politics and economics (Weber, 1971, pp. 14–15). He went on to argue that following the creation of a German national state by the preceding generation the supreme task facing his own generation was to promote the expansion of German power and influence, and as a means to that end to help create a capable and vigorous political leadership; for 'we should realize that the unification of Germany was a youthful folly committed by the nation in the old days, which it would have been better not to undertake at all, in view of its cost, if this was to be the conclusion, and not the starting point, of Germany's striving to become a world power' (1958, p. 23).

In his later political studies Weber never abandoned this criterion of the interests of the German state, and the value–

laden notion of 'effective political leadership' which he constantly invoked, always meant that kind of political leadership which would most successfully promote, in the given international conditions, the interests of Germany as a world power. Thus, in his monograph of May 1918 on 'Parliament and Government in a Reconstructed Germany' (1958, pp. 306–443) he analyzed bureaucracy and democracy primarily in relation to the need for strong political leadership, and he concluded his lecture on socialism, delivered in June 1918 to a group of army officers in Vienna, by saying: 'The question is only whether this socialism will be of such a kind that it is bearable from the standpoint of the interests of the state, and in particular at the present time, of its military interests' (1924, p. 517). During the last two years of his life Weber's attitude to the revolutionary movement in Germany was determined by the same considerations, namely, that a revolution would weaken Germany still further in relation to the victorious allied powers, whereas the most urgent need was to reestablish a strong state.[1]

Weber was the intellectual voice of the German bourgeoisie[2] in the period of rapid growth of German capitalism between the 1880s and 1914. His theory of the modern state is a theory of the capitalist nation state in the age of imperialism; not only, or even mainly, in the sense of analyzing the social and historical characteristics of this form of state,[3] but in the sense of formulating as the central problem of political sociology the most effective possible development of bourgeois rule and of German participation in the struggle for world power. In short, Weber's model of the nation state is also an ideal. This appears most clearly if we contrast his analysis with that of Rudolf Hilferding, who examined from a very different standpoint the same phenomenon of German capitalist development. In the final part of *Finance Capital* (1910) Hilferding analyzed the 'struggle for economic territory' resulting from the growth of capitalist monopolies, and observed in particular the rivalry between Britain and Germany in the export of capital to colonial or dependent countries, a rivalry which was the principal factor creating the danger of a European war. For Hilferding, therefore, rational and effective political leadership did not consist in strengthening the power position of Germany in world politics, but, on the contrary, in organizing working–class opposition to the militarist and expansionist orientation of the German bourgeoisie—which Weber's doctrine helped to reinforce—and formulating a strategy to achieve a new international economic order which would be both pacific and just.

It is in no way surprising, given the character of Weber's basic model, that in discussing bureaucracy and democracy he should have concentrated his attention almost entirely upon their relation to the interests of the nation state. In the case of bureaucracy, it is true, there is also a larger theme concerning the rationalization and 'disenchantment' of the modern world brought about by the development of capitalist production with its increasing specialization of tasks, and an ever more pervasive and sophisticated money economy, which diffuses the 'specifically modern calculating attitude' through all spheres of social and cultural life.[4] But in examining the political context of bureaucracy, Weber was concerned only with two questions: the extent to which the power of the state bureaucracy impeded the development of an 'effective political leadership' serving German national interests; and the significance which could be attributed to bureaucracy in his general argument against the socialists.

For Weber, the political problem in Germany consisted in the fact that since Bismarck's eclipse (but also because Bismarck had left Germany in a condition of complete political immaturity[5]) the direction of the nation's affairs had fallen into the hands of the state bureaucracy, which had become a distinct social stratum with its own particular interests and values, while on the other hand the bourgeoisie had been excluded from political involvement and rendered incapable of assuming a leading political role. Hence Germany, largely as a result of the alliance between the emperor and the high officials against parliament, presented an extreme example of bureaucratic domination or rule by officials (*Beamtenherrschaft*), where officials had assumed functions (in particular as cabinet ministers) for which, in Weber's view, they were quite unsuited. The absence of real political leadership was responsible, Weber later argued, for the disastrous foreign policy pursued from the end of the nineteenth century up to 1914, which 'helped to create a world coalition against Germany' (1958, pp. 369–82). It was largely as a response to this bureaucratic domination that Weber formulated the alternative of charismatic leadership, but this idea was closely related to his peculiar conception of democracy and will be better examined in that context.

The growth of bureaucracy also provided the ground for one of Weber's principal objections to socialism.[6] In his view a socialist regime would be obliged to rely, as did capitalism, upon an extensive bureaucracy as the most rational form of administration, and bureaucratic domination would in fact be strengthened by the merging of public and private bureaucracies.

'A progressive elimination of private capitalism is no doubt theoretically conceivable . . . although it will certainly not be the outcome of this war. But assuming that it eventually happens, what would that mean in practice? The destruction of the iron cage of modern industrial labour? No! Rather that the administration of nationalized or 'socialized' enterprises too would become bureaucratic . . . If private capitalism were eliminated the state bureaucracy would rule *alone*. The public and private bureaucracies which can now, at least in principle, counterbalance each other and hold each other in check, would then be welded into a single hierarchy' (1958, pp. 331–2).

The changes taking place in modern society, according to Weber, indicated an advance towards the 'dictatorship of the official' rather than the 'dictatorship of the proletariat' (1924, p. 508).

This interpretation of the relation between bureaucracy and socialism is open to criticism on several counts. First, it is only 'in principle', as Weber himself says, that the public and private bureaucracies in a capitalist society counterbalance each other; in practice, in the conditions of advanced capitalism where the economy is dominated by large corporations (including the banks), it is much more likely that the two sectors will reinforce each other, and the situation is made worse by the fact that private bureaucracies elude any effective democratic control. Second, the historical experience of the USSR since 1917 and of the state socialist societies in Eastern Europe since 1945 indicates clearly, in my view, that they have been dominated, not by a bureaucracy, but by a

political party which possessed at various times the charismatic leadership qualities which Weber saw as the alternative
to bureaucratic domination. If those societies are to become
less authoritarian in the future it will not be through the
restoration of large–scale private ownership of productive
resources, and the recreation of private bureaucracies, but
through the decentralization of political power, the emergence of independent centres of political thought and action,
and the restoration of democratic control over policy–
making. Finally, it seems scarcely plausible any longer to
contrast 'dynamic capitalism' with 'bureaucratic socialism', as
Mommsen (1974, chap. III) suggests that Weber was doing.
For the present–day western capitalist societies are anything
but dynamic, in either an economic or a cultural sense; on the
contrary, they are now characterized by economic stagnation
and cultural decline, while dynamism in the assertion of new
values and commitment to political ideals, sometimes in
opposition to the authoritarianism of the ruling groups, has
been more evident in some socialist countries (in China at
least until the death of Mao Tse Tung, Yugoslavia, Czechoslovakia until the military occupation of August 1968, Poland
until the imposition of martial law in December 1981) as well
as in a number of socialist–oriented, developing countries.

Weber's own solution to the problem of bureaucratic
domination had two elements: the first—which I have just
discussed—was the strengthening of private capitalism
against the encroachment of socialism; the second, the
creation of conditions in which it would be possible for
'charismatic' political leaders to emerge within the framework
of a limited democratic system. Mommsen has suggested that
'Weber's charismatic personalities have much in common
with Nietzsche's great individuals who set new values for
themselves and for their followers' (1974, p.79); and it is
undoubtedly the case that Weber's later thought was strongly
influenced by Nietzsche.[7] But this influence is most apparent
in the emphasis which he placed upon the 'will to power' and
the inevitability of struggles for power (which he interpreted
almost exclusively in terms of the conflicts among nation
states). On the other hand, Weber's conception of charismatic leaders is very much narrower than Nietzsche's idea of

'superior individuals' who would bring about a 'transvaluation of all values'; for the role of Weber's political leaders is not so much to create new values as to uphold effectively traditional bourgeois values—private capitalism and the power interests of the capitalist nation state.[8] Sorel's vision of the proletariat as the creator of new values, 'confronting the bourgeois world as an irreconcilable adversary, threatening it with a moral catastrophe much more than with a material catastrophe' (Sorel, 1898) might be interpreted as a more authentic expression of the Nietzschean doctrine.

It is in his discussion of democracy, mainly in the writings of his last years, that Weber reveals most clearly his obsession with political leadership by exceptional individuals. Western democracy, for Weber, is in no sense rule *by* the people,[9] but simply a useful arrangement, in the form of parliamentary government, for the recruitment and training of political leaders. In *Economy and Society* he argues that 'direct democracy' (i.e. effective rule by the people) is only possible in associations or societies which are small (not more than a few thousand members), have no need for specialized administration, and have no permanent party organizations engaged in a struggle for offices (1921, pp. 170–1). Beyond this stage some kind of representation is unavoidable, and in the case of the modern western societies Weber conceives it as a 'representation of interests' which has to be analyzed largely in terms of the situation of various classes and status groups (1921, pp. 171–6). At the same time, representation produces a sharp distinction between leaders and followers, and the subordination of the latter (1921, pp. 667–8).

Consequently, according to Weber, the modern 'mass democracies' can only take the form of 'plebiscitarian leader democracies'; that is to say, political regimes in which charismatic leaders of party organizations compete for the popular vote: 'There is only a choice between leader–democracy with a "machine" and leaderless democracy—that is to say domination by professional politicians without a calling, without the inner charismatic qualities which make a leader' (1919, p. 544). In the whole of Weber's discussion of plebiscitarian leader–democracy there is an ambiguity about the basis of legitimacy in such a regime; whether what exists is rational—legal domination (depending upon the popular vote) or charismatic domination (depending upon the personal qualities of the leader). But Weber's inclination was to emphasize the latter. In *Economy and Society* he observed that ' "Plebiscitarian democracy"—the most important type of leader democracy—is, in its genuine sense, a kind of charismatic domination which conceals itself behind a legitimacy that is formally derived from and sustained by the will of the governed. The leader (the demagogue) rules in fact by virtue of the devotion of his followers and their trust in him as a person' (1921, p. 156); and in his articles on the future form of the German state he expressed himself in favour of a *plebiscitarian* President of the Reich as head of the government (1971, p. 482), rather than a purely parliamentary system.

Weber's preoccupation with charismatic leaders— politicians *with* a 'calling'—had two main sources. One was his concern with the 'overwhelming tendency towards bureaucratization' (1971, p. 333)—in political parties as well as in the state and the economy—and its probable outcome in a severe restriction of the sphere of free individual activity and an ossification of western society, which he saw both as an eclipse of 'dynamic capitalism' and as a cultural decline, a routinization and disenchantment of the world. But the second source, as I have argued above, was his conviction that Germany needed political leaders who, unlike the bureaucracy, would effectively promote the power interests of the nation state. Many commentators on Weber's political theory have drawn attention to the vague and unsatisfactory character of his conception of a 'charismatic leader', whose personal qualities—which are supposed to entitle him to this exalted role—are left entirely undefined and unanalyzed. In fact, the normally hidden content of this notion was from time to time revealed when, as in his Freiburg lecture or in the lecture on socialism, Weber related the political capacity of various classes and status groups, and of the leaders who rose to prominence within them, solely to the probable consequences of their actions for the interests of the nation state. The 'charismatic leader' is the politician who can most effectively arouse nationalist fervour and set, or keep, the nation on its path to glory.

Democracy as a political ideal, and as a social movement inspired by that idea, which is valuable in its own right, finds no place whatsoever in Weber's thought. A sharp contrast is drawn between 'direct democracy' which can exist only in small–scale, undifferentiated societies, and modern 'mass democracies' in which the people cannot possibly govern themselves and the only feasible system is 'leader democracy'. Any intermediate position is ignored, as is the idea of a gradual broadening of democracy which was historically the fundamental element in the whole modern democratic movement, culminating in the social democracy of the socialist movement. Democracy is thus reduced to a mechanism for the selection and training of political leaders through a competitive struggle for the popular vote,[10] and any other view of a democratic political system is dismissed as 'utopian'—utopian because, according to Weber, there is no way in which the people can effectively control either the leaders for whom they have voted or the expert officials who administer the complex apparatus of a modern industrial society.

But even leaving aside any consideration of the intrinsic value of such utopian thought which, while it may never lead to a complete attainment of its goal, may none the less push society closer to the goal, it is not difficult to criticize Weber's sweeping denial of the possibility of any real and direct democratic participation in policy–making. In the first place, democratic organizations in many different spheres, and at different levels, can and do control the actions of their officials in a more or less effective way, though there is undoubtedly scope for much more extensive study (which a Weberian stance on the issue would systematically discourage) of how democratic control can be progressively improved in large organizations. Furthermore, as Paul Hirst has suggested in a discussion of this question, democratic participation may not only provide adequate control, but may actually increase the efficiency of bureaucratic administration, particularly in the sphere of production; as he argues (and the argument applies more widely) 'the more antagonistic the separation between manager and managed, the greater the labour devoted to supervision and the less efficient the means of coordina-

tion. . . In contradiction to Weber, efficiency is only possible
when the production workers do *not* play the part of cogs in a
wheel' (1976, pp. 120–1). No doubt at the level of national
government (and of regional and international organizations)
it is much more difficult for the people and their elected
representatives to ensure that it is their own policies which are
carried out rather than those of the permanent high officials,
who are certainly able to exert a very great influence on policy
making,[11] but the problem is widely recognized, and there are
numeous ways in which control over the actions of officials
can be strengthened, among them being, again, greater direct
participation by the people who are the consumers of public
services.

The second important issue concerns the degree of control
which the people can exercise over their elected representatives and party leaders. Here Weber took the same one–sided
view as was expounded by Michels (1911) in his formulation of
the 'iron law of oligarchy', according to which a small group of
leaders is bound to dominate the unorganized majority of the
party members or the electorate.[12] Robert Brym (1980), however, has recently noted that 'Michels, of course, never
bothered to specify those forces which might counteract the
iron law of oligarchy', and has proposed an alternative conceptualization which 'transforms a constant (the "inexorable"
drift toward oligarchy and élitism) into a variable (the ebb and
flow of oligarchical and democratic tendencies)', bringing
evidence to demonstrate 'that in some cases the iron law of
oligarchy does not apply, and even that the distribution of
power within political organizations may on occasion be such
as to allow us to speak of an "iron law of democracy" ' (pp.
41–2). The conceptions of Michels and Weber were probably
influenced very greatly by the generally authoritarian climate
of German politics, but in Weber's case something more is
involved too; he espoused as a value commitment the idea of a
strong authoritarian capitalist nation state, and spoke with
contempt of 'leaderless democracy', such as he thought was
implicit in the aims of the German revolutionary movement.
Yet the cult of leaders which he expounded is itself an indication of political immaturity and a servile cast of mind; and the
advocacy of strong 'charismatic' leadership itself operates as a

social psychological force which increases the propensity to authoritarianism on one side, servility and political irresponsibility on the other. In practice, there are many methods—all of which could be greatly improved beyond their present effectiveness—by which the power and pretensions of political leaders can be regulated: elections, scrutiny of the performance of elected representatives (as is suggested in recent Labour Party discussions on the reselection of MPs), a free and critical press and television (such as exists as yet only imperfectly even in the western countries), and the deliberate encouragement and extension of practices of self–management in all spheres of society, from the economic to the cultural. These matters—involving a continual struggle to achieve an ever greater degree of genuine rule *by* the people—are infinitely more significant for the well–being, and indeed the survival, of humanity in the next few decades than is Weber's obsession with charismatic leaders and the power of the nation state, which in the present age is little more than a dangerous irrelevance.

It is astonishing to my mind that after the horrible and senseless slaughter of the first world war, Weber himself should not have felt a need to reconsider his early beliefs about the paramountcy of national interests and of the 'struggle for existence' among nation states. In fact, he clung to these beliefs, retained his faith in bourgeois values, and by his interpretations of the post–war political situation in Germany helped to sustain that conservative nationalism and militarism which in due course destroyed the Weimar Republic. He remained to the end a fervent nationalist, a half–hearted democrat, and an implacable opponent of socialism.

NOTES

1. Weber is said to have replied to a student who asked him what his political plans were after the signing of the Versailles peace treaty and its ratification by the National Assembly in July 1919: 'I have no political plans except to concentrate all my intellectual strength on the one problem, how to get once more for Germany a great general staff' (quoted in Mayer, 1956, p. 107).
2. He himself made this clear in his Inaugural Lecture of 1895: 'I am a

member of the bourgeois class, regard myself as a member, and have been educated in its view and ideals.' His criticism of the bourgeoisie was that it had not yet demonstrated its political capacity to rule and to direct national policy effectively towards making Germany a world power.

3. There is indeed very little critical or comparative analysis of the modern nation state in Weber's political writings, and as Mommsen suggests he largely took for granted the late nineteenth–century world of imperialist rivalries.

4. From the standpoint of an interpretation of modern culture in the capitalist world the concept of rationalization is no doubt a fundamental theme in Weber's work, as Karl Löwith argued in his monograph on Weber and Marx (Löwith, 1932). A similar theme occupies a prominent place in Simmel's analysis of modern culture, especially in his study of money (Simmel, 1900).

5. See Weber's analysis of Bismarck's 'political legacy' in 'Parliament and Government in a reconstructed Germany' (1958, pp. 311–19).

6. Weber's general argument against socialism—which is set out in fragmentary form in several of his political essays (1958) and in a more connected way in *Economy and Society* (1921) and the lecture on socialism (1924)—had three main elements: (i) that a socialist economy would be deprived of the means of rational calculation, in so far as it involved physical allocation of resources rather than the use of money and a price mechanism (1925, esp. pp. 53–8); (ii) that socialism would result not in government by the people, but in an extension of bureaucratic power; and (iii) that the existing socialist movement in Germany was incapable of providing competent and effective political leadership for the nation. In the present context I am concerned only with the second element.

7. See especially E. Fleischmann (1964).

8. H.P. Bahrdt notes, quite correctly in my view, that Weber's fundamental conviction, as expressed for example in his lecture on socialism, was that 'the property–owning entrepreneurial bourgeoisie was the only group capable of providing the leadership to maintain a dynamic society' (Bahrdt, 1965, p. 126).

9. Already in a letter of 1908 to Roberto Michels (cited in Mommsen, 1959), Weber asserted that 'any idea which proposes to eliminate the domination of man by man through an extension of "democracy" is utopian', and further 'Such concepts as "will of the people", authentic will of the people, have long since ceased to exist for me; they are *fictions.*'

10. This view was later elaborated by Schumpeter (1976. Part IV) in his study of capitalism, socialism and democracy.

11. Their influence is generally greater when governments themselves are weak and short–lived; hence the considerable discussion about the role of high officials during the period of the Third Republic in France. However, there may well be a tendency for the power of officials to increase steadily, unless checked, in present–day societies, as is suggested by critical accounts of the 'rule of the *Énarques*' (high officials trained since the war at the National School of Administration, ENA) in France, and by Mr Tony Benn's recent comments on the role of higher civil servants in Britain.

12. Roberto Michels, *Political Parties* (1911, English trans. 1962). On the relations between Weber and Michels, see Mommsen, Wolfgang J., 'Max Weber and Roberto Michels', *European Journal of Sociology*, XXII, 1 (1981), pp. 100–16; and on the development of Michels' own views, see Beetham, David, 'Michels and his critics', ibid., pp. 81–99.

BIBLIOGRAPHY

Bahrdt, H.P., 'Contribution to Discussion on "Max Weber und die Machtpolitik" ', in Stammer, Otto, (ed.), *Max Weber und die Soziologie heute* (Tübingen: J.C.B. Mohr (Paul Siebeck), 1965), pp. 124–30.

Brym, Robert J., *Intellectuals and Politics* (London: Allen & Unwin, 1980).

Fleischmann, E., 'De Weber à Nietzsche', in *Archives Européennes de Sociologie* V (1964) pp. 190–238.

Hilferding, Rudolf, *Finance Capital: A Study of the Latest Phase of Capitalist Development* (1910) (English trans, London: Routledge & Kegan Paul, 1981).

Hirst, Paul Q, *Social Evolution and Sociological Categories* (London: Allen & Unwin, 1976).

Löwith, Karl, 'Max Weber und Karl Marx', in *Archiv für Sozialwissenschaft und Sozialpolitik*, LXVI (1932), pp. 53–99, 175–214. (English trans. London: Allen & Unwin, 1982).

Mayer, J.P., *Max Weber and German Politics: A Study in Political Sociology*, 2nd rev and enlarged edn (London: Faber & Faber, 1956).

Michels, Roberto, *Political Parties* (1911) (English trans. New York: The Free Press, 1962).

Mommsen, Wolfgang J., *Max Weber und die deutsche Politik 1890–1920* (Tübingen: J.C.B. Mohr (Paul Siebeck), 1959).

Mommsen, Wolfgang J., *The Age of Bureaucracy: Perspectives on the Political Sociology of Max Weber* (Oxford: Basil Blackwell, 1974).

Schumpeter, J.P., *Capitalism, Socialism and Democracy* (1942), 5th edn with a new introduction (London: Allen and Unwin, 1976).

Simmel, Georg, *Philosophie des Geldes* (1900), 2nd enlarged edn (Munich and Leipzig: Duncker & Humblot, 1907; English trans. London: Routledge & Kegan Paul, 1978).

Sorel, Georges, Preface to Saverio Merlino, *Formes et essence du Socialisme* (Paris, 1898).

Weber, Max, 'Der Nationalstaat und die Volkswirtschaftspolitik [Inaugural Lecture at the University of Freiburg]' (1895), in *Gesammelte Politische Schriften*, 3rd enlarged edn (Tübingen: J.C.B. Mohr (Paul Siebeck), 1971), pp. 1–25.

Weber, Max, 'Parlament und Regierung im neugeordneten Deutschland' (1918), in *Gesammelte Politische Schriften* (1971), pp. 306–443. (English trans. in *Economy and Society*. 3 vols. New York: Bedminster Press, 1968. Appendix to Vol. III).

Weber, Max, 'Der Sozialismus' (1918), in *Gesammelte Aufsätze zur Soziologie und Sozialpolitik* (Tübingen: J.C.B. Mohr (Paul Siebeck),

1924), pp. 492–518.

Weber, Max, 'Deutschlands künftige Staatsform' (1918) in *Gesammelte Politische Schriften* (1971). pp. 448–83.

Weber, Max, 'Politik als Beruf' (1919), in *Gesammelte Politische Schriften* (1971), pp. 505–60. (English trans. in Gerth, H.H. and Mills, C.W. (eds.), *From Max Weber: Essays in Sociology*, New York: Oxford University Press, 1947. pp. 77–128).

Weber, Max, *Wirtschaft und Gesellschaft (Tübingen:* J.C.B. Mohr (Paul Siebeck), 1921; English trans. *Economy and Society*, 1968).

8 The Decline of Capitalism

PRESENTATION OF THE PROBLEM

In this essay I propose to examine from a sociological perspective Schumpeter's predictions concerning the decline of capitalism and the advent of socialism. I use the term 'prediction' here in the highly qualified sense which Schumpeter himself gave to it in his paper 'The March into Socialism', which was appended to the third edition of *Capitalism, Socialism and Democracy* (1950):

I do not advocate socialism . . . More important . . . I do not 'prophesy' or predict it. Any prediction is extrascientific prophecy that attempts to do more than to diagnose observable tendencies and to state what results would be, if these tendencies should work themselves out according to their logic. In itself, this does not amount to prognosis or prediction because factors external to the chosen range of observation may intervene to prevent that consummation; because, with phenomena so far removed as social phenomena are from the comfortable situation that astronomers have the good fortune of facing, observable tendencies, even if allowed to work themselves out, may be compatible with more than one outcome; and because existing tendencies, battling with resistances, may fail to work themselves out completely and may eventually 'stick' at some halfway house (*CSD*, 1950 and subsequent editions, p. 422).

Thus Schumpeter's general prognosis, which is also expressed in a qualified form in the third edition as a belief 'that the capitalist order tends to destroy itself and that centralist socialism is—with the qualifications mentioned above—a likely heir apparent' (p. 423), has to be considered from two aspects. First, is his diagnosis of the 'observable tendencies' sound? And if so, have any new countervailing tendencies emerged, during the thirty years since the third edition of his book was published, which suggest a different outcome, and possibly some kind of 'sticking' at a halfway house? Schumpeter made clear that he did not think capitalism would disappear as a result of economic failure or breakdown. On the contrary, he claimed that it would be destroyed by its economic success, which was bringing about social and cultural conditions inimical to its own survival. These conditions were, in his view, the obsolescence of the entrepreneurial function; the destruction of the protecting strata constituted by pre–capitalist social groups; the destruction of the institutional framework of individual proprietorship; and a growing hostility to the social system and culture of capitalism, which is widely diffused by a large stratum of critical intellectuals. Let us consider these various tendencies in turn.

THE VANISHING ENTREPRENEUR

Schumpeter argued that the social function of the entrepreneur is being steadily undermined as 'economic progress tends to become depersonalized and automatized', and 'bureau and committee work tends to replace individual action' (p. 133), and that this process

affects the position of the entire bourgeois stratum . . . Economically and sociologically, directly and indirectly, the bourgeoisie therefore depends on the entrepreneur and, as a class, lives and will die with him . . . The perfectly bureaucratized giant industrial unit not only ousts the small or medium–sized firm and 'expropriates' its owners, but in the end it also ousts the entrepreneur and expropriates the bourgeoisie as a class (p. 134).

This process of eliminating the entrepreneur, through the growth of large corporations in which management and administration are bureaucratized, while scientific and technological progress is routinized, is reinforced by the increasing intervention of the state in economic life. Schumpeter summed up the latter tendency by noting the extent to which, in the years immediately following the second world war, the business class, as well as many economists, accepted approvingly a large amount of public management of business situations, redistributive taxation, price regulation, public control over the labour and money markets, indefinite growth of the sphere of wants to be satisfied by public enterprise, and extensive social security legislation (p. 424).

Hence, in Schumpeter's view, the economic process tends to socialize itself, and the development of the western industrial societies can be regarded as passing through the three stages of entrepreneurial capitalism, organized or bureaucratic capitalism and socialism. This view is not unlike that of the Austro–Marxist thinkers with whom Schumpeter was acquainted in his student days (Smithies, 1951, p. 11) and whose work influenced him in several respects. Karl Renner, for example, drew attention during the first world war to the significance of what he called the 'state penetration' of the economy:

> The epoch of the individual entrepreneur operating in a situation of completely free competition is already farther away than we think. Here I am not so much concerned with the fact of the numerous nationalizations, which only make the state a private owner and change little or nothing in its social character. It is a question rather of the penetration of the private economy down to its elementary cells by the state; not the nationalization of a few factories, but the control of the whole private sector of the economy by willed and conscious regulation and direction . . . The enterprise takes the place of the entrepreneur and becomes semi–public (Renner, 1916).

Similarly, Rudolf Hilferding, in *Finance Capital* (1910) and in subsequent writings (Hilferding, 1915, 1924), analyzed in detail the concentration of capital in large corporations, and the changing economic role of the state, which were bringing into existence a new kind of economic and social order, namely 'organized capitalism'.

The growth of corporations and the increasing state regulation of the economy have continued unabated over the past thirty years. In the 1950s and 1960s there was a wave of mergers, comparable with that which took place around the turn of the century when the early trusts and cartels were formed (Hannah, 1975), and large corporations have become increasingly dominant in the economy as a whole (for the USA see Miller, 1975). At the same time, state intervention has continued to grow in the provision of infrastructural

services (welfare and the education and training of the labour
force), in the management of demand, intended to maintain
economic growth and a high level of employment, and in a
more general planning of the economy. State expenditure has
increased in all the western capitalist countries and now represents between 40 and 50 per cent of gross national product in
most of them. It is evident that the health of the economy now
depends overwhelmingly not upon entrepreneurship but
upon regular, efficient activity in the major spheres of
industry, food production, distribution, transport, communi-
cation and finance, which is assured by large corporations—
both public and private—and by state regulation. Innovation
and economic development now result much more from
scientific research programmes, largely sponsored and
financed by the state, and from a massive investment of public
funds, than from the activities of individual inventors and
entrepreneurs.

  The question is how far this socialization is likely to proceed
in the next few decades. Schumpeter, as we have seen,
thought that the decline of the entrepreneur would weaken
the position of the whole bourgeois class, and presumably
lead to the social and political dominance of new social
groups. I shall consider the situation and role of various
classes more fully later, but first it should be observed that in
the present–day, 'mixed economies' the power of private
capital is still very great and there is a close relation between
business and the state (Domhoff, 1967; Johnson, 1973). It is
indeed the contradiction between the private appropriation of
profits and the socialization of costs (of unemployment,
research and development, unprofitable or excessively risky
undertakings) which is considered by some writers to be the
main cause of the 'fiscal crisis of the state' (O'Connor, 1973)
or of a more general 'legitimation crisis' (Habermas, 1973).
Since it is very doubtful that a modern economy could continue to function effectively without this 'socialization of
costs'—that is to say, if public expenditure were substantially,
or perhaps even marginally, reduced—the most likely outcome of the present economic crisis is a further extension of
public control and planning of the economy. Undoubtedly,
one major way out of the fiscal crisis would be for the state to

socialize profits as well as costs, and thus to derive a larger proportion of its revenues from profit–generating activities— in the oil industry, automobiles, insurance, banking—as against taxation. However, this postulated tendency towards an extension of public control depends for its actualization upon a great many other social and cultural factors, and in the first place upon the orientation and strength of various economic and political interests, which we now need to consider.

THE CHANGING CLASS STRUCTURE

Although Schumpeter himself wrote an original and illuminating study of social classes (Schumpeter, 1927)—concerning which he observed that 'the subject . . . poses a wealth of new questions, offers outlooks on untilled fields, foreshadows sciences of the future. Roaming it, one often has a strange feeling, as though the social sciences of today, almost on purpose, were dealing with relative side–issues'—he did not in fact assign a very large place to the actions of classes in his analysis of the developmental tendencies of modern capitalist society in *Capitalism, Socialism and Democracy*. To be sure, he discussed briefly, as we have seen, the disappearance of the entrepreneur and what he took to be its consequences for the whole bourgeois class (pp. 131–4); and he went on to note (pp. 134–42) the 'destruction of the protecting strata', that is to say, of those social groups surviving from feudal society— aristocracy and gentry, small traders, artisans and peasants— which had provided a political protective framework for the bourgeoisie, as well as the decline of the bourgeoisie as a cohesive and distinctive property–owning class with the growth of the joint stock company and the emergence of a more diffuse pattern of ownership which, he argued, 'takes the life out of the idea of property'.

But Schumpeter did not examine in any detail the changes in the class structure, and in particular he did not associate the advent of socialism with the politics of a class. The development of capitalism, as he portrayed it here, is conceived as a purely economic and impersonal process, and socialism—

defined only in economic terms, as a system in which 'the economic affairs of society belong to the public and not to the private sphere'—is represented as the most probable outcome of that process. In short, the economy socializies itself. There is expressed here an implicit economic determinism—qualified by Schumpeter's remarks on prediction in the social sciences[1]—which has a close kinship with those deterministic forms of Marxist theory that envisaged an inevitable economic breakdown of capitalism; above all in its disregard of the mediating influence of ideological and political struggles among classes and other groups. On the other side, this view contrasts strongly with another form of Marxist theory, well represented by Hilferding who also worked out, as I have indicated, a conception of 'organized capitalism', but regarded the transition from capitalism to socialism as being a question of political struggle between classes, not an ineluctable outcome of economic development.

Even a brief consideration of the changing class structure in advanced capitalist societies will provide a vantage point from which to criticize much of Schumpeter's argument about the necessary, or probable, transition to socialism. Let us consider first the position of the bourgeoisie. Schumpeter envisaged its demise ensuing from the disappearance of the entrepreneur; but what has occurred can more plausibly be interpreted as a change in its composition, and in the specific manner in which it dominates the economic system, while at the same time a historical continuity is maintained. We need to examine two aspects of these changes. One is the emergence, in the period of organized capitalism, of much larger and more influential groups of technologists, managers and officials who play a major part in the control and planning of the economy, whether in the public or private sphere. The rise to prominence of these social groups was analyzed several decades ago in terms of a 'managerial revolution' (Burnham, 1941); and since that time it has been frequently discussed as an indication of the formation of a 'new class', comprising technocrats and bureaucrats, in both capitalist and socialist societies (Gurvitch, 1949, 1966; Djilas, 1957; Meynaud, 1964). More recently, the same theme has assumed a central importance in various conceptions of 'post–industrial society'. Thus Touraine writes, in a discussion of 'old and new social classes', that:

The new ruling class can no longer be those who are in charge of and profit from private investment; it can only be all those who identify themselves with collective investment and who enter into conflict with those who demand increased consumption or whose private life resists change [and] . . . If property was the criterion of membership in the former dominant classes, the new dominant class is defined by knowledge and a certain level of education (Touraine, 1969).

What is common to these studies is the idea that a new dominant class has emerged, or is emerging, in the advanced industrial societies. Thus in the case of the western countries the most likely path of social development is no longer visualized, at least in the medium–term future, as a transition from capitalism to socialism in the sense of the advent of a classless society, or even in Schumpeter's narrower sense of the more or less complete substitution of public for private ownership and control of production (although the enhanced role of the state in the economy is recognized), but rather as a consolidation of 'organized capitalism' or 'state capitalism'. Where the analyses differ is in the account they give of the relation between the new dominant class and the traditional bourgeoisie. Touraine asserts a more or less total separation when he claims that property is no longer a criterion for membership of the dominant class. Marxist writers, on the other hand, emphasize the continued dominance of private capital—and indeed its increasing power, with the concentration of capital in giant corporations, including the transnational corporations[2]—and conceive the western economies as being still essentially capitalist market economies. At the same time they recognize the changing character of 'late capitalism' (Mandel, 1972), and some Marxist interpretations come close to those proffered by social scientists who, while acknowledging the significance of the 'techno–bureaucracy' (Gurvitch, 1949), see these new social groups as being largely assimilated to, or merging with, the old bourgeoisie.

The second aspect of this question, therefore, concerns the extent to which there is a historical continuity between the traditional bourgeoisie and the dominant class in the present–

day western societies. My own view is that the element of continuity is very great, being sustained both by the considerable overlapping of ownership and management of productive capital and by the ideological commitment of a large proportion of those managers, technocrats and bureaucrats who are not substantial owners of capital to the bourgeois conception of a capitalist market economy, although this does not exclude the possibility of diverse, and even contradictory, interests and values within the dominant class, or the existence, for example, of important similarities between western and Soviet societies in the functions, and to some extent in the outlook, of techno–bureaucratic groups. I conclude, therefore, that Schumpeter was mistaken in arguing that the decline of the entrepreneur would necessarily entail the decline of the whole bourgeois class.

This criticism of Schumpeter is strengthened, I believe, by consideration of another feature of the class structure in present–day western societies; namely, the growth of the 'new middle class'. This has been seen as a major factor in the development of western capitalist societies ever since Bernstein (1899) in his reassessment of Marxist theory and social democratic politics in Germany drew attention to the fact— among other things—that the middle class was not disappearing, and that the polarization of modern society into two great classes, which Marx had envisaged, was therefore not taking place. During the present century, and especially in the past three decades, sociologists of all persuasions have had to reckon, not simply with the non–disappearance of the middle class, but with its sustained expansion, as white–collar occupations of all kinds have proliferated, and to explore the social and political consequences of this development.

Broadly speaking three different views have been adopted. The first suggests that the middle class, or at any rate large sections of it, align themselves ideologically and politically with the bourgeoisie; and one reason for this tendency was indicated by Hilferding (1910) in his analysis of the changes in class relations accompanying the development of 'organized capitalism', when he observed that the growth of salaried employment has created a new hierarchical system in which 'The interest in a career, the drive for advancement which develops in every hierarchy, is thus kindled in each individual employee and triumphs over his feeling of solidarity. Everyone hopes to rise above the others and to work his way out of his semi-proletarian condition to the heights of capitalist income' (p. 347).

A second view conceives the middle class, notwithstanding its diversity, as possessing some common characteristics which give it a distinctive and independent political role, between the bourgeoisie and the working class.[3] The post–war expansion of the middle class has reinforced this idea, and has given rise to a conception of 'middle–class societies' in which the political conflict between bourgeoisie and working class is likely to abate, or even disappear, and to be replaced by a style of consensus politics based upon commitment to a mixed economy and the welfare state (Aron, 1968; Bell, 1973).[4]

Third, however, some social scientists, from a standpoint quite opposed to the foregoing, have conceived white–collar and professional workers in the present–day capitalist societies as constituting elements of a 'new working class' (Mallet, 1963; Touraine, 1968),[5] or at least as being potential allies of the working class and the socialist movement (Poulantzas, 1974). Such interpretations can be supported by some empirical evidence; notably the rapid expansion of white–collar trade unionism, the increasing militancy of white–collar unions, and on occasion (as in France in May 1968) some manifestations of political radicalism. Nevertheless, electoral data and surveys of political attitudes over longer periods indicate clearly that a very large part of the middle class, in spite of variations among different sections of it—small businessmen/women, shopkeepers, professional and technical employees, clerical workers, etc.—has maintained a political orientation which is much more favourable to parties of the Right and the Centre than to those of the Left. This outlook might be encapsulated in the fairly obvious comment that an overwhelming majority of the middle class is much more strongly attracted by policies which would reduce taxation and diminish public expenditure than by any projects for extending public ownership or industrial democracy, or, in general, for bringing about greater equality.

Hence it may be claimed that the position of the bourgeoisie in present–day capitalist societies has been strengthened rather than weakened by the growth of the middle class. Concomitantly, the traditional working class has declined, both relatively (as a proportion of the employed population) and, in some cases, in absolute numbers; and these changes in its economic and social situation, which are likely to continue in the same direction with the further progress of technology and automation, must necessarily diminish its political influence. So far, this political decline has been counteracted to some extent by other factors, and in some countries, for example, labour and socialist parties have been more successful in gaining working–class votes since the war than they were in earlier periods, or have regained their electoral strength after a period of decline. In effect, such parties have gained a greater degree of support from a smaller working class, and in this respect perhaps it can be argued that there has been a development of working–class consciousness, and a more pronounced polarization of society, at least since the end of the 1950s.

But is the working–class vote a vote for socialism? The answer to this question is far from clear, but I think it may reasonably be argued that for most of the social democratic labour parties in Western Europe—and they are the pre–eminent political representatives of the western working class—the goal of socialism has been relegated to a distant future, if it is seriously entertained at all, while the practical, effective political aim is to consolidate and improve the existing system of a mixed economy and a welfare state. Of course, there are considerable differences among countries even in Europe, and in Sweden, for example, where the social democratic movement has been a dominant force in politics for a much longer time than elsewhere, it has been suggested that the *political* levels of aspiration of wage–earners are likely to rise in the medium–term future, extending increasingly to issues of control over work and production (Korpi, 1978). But changes in the opposite sense seem to have been taking place in some of the communist parties of Western Europe, and some observers have seen in the Eurocommunist movement a distinct trend towards a more reformist outlook, closer to that of the social democratic parties. Outside Europe, the socialist movement is particularly weak in North America; in the USA there is no independent labour or socialist party of any significance, and in Canada the labour party (the New Democratic Party) has nothing like the strength of similar parties in Europe.

If the commitment of working–class political parties to socialism is thus questionable, this is even more clearly the case with the mass organizations of workers, the trade unions. As I have argued elsewhere (Bottomore, 1979), the link between the trade unions and socialism seems, in the post–war period, to have become more tenuous, or at any rate ambiguous; though again there are important variations between countries. Undoubtedly, the economic power of trade unions (both working–class and white–collar unions) has increased considerably over the past few decades, but the exercise of this power takes place very largely in the context of an acceptance of the capitalist market economy, as modified and regulated by the present degree of state intervention. This is notably the case in Britain, where the enormous importance attached to free collective bargaining by much of the trade union leadership and membership represents both an accommodation to a market economy and an abandonment of wider political aims. More generally, the dominant tendency in the European trade union movement—with some exceptions where unions or federations are still closely allied with more radical socialist parties—seems to be a development towards a form of 'business unionism' within the existing economic and social framework, and in this sense a 'depoliticization' of the unions.

From this brief account of the class structure, and of what appear to be the political orientations of the major classes, it may be concluded that the 'march into socialism' has been much less vigorous and rapid than Schumpeter expected. The development of the modern capitalist societies does indeed seem to have stuck at some kind of halfway house—or perhaps it would be more accurate to say, at a point which is a quarter or a third of the way—along the road to socialism. But this is not to claim that a position of stable equilibrium has been reached. Clearly, the present form of society is still contested—from both sides. In Britain at present a vigorous attempt is being made to reduce state intervention and augment the role of capitalist enterprises and the market economy. On the other side, the worsening economic crisis may well lead to an extension of public planning of the economy, and to a reanimation of the socialist movement, in many countries. Before considering these possibilities more fully, however, it is necessary to look at some other aspects of the decline of capitalism as Schumpeter envisaged it.

CAPITALIST VALUES

Just as Schumpeter saw the economic trend towards socialism as being facilitated by the destruction of the institutional framework of capitalism and the decline of the bourgeoisie as a class, so also he thought that the assault upon, and the decay of, capitalist values would give a further impetus to this trend. Capitalism, he argued,

'creates a critical frame of mind which, after having destroyed the moral authority of so many other institutions, in the end turns against its own; the bourgeois finds to his amazement that the rationalist attitude does not stop at the credentials of kings and popes but goes on to attack private property and the whole scheme of bourgeois values. The bourgeois fortress thus becomes politically defenceless' (p. 143).

But Schumpeter devotes only a few pages to this issue, and his analysis is quite inadequate. Let us, therefore, examine more closely the capitalist ideology, and the counter–ideology of socialism, and try to assess their development in the post–war period. By an ideology I mean here the body of ideas in which the values and aspirations of a social class (or other social group) are expressed in a more or less systematic and coherent way.[6] In the case of a dominant class its ideology does not only serve to systematize its values, and in this way reinforce the cohesion of the class, but is also a means of legitimating—and is at least in part consciously intended to legitimate—its domination, by ensuring as far as possible the support or acquiescence of other classes.[7] For a subordinate class ideology also has this systematizing and unifying role, and it provides at the same time the ground for a critical assault upon the ideology of the dominant class. Clearly, it is this kind of ideological conflict which Schumpeter had in mind in discussing the cultural aspects of the decline of capitalism, but he referred to the capitalist ideology only in vague general terms as the 'scheme of bourgeois values', and largely ignored the role of a counter-ideology as expounded by representatives of a subordinate class. The dissolution of bourgeois values was presented by Schumpeter as the outcome of a purely intellectual process of rational criticism.

What then are the principal elements of the capitalist ideology, and how have they fared over the past few decades? The fundamental components—which may be related in diverse ways and have varying degrees of importance in particular formulations of the ideology—are, I would suggest, the ideas of private property, individualism, achievement and nation. When Schumpeter argued that corporate ownership 'takes the life out of private property' he expressed in a one–sided and inadequate form an important observation which has been more clearly and comprehensively formulated by socialist thinkers in their criticism of individualistic interpretations of property as applied to the modern system of industrial production.[8] The underlying theme of this criticism has been concisely stated as follows:

Property rights can no longer be defined as a relation between the individual and the material objects which he has created; they must be defined as social rights which determine the relations of the various groups of owners and non–owners to the system of production, and prescribe what each group's share of the social product shall be (Schlatter, 1951).

The important question to consider is whether the undoubted expansion of social or collective property—in the form either of capitalist corporate property or of public property—has actually weakened the idea of private property as an ideological influence. The answer, it seems to me, is that it has not done so to any significant degree. No doubt there is now a greater acceptance of fairly extensive public ownership, particularly in connection with the provision of infrastructural services, and even to a limited extent in the sphere of production, but the idea of private ownership and control of productive resources is still pre–eminent. There is no evidence that shareholding, as distinct from the direct ownership of physical plant, has attenuated the sense of private property in the very small section of the population who actually own shares, as Schumpeter thought it would. On the other hand, those who run the large corporations as directors are still engaged, and know that they are engaged, in the productive use of private property, some of which they 'own' in the legal sense, while the rest of it they collectively 'possess' in the sense that they can effectively decide, within very wide limits, how, when and where to use the property in production, and upon the disposition of the profits.[9] In addition, it should be remembered that a large part of production in the most advanced economies is still carried on by businesses in which the capital is owned directly by individuals, families or partnerships. Finally, it is important to recognize that the socialist criticism of private property has evoked a powerful counter–criticism of collective, or public, property, based largely upon arguments about the inefficiency of state–owned enterprises and about the threat to individual freedom where property ownership becomes concentrated in the state. Hence, although property relations have certainly been modified, and have become more complex, in the advanced capitalist societies, I do not think there is any evidence to support the view that private property in the sphere of production, either as a fact or as an ideology, has been steadily and continuously eroded over the past few decades. In this case too, a halfway (or quarter–way) house seems to have been reached, where there is a precarious and contested balance between private and collective property, with conflicting movements to change the balance in one direction or the other.

Individualism, of course, has always been closely associated with the idea of private property in the bourgeois scheme of values, most evidently in the individualistic theories of property mentioned earlier. But this association, which was relevant at any time only to a minority of the population, has become increasingly anachronistic, as far as the ownership of industrial property is concerned, with the economic dominance of large corporations. As C. Wright Mills (1951) observed with respect to American society, the prevailing ideology, with its emphasis on independence, individualism and mobility, which may have been appropriate to the small–propertied world of the early nineteenth century, was only a mystification in the conditions of the mid–twentieth century when most Americans had become 'hired employees' (and still more so today, we might add). The persistence of this ideology, not only in the USA, although it has doubtless been strongest there, is due in large measure to a confusion between private property in the sense of ownership of means of production—which may be considered to confer a certain economic, and hence political, independence—and 'personal' property. No doubt, a sufficient amount of personal property, even without any direct ownership of means of production, also makes possible a greater independence of the individual; but the notion then does not apply to the vast majority of people in any modern capitalist society, whose 'ownership' consists for the most part of 'owning' a mortgage on their dwelling, in the case of those (50 per cent or less) who are owner–occupiers, and a substantial amount of hire–purchase debt.

None the less, the ideology of individualism remains strong, and continues to sustain the capitalist order. One important factor in addition to the confusion just considered is the widespread apprehension about the increasing power of the state, the invasion of privacy (though this is by no means due only to the activities of the state), and a general sense of living in 'over–regulated' societies. Such views seem to reinforce the prevailing capitalist version of individualism,[10] in spite of the fact that the extension of the state's activities has not been primarily associated with the advance of socialism in the western capitalist countries, but may be regarded as essential to the functioning and continuance of modern capitalism itself, and also as a consequence of international rivalries and conflicts, including two world wars. And oddly enough, the idea that a capitalist market economy (and hence strict limits to state intervention) is essential for individual liberty to flourish has remained very persuasive in spite of the fact that our 'over–regulated' societies are at the same time characterized as 'permissive', and that the 'march into socialism' has actually been accompanied by greatly expanded opportunities for large numbers of people to choose more freely their individual style of life.

The third element in the capitalist ideology, the idea of 'achievement', is also quite closely related to individualism, and it has been regarded by some socialist critics as the major factor which legitimates and sustains the present–day capitalist order. Thus Claus Offe (1970) writes: 'In contemporary capitalist industrial societies, the system of official self–imagery and self–explanation is dominated by the concept of the achieving society.' This 'achievement principle', he goes on to argue, legitimates differences of social status and reward by attributing them to individual differences in achievement or 'merit', and represses alternatives to the existing arrangements. An effective criticism of the prevailing ideology in modern capitalist societies therefore requires above all a criticism of this particular principle, which he attempts to provide, not by showing that it is incompletely realized in practice (as is evidently the case), but by demonstrating the consequences of its success, in as much as 'these consequences conflict with existing interests and values', and by pointing out 'the "costs" that a society must be prepared to pay if it accepts the achievement principle as a "just" mechanism by which to distribute status' (Offe, 1970, p. 137).

Finally, the 'nation' and nationalism play an important part in bourgeois ideology; both positively, in fostering a sense of unity and an attachment to traditional values, and negatively, in countering the divisiveness implied by ideas of class differences and class conflict, which are especially prominent in Marxist socialism. In some periods nationalism has been expressed with particular intensity, in the form of imperialism, by the dominant groups in capitalist countries.[11] Such nationalism contrasts sharply with the internationalism which has been an important feature of socialist ideology from the beginning, and has assumed a variety of institutional forms since the creation of the 1st International in 1864. The fact that internationalism has been relatively ineffectual in practice is in part an indication of the continuing strength of nationalist ideology, which remains one of the mainstays of the bourgeois scheme of values.

As I suggested earlier, the specific form taken by the capitalist ideology at any given time and place involves diverse combinations of the various elements which compose it. During the past three decades, rapid economic growth and increasing prosperity seem to have linked together the ideas of private property, individualism and achievement in a social outlook which can best be characterized as one of unrestrained acquisitiveness—as R.H. Tawney (1921) described it more than half a century ago in a work which has lost none of its relevance—notwithstanding the fact that there has also been, during the same period, some movement towards more extensive collective provision of basic social services. An analysis of present–day culture suggests, therefore, that the economic successes of capitalism—the 'managed capitalism' of the post–war period—far from killing it, as Schumpeter predicted, have greatly strengthened it. On the other side, its possible economic failures now loom larger again (as in the 1930s), not only because of the immediate crisis, with declining rates of growth and rising unemployment, but because of the longer–term problems associated with the natural and social limits to growth, and with the impact upon the whole labour process of advanced technology. These prospects have already given rise, since the late 1960s, to new social movements, such as the ecology movement, which perhaps mark the beginning of a significant change in the cultural orientation of western capitalist societies. Whether they also indicate a possible resumption of the 'march into socialism', a revival and renewal of the socialist movement, still needs to be considered in a wider context.

THE INTELLECTUALS AND SOCIAL CRITICISM

There was one social group to which Schumpeter attached particular importance in his account of the growing climate of hostility to capitalism; namely, the intellectuals. Capitalism, he argued, 'unlike any other type of society . . . inevitably and by virtue of the very logic of its civilization creates, educates and subsidizes a vested interest in social unrest'

(*CSD*, p. 146). But in this case Schumpeter was undoubtedly too greatly influenced by the particular circumstances of the 1930s; by the notoriety given to what were in fact relatively small groups of radical intellectuals in most countries, and by the phenomenon of 'intellectual unemployment' which produced, in his view, large numbers of discontented and resentful individuals. The intellectuals, he argued, had 'invaded labour politics' and radicalized it, 'eventually imparting a revolutionary bias to the most bourgeois trade union practices . . . Thus, though intellectuals have not created the labor movement, they have yet worked it up into something that differs substantially from what it would be without them' (p. 154).

This account exaggerates both the radicalism and the social influence of intellectuals in modern societies. If we take a longer historical view it soon becomes apparent that there are major fluctuations in the radicalism of intellectuals over time, as well as important differences among the various categories of intellectuals (for example, between social scientists and natural scientists, and between different intellectual professions, with university teachers probably being more radical, in general, than lawyers). One significant factor in the historical fluctuations is undoubtedly the degree of overproduction of educated persons (and hence intellectual unemployment), as Schumpeter suggested, and as a recent study largely confirms while introducing some important qualifications (Brym, 1980). But even in periods when intellectual radicalism appears to be flourishing, as in the 1930s and 1960s, it is hard to demonstrate that even a majority of intellectuals adopt a radical orientation; and there are certainly very great differences between countries.[12] Moreover, such periods have almost always been followed by a conservative reaction among intellectuals (the 1950s, the 1970s), so that it would in any case be invalid to argue that a consistent and progressive radicalization of intellectuals has been taking place which, in itself, tends to undermine capitalism.

But Schumpeter also attributes too great an influence to intellectuals even when large numbers of them are radical. What is much more evident, I think, is the relative social isolation of intellectuals, and their incapacity to exercise any profound effect upon social and political life, though here too there are considerable differences between countries, with intellectuals having probably a greater political role in France than in Britain or the USA. The following comments on the American situation in the 1930s seems to me to present a more truthful picture than the one conveyed by Schumpeter:

While novelists, in the main, fought shy of the proletarians, critics in some cases welcomed the new literary credo [the idea of 'proletarian literature'] . . . In Greenwich Village the revolution seemed about to burst forth at any moment . . . After election day, when noses were counted, it was discovered that about one hundred thousand Americans had voted red—1/4 of 1 per cent of the electorate. The millions of unemployed, the dispirited of the breadlines and flophouses, had voted for either Hoover or Roosevelt. Even the mild Socialist programme suffered overwhelming defeat. (Harrison, 1933).

Similarly, in 1968 and again in 1972, after several years of intellectual ferment, and an apparent upsurge of radicalism, the American electorate voted for Richard Nixon as President, while in France, after an even more turbulent and dramatic display of intellectual radicalism, culminating in the events of May 1968, the electorate gave overwhelming support to the regime of General de Gaulle.

Against Schumpeter's conception of the more or less autonomous, and generally radical, social and political orientation of intellectuals, I think it is more convincing (i.e. better supported by empirical evidence) to argue that the politics of intellectuals are primarily determined by the direction of their 'ties with society's fundamental classes and groups' (Brym, 1980, p. 71), and that the rate and level of intellectual radicalism 'vary proportionately with the size, level of social organization and access to resources of both radical intellectual groups themselves, and other radical groups which can sustain them' (Brym, p. 72). It is not, therefore, intellectuals who radicalize the labour movement (or other social movements), but social movements which, in certain circumstances, radicalize the intellectuals. This enables us to explain why it is that the main elements of the culture of capitalism, as I indicated in the preceding section, have retained their vitality and their dominant position through the postwar period. Economic growth and the consequent changes in class structure and class relations have been the main factors restricting the growth and influence of intellectual radicalism; although as we shall see there are also other forces at work, quite neglected by Schumpeter, in the continuing contest between capitalism and socialism.

SCHUMPETER'S CONCEPTION OF SOCIALISM

The major weakness in Schumpeter's account of the probable transition from capitalism to socialism is that the process itself, and the end result, are defined too exclusively in economic terms. By 'centralist' socialism Schumpeter understood 'that organization of society in which the means of production are controlled, and the decisions on how and what to produce and on who is to get what, are made by public authority instead of by privately–owned and privately–managed firms'; and by the 'march into socialism', 'the migration of people's economic affairs from the private into the public sphere' (*CSD*, p. 421). He deliberately excluded the idea of socialism as a class movement expressing broad political and cultural goals, among which the reorganization of the economy is only one, though a crucial, element; and while recognizing that for many people socialism 'means a new cultural world', he argued that its 'cultural indeterminateness' is so great that it cannot be given any precise definition in these terms (pp. 170–1). In practice Schumpeter took as his principal model of a centralist socialist society the USSR in the 1930s, although in a new chapter on 'the consequences of the second world war', added to the second edition (1947), he also considered very briefly the kind of socialism which might emerge in Britain and elsewhere in Western Europe.

But the cultural 'indeterminateness' or diffuseness of socialism should not be exaggerated. In just the same way as bourgeois ideology, the socialist ideology incorporates various distinctive conceptions, which may be combined in different ways in specific formulations of the doctrine. Among the most important underlying conceptions are those of the collective ownership and use of the major physical productive resources of society; the emancipation of subordinate or oppressed groups; the eventual attainment of a classless society in which all individuals would be able to participate fully, on broadly equal terms, in social and cultural life, and more particularly in major decisions affecting work and community life;[13] and finally, internationalism.

Whether or not there will be a sustained movement towards socialism in the above sense depends ultimately upon the extent to which the socialist scheme of values can establish its pre–eminence over the bourgeois scheme of values, and gain the support of large social groups for its realization in practice. The process in which, according to Schumpeter, the economy 'socializes itself'—through the growth of large corporations and increasing state regulation—is undoubtedly one very important element in this movement, establishing some of the essential preconditions for socialism, as Hilferding (1910) saw clearly; but by itself it may lead just as easily to some form of 'state capitalism' or a 'corporate state' in which the same social groups remain dominant, gross inequalities persist, and nationalism flourishes. In earlier sections of this chapter I have argued, against Schumpeter's view, that bourgeois values are still predominant in the present–day 'organized' or 'managed' capitalist societies, and the principal question we have to consider is why it is that socialist values have made so little progress over the past three decades.

A part of the answer lies in the changes in class structure and class relations which I discussed earlier. From the outset socialism was the doctrine of a particular class, the industrial working class (most obviously when it was expressed in a Marxist form); and in so far as that class has become less powerful, especially in numerical terms, as an economic and political group, is less clearly delineated, and is more integrated into the existing society, the main social base of socialism has been attenuated. In consequence, the socialist ideology itself has become less sharply defined, less vigorous and challenging, more apt to be expressed in diverse, fragmented, and often sectarian views, as happens with all social doctrines which lose their connection with the interests of some major group in society which can claim at the same time to represent a general human interest. As Marx (1844) wrote, in the years which led up to the revolutions of 1848:

No class in society can play this part [as the leader of a movement of emancipation] unless it can arouse, in itself and in the masses, a moment of enthusiasm in which it associates and mingles with society at large, identifies itself with it, and is felt and recognized as the *general representative* of this society. Its aims and interests must genuinely be the aims and interests of society itself, of which it becomes in reality the social head and heart.

It is all too evident that socialism and the working class are not now the 'social head and heart' of any such movement: evident in the reformism of the European social democratic and labour parties, which no longer look beyond an ameliora-tion of conditions for the most deprived social groups within the existing, largely accepted, economic and social system; and in a different form, in the defensive and uninspiring outlook of the Eurocommunist movement. In Western Europe the socialist press has declined in readership and influence,[14] and the mass media as a whole are now more or less uniformly liberal or conservative in oreintation. The expansion of the media, and especially television, has pro-vided new careers for intellectuals, and the high levels of economic growth and more widespread prosperity of the 1950s and 1960s made it possible to assimilate them more fully into bourgeois society, with the result that the edge of radical social criticism has been blunted.

But it is not only these internal social changes which have diminished the appeal of socialism. One of the major blows to its intellectual and political influence has come from the experience of socialism in Eastern Europe, and above all in the USSR. There, 'centralist' socialism, in Schumpeter's sense, has produced regimes which were, in the Stalinist period, despotic and have remained authoritarian. In no sense can these regimes be said to have achieved either the social equality or the emancipation of the individual which are essential aims of the socialist movement; yet they proclaim themselves socialist and they are widely regarded as models of what a socialist society would be like.[15] Their character and policies have unquestionably bred scepticism about socialism as a political goal, or in many cases outright rejection of it; and in this sense they have greatly strengthened the attachment to capitalism, and facilitated the task of its ideological defenders. It has become a matter of 'keep a–hold of nurse, for fear of finding something worse'.

Even if we disregard the extreme authoritarianism of the regimes in Eastern Europe—which may be held to have developed in part, or even mainly, from particular historical conditions, and hence not to demonstrate a necessary connection with socialism—there are other problems in the functioning of a socialist society which have become more apparent as a result of the limited growth of a socialized economy within capitalism. One such problem, frequently raised by the opponents of socialism, is that of bureaucracy, but here Schumpeter seems to me to have taken a more realistic sociological view—clearly influenced by Max Weber's analysis of bureaucracy as a system of rational administration which is in fact inseparable from the development of capitalism—when he wrote that:

> I for one cannot visualize, in the conditions of modern society, a socialist organization in any form other than that of a huge and all-embracing bureaucratic apparatus . . . But surely this should not horrify anyone who realizes how far the bureaucratization of economic life—of life in general even—has gone already . . . We shall see in the next part that bureaucracy is not an obstacle to democracy but an inevitable complement to it. Similarly it is an inevitable complement to modern economic development and it will be more than ever essential in a socialist commonwealth (p. 206).

Nevertheless it may be argued that there are particular dangers to the liberty of the individual in the emergence of a huge, more or less unified, and omnicompetent *state* bureaucracy; and these dangers have been widely discussed by social critics in both capitalist and socialist societies.[16]

A second problem, related in certain aspects to that of bureaucracy, concerns the social and political consequences of centralized economic planning, which Schumpeter took to be the crucial feature of socialism (he always referred to 'centralist socialism'). Here two separate issues must be distinguished: that of economic efficiency and that of the concentration of power in the hands of a small élite who make all major decisions of economic and social policy without being subject to effective public democratic control. Both issues have been widely discussed in recent years, inside and outside the socialist countries, and the debates have become largely focused upon the idea of a 'socialist market economy'. The principal model for such an economy has been the Yugoslav system of self–managed enterprises and institutions within the framework of an overall plan, involving a considerable degree of decentralization of decision–making; and there has been a distinct movement towards such a system in other East European societies, although it has been limited by Soviet control, and sometimes arrested by direct intervention, as in Czechoslovakia in 1968. Some of the major issues involved have been well analyzed by Wlodzimierz Brus (1961, 1973) who examines carefully the difficulties which emerge in the process of socialization of ownership and argues that, in the socialist countries, 'the system for the exercise of state power must evolve so that there is a constant real growth in the influence of society on politico–economic decisions at all levels and an increase in social self–government in all areas of life, especially in economic activities' (1973, p. 99).

The experiences of the socialist countries in respect of the effective implementation of social ownership and of self–management in relation to central planning lend some support to the arguments (which I discussed earlier) of those sociologists who see in the development of advanced industrial societies a trend towards the formation of a new ruling group of technocrats and bureaucrats, and a probable transition, not from capitalism to socialism, but from 'organized capitalism' to some still more organized and regulated form of society, clearly differentiated into dominant and subordinate groups and highly inegalitarian, for which no better name has yet been invented than 'post–industrial society'. Whatever judgement may be made on the plausibility of these interpretations it is certainly the case that no serious student of society can any longer envisage a possible transition from capitalism to socialism in terms of a sudden and dramatic leap from a 'realm of necessity' into a 'realm of freedom'. The contrast between social ownership in practice, as the implementation of a central economic plan, and the ideas of 'classlessness', participation, and self–determination or self–government; the complex difficulties which the achievement of socialism in the latter sphere can now be seen to confront; these have contributed greatly, together with the other tendencies in the development of present–day societies that I described earlier, to diminishing the vigour of the drive towards socialism.

My own evaluation of the situation in the western capitalist countries, forty years on, is therefore just the opposite of that which Schumpeter expressed. He thought that the 'march into socialism' was well–nigh irresistible, and deplored the fact. I, on the contrary, think that this 'march' has come to an untimely halt, and regret the eclipse of the highest ideal that has emerged in modern western culture. With this eclipse the prospect for western capitalism has become more opaque than it was when Schumpeter embarked on his analysis. Two main possibilities present themselves: one is that the western societies will continue to drift aimlessly and dully within the confines of the present status quo; the other that nationalist fervour (by no means ony in the West) and the struggle for the world's limited resources will end in a nuclear conflict and the extinction of any kind of civilized society. Finally, there is a more remote and speculative chance that the economic cr̀isis, and the tedium of our culture, will eventually provoke a revival of socialism, or some new form of radicalism, and with it a new conviction of the possibilities for human progress.

NOTES

1. See p. 136 above. In the preface to the first edition of the book this deterministic view was more forthrightly expressed: 'I have tried to show that a socialist form of society will inevitably emerge from an equally inevitable decomposition of capitalist society.'
2. See p. 138 above.
3. This view is discussed critically in Mills (1951); see also Lockwood (1958).
4. See also the discussion of 'non-egalitarian classlessness' in Ossowski (1963), chap. VII.
5. Mallet argues that the 'new working class' comprises technically-trained manual workers, technicians and some cadres of managers and engineers in the technologically advanced and automated industries, while Touraine observes that in the May 1968 movement in France 'sensibility to the new themes of social conflict was not most pronounced in the most highly organized sectors of the working class. The railroad workers, dockers and miners were not the ones who most clearly grasped its most radical objec-

tives. The most radical and creative movements appeared in the economically advanced groups, the research agencies, the technicians with skills
but no authority, and, of course, in the university community' (1968, p.
18). These views are critically examined in Mann (1973). In his later writing,
Touraine has somewhat modified his views, and he now conceives the main
oppositional groups in the 'post–industrial societies' as being, not 'new
classes', but the new social movements (e.g. the women's movement, the
ecology movement). See Touraine (1980).

6. I am not concerned here with the specifically Marxist concept of ideology,
in which ideology is seen as a distorted world view arising from a 'false
consciousness', strictly related to social classes; and is contrasted with
science. For an account of the different conceptions of ideology, see Jorge
Larrain (1979).

7. In this respect 'ideology' has the same significance as what Mosca (1896)
called the 'political formula', which represents the essential element of
persuasion and legitimation, as against coercion, in the dominance of a
ruling group.

8. See, for an interpretation of the individualist theories, Macpherson
(1978).

9. On the various distinctions which need to be made in considering the
sociological meaning of 'property', see especially Hegedus (1976).

10. For a broader discussion which brings out the diverse meanings of
individualism, see Lukes (1973).

11. Schumpeter himself recognized this phenomenon in his monograph on
imperialism (1919), although he did not accept the view that imperialism is a
necessary stage in the development of capitalism. It should be added that a
Marxist conception of the relation between modern capitalism and imperialism does not exclude the possibility that there are other sources and forms
of imperialist expansion.

12. In the USA, for example, during the 1930s, radicalism, and in particular
Marxism, seem to have had their greatest influence among small groups of
literary intellectuals, while the social sciences, and still more other spheres
of intellectual activity, remained largely unaffected (Bottomore, 1968,
chap. 3).

13. The idea of 'participatory democracy', which was formulated in some of
the radical movements, and notably in the student movement, of the 1960s,
is an important restatement of the socialist conception. It has also a close
affinity with the idea of 'self–management' which is the most distinctive
feature of Yugoslav socialism. There is not yet, I think, a comprehensive
study of the development of this body of related ideas, but a useful introduction to the subject will be found in Carole Pateman (1970).

14. It is worthy of note here that in the post–war period, when the British
Labour Party substantially increased its electoral support, its daily news-
paper eventually had to cease publication (in 1964).

15. There exists in Yugoslavia a form of socialism which is much closer to the
idea embodied in socialist ideology, but it has been obscured by the prominence of the Soviet model and has had an influence only upon relatively
small numbers of socialists.

16. On the latter, see especially Andras Hegedus (1976).

BIBLIOGRAPHY

Publication dates given below refer to the most recent edition.

Aron, R, *Progress and Disillusion* (London: Pall Mall Press, 1968).
Bell, D., *The Coming of Post−Industrial Society* (New York: Basic Books, 1973).
Bernstein, E., *Evolutionary Socialism* (English trans. New York: Huebsch, 1909).
Bottomore, T.B., *Critics of Society* (London: Allen & Unwin, 1968).
Bottomore, T.B., *Political Sociology* (London: Hutchinson, 1979).
Brus, W., *The Market in a Socialist Economy* (English trans. London: Routledge & Kegan Paul, 1972).
Brus, W., *The Economics and Politics of Socialism* (London: Routledge & Kegan Paul, 1973).
Brym, R., *Intellectuals and Politics* (London: Allen & Unwin, 1980).
Burnham, J., *The Managerial Revolution* (New York: John Day, 1941).
Djilas, M., *The New Class* (London: Thames & Hudson, 1957).
Domhoff, G.W., *Who Rules America?* (Englewood Cliffs, NJ: Prentice–Hall, 1967).
Gurvitch, G., (ed.), *Industrialisation et technocratis* (Paris: Armand Colin, 1949).
Gurvitch, G., *The Social Frameworks of Knowledge* (English trans. Oxford: Basil Blackwell, 1971).
Habermas, J., *Legitimation Crisis* (English trans. London: Heinemann, 1976).
Hannah, L., *The Rise of the Corporate Economy* (London: Methuen, 1975).
Harrison, C.Y., in *The Nation*, 22 March, 1933.
Hegedus, A., *Socialism and Bureaucracy* (London: Allison & Busby, 1976).
Hilferding, R., *Finance Capital* (English trans. London: Routledge & Kegan Paul, 1981).
Hilferding, R., 'Arbeitsgemeinschaft der Klassen?', *Der Kampf*, VIII, 1915.
Hilferding, R., 'Probleme der Zeit', *Die Gesellschaft*, I, 1924.
Johnson, R.W., 'The British political élite 1955–1972', *European Journal of Sociology*, XIV, 2, 1973.
Korpi, W., *The Working Class in Welfare Capitalism* (London: Routledge & Kegan Paul, 1978).
Larrain, J., *The Concept of Ideology* (London: Hutchinson, 1979).
Lockwood, D., *The Blackcoated Worker* (London: Allen & Unwin, 1958).
Lukes, S., *Individualism* (Oxford: Basil Blackwell, 1973).
Macpherson, C.B., *The Political Theory of Possessive Individualism* (Oxford: Oxford University Press, 1962).

Macpherson, C.B. (ed.), *Property: Mainstream and Critical Positions* (Oxford: Basil Blackwell, 1978).

Mallet, S., *The New Working Class* (English trans. Nottingham: Spokesman Books, 1975).

Mandel, E., *Late Capitalism* (English trans. London: New Left Books, 1975).

Mann, M., *Consciousness and Action Among the Western Working Class* (London: Macmillan, 1973).

Marx, K., 'Contribution to the Critique of Hegel's Philosophy of Right. Introduction,' English trans. in Bottomore, T.B. (ed.), *Karl Marx: Early Writings* (London: C.A. Watts, 1963).

Meynaud, J., *Technocracy* (English trans. London: Faber & Faber, 1968).

Miller, S.M., 'Notes on neo–capitalism', *Theory and Society*, **II**, 1, 1975.

Mills, C.W., *White Collar* (New York: Oxford University Press, 1951).

Mosca, G., *The Ruling Class* (English version, compiled from the original edition and the 2nd ed. (1923), by Livingston, A., (ed.), New York: McGraw-Hill, 1939).

O'Connor, J., *The Fiscal Crisis of the State* (New York: St Martin's Press, 1973).

Offe, C., *Industry and Inequality* (English trans. London: Edward Arnold, 1976).

Ossowski, S., *Class Structure in the Social Consciousness* (London: Routledge & Kegan Paul, 1963).

Pateman, C., *Participation and Democratic Theory* (Cambridge: Cambridge University Press, 1970).

Poulantzas, N., *Classes in Contemporary Capitalism* (English trans. London: New Left Books, 1975).

Renner, K., 'Probleme des Marxismus' *Der Kampf*, **IX**, 1916. Excerpts translated in Bottomore, T. and Goode, P. (eds.), *Austro–Marxism* (Oxford: Oxford University Press, 1978), pp. 91–101.

Schlatter, R., *Private Property: The History of an Idea* (London: Allen & Unwin, 1951).

Schumpeter, J.A., *The Sociology of Imperialisms* (English trans. in *Imperialism and Social Classes*, Oxford: Basil Blackwell, 1951).

Schumpeter, J.A., *Social Classes in an Ethnically Homogeneous Environment* (English trans. in *Imperialism and Social Classes*. Oxford: Basil Blackwell, 1951).

Schumpeter, J.A., *Capitalism, Socialism and Democracy*, (1942) (5th edn with a new introduction, London: Allen & Unwin, 1976).

Smithies, A., 'Memorial: Joseph Alois Schumpeter, 1883–1950', in Harris, S.E. (ed.), *Schumpeter, Social Scientist.* (Cambridge, MA: Harvard University Press, 1951).

Tawney, R.H., *The Acquisitive Society*. (London: Bell, 1921).

Touraine, A., *The May Movement* (English trans. New York: Random House, 1971).

Touraine, A., *The Post–Industrial Society* (English trans. London: Wildwood House, 1971).

Touraine, A., *L'Après–Socialisme* (Paris: Bernard Grasset, 1980).

9 Socialism and the Division of Labour

'I don't like work—no man does—but I like what is in the work—the chance to find yourself. Your own reality—for yourself, not for others—what no other man can ever know.'

(Joseph Conrad, *Heart of Darkness*)

'Perhaps after all the division of labour is a necessary evil . . . Let us then accept the division of labour where it is proved necessary, but with the hope that the machine will increasingly take over all simplified jobs; and let us insist with the same urgency as for the workers in other classes, that the workers of this class should receive an education not only saving them from mental torpor, but also stimulating them to find a way of controlling the machine instead of being themselves the machine—controlled.'

(Anthime Corbon, *Worker, Vice-President of the Constituent Assembly of 1848*[1])

Few socialist thinkers have been ready to accept the division of labour, at any rate in the forms which it has assumed in the industrial capitalist societies, as an unalterable condition. In one way or another they have been concerned to find some means of modifying its operation, mitigating its effects, or even 'abolishing' it. Marx formulated, at different times, ideas about the division of labour which have played a major part in all later criticism and have found, in diverse guises, a practical application.

In *The German Ideology*, Marx outlined a broad criticism, and an equally sweeping alternative:

'as soon as the division of labour begins each man has a particular, exclusive sphere of activity, which is forced upon him and from which he cannot escape. He is a hunter, a fisherman, a shepherd, or a critical critic, and must remain so if he does not want to lose his means of livelihood; whereas in communist society, where nobody has one exclusive sphere of activity but each can become accomplished in any branch he wishes, production as a whole is regulated by society, thus making it possible for me to do one thing today and another tomorrow, to hunt in the morning, fish in the afternoon, rear cattle in the evening, criticise after dinner, in accordance with my inclination, without ever becoming hunter, fisherman, shepherd or critic.'

Later on Marx expressed alternative, or at least modified ideas about how the division of labour might be changed or superseded. In *Capital*, vol 1, he argued that, in a future condition of society, 'the detail worker of today, the limited individual, the mere bearer of a particular social function, will be replaced by the fully developed individual, for whom the different social functions he performs are but so many alternative modes of activity'; and he went on to suggest that the development of education, especially scientific and technical education, would help to accomplish these ends in a socialist society. But in a later discussion, in *Capital*, vol. III, Marx emphasized more strongly that man's struggle with nature in order to maintain and reproduce his life, which he must undertake 'under any possible mode of production', remains always a realm of necessity: 'Beyond it begins that development of human potentiality for its own sake, the true realm of freedom, which however can only flourish upon that realm of necessity as its basis. The shortening of the working day is its fundamental prerequisite.'

These different judgements are not, however, contradictory. They embody diverse approaches to a problem which Marx treats in a consistent and systematic way. In the first place, Marx's concern is always the same: it is a concern with human liberation, with the possibility of constructing, and the means of achieving, a form of society in which each individual would be able to develop to the fullest extent his own talents and interests, instead of being confined within a narrow and imposed sphere of labour. The ideal is a society in which free, creative activity, as against *forced* labour, predominates. Throughout all his work, and not only in his early writings, Marx was guided by this vision of a liberated society, in which the division of labour too would be subjected to rational human control instead of developing as an apparently objective necessity determined by economic and technological imperatives. In the first drafts of *Capital*[2] Marx returns frequently to this theme: he writes, for example:

In fact, however, when the limited bourgeois form is stripped away, what is wealth other than the universality of individual needs, capacities, pleasures, productive forces, etc., created through universal exchange? The full development of human mastery over the forces of nature, those of so–called nature as well as of humanity's own nature? The absolute working out of his creative potentialities, with no presupposition other than the previous historic development . . . Where he does not reproduce himself in one specificity, but produces his totality? Strives not to remain something he has become, but is in the absolute movement of becoming?[3]

Secondly, Marx always analyzed the division of labour in a more general economic and social context, and with reference to particular forms of society. In *The German Ideology*, he observed that:

The division of labour implies from the outset the division of the *prerequisites of labour*, tools and materials, and thus the partitioning of accumulated capital among different owners. This also involves the separation of capital and labour and the different forms of property itself. The more the division of labour develops and accumulation increases, the more sharply this differentiation emerges.

Hence, Marx analyzed not only the division of labour, in the narrower sense of the specialization of tasks within a produtive enterprise, but also the differentiation of social functions which made one individual a landowner or capitalist, another an agricultural labourer or factory worker. The division of labour, in its more restricted sense, is only one aspect of this larger differentiation of functions, and the specific form that it takes is influenced not merely by the development of technology (which results in the creation of new occupations and new ways of organising the productive process), but also by the particular interests, objectives and tendencies within a given social mode of production.

It also follows from Marx's historical treatment of the division of labour that it is only with the rise of modern capitalism, the rapid growth of productive forces and the systematic application of science to production, that it becomes possible to think realistically of a new type of society in which men would not simply accept their ascribed social roles within a system that appears to exist and function on a basis of natural necessity, but would organise their production for definite social objectives and seek to achieve a balance between the need for specialized labour in production and the claims of individuals to develop freely and fully their personal talents and capacities. To use Marx's own phrase, the post–capitalist society would be one in which men could 'regulate their interchange with nature rationally, bring it under their common control, instead of being ruled by it as by some blind power.'

It is worthwhile to note here that Durkheim, who attributed a greater significance, and paid more attention, to the division of labour than did any other modern social thinker, although he approached the subject in a very different spirit from Marx arrived at conclusions which are not entirely divergent. Durkheim regarded the division of labour as a beneficent element in social life, as being essentially a source of solidarity;[4] but what he presented as its 'natural course' was a highly idealized picture, and only when he turned to discuss, in the third part of his book, the 'abnormal forms' of the division of labour did he seem to be describing its real features and effects in modern capitalist society. The two principal abnormal forms that he distinguished were the 'anomic' division of labour characterized by an insufficient regulation of the diverse functions, which resulted in economic crises and the conflict between capital and labour; and the 'forced' division of labour, in which the crucial element was the existence of class inequalities, which brought about a discordance between the distribution of social functions and the distribution of natural abilities, and unjust contractual relationships.

Thus Durkheim, like Marx, recognized the profound importance of class structure and class conflict in the actually existing division of labour, but he assumed that this is a temporary deviation from the inherent, natural tendency of the division of labour which will somehow bring about, through the progress of the collective consciousness and the activities of an impartial state embodying this consciousness, a condition of social harmony and solidarity. But this is no more than a vaguely formulated hope, and, as Bouglé observed in a comprehensive review of the theories about the division of labour, 'there emerges from Durkheim's apologia an impression which is very nearly as pessimistic as that which the socialist critics attempted to give.'[5] Later critics of Durkheim have pointed out that the increased coordination of functions in an enterprise, in accordance with doctrines of 'scientific management', does not necessarily enhance solidarity; and Georges Friedmann, in particular, has noted that two different kinds of solidarity may be engendered by the capitalist system of production—either the solidarity of all those engaged in production in an enterprise or branch of industry, or the solidarity of workers as a class.[6] In fact, it is the second type of solidarity which has grown most notably up to the present time.

Let us now examine more closely Marx's ideas about how the division of labour might be transformed in a socialist society, and consider how relevant these ideas are to present day conditions. The passage in *The German Ideology*, where Marx talks about hunting, fishing, etc. has sometimes been ridiculed by anti–socialist writers, but the notion it expresses is by no means so foolish and impractical as they suggest, although it needs to be put in a less romantic and archaic form. Of course, in an advanced industrial society a man cannot be an airline pilot in the morning, a nuclear physicist in the afternoon, and so on, but it is not altogether out of the question that many people, whatever their principal occupation might be, could become 'critical critics' in the evening; and the progress of a society in liberty and civilization might well be gauged by the numbers of citizens who participate significantly in its intellectual life and become, for at least a part of their lives, 'intellectuals'.

There is another social function which could also, with great benefit, be much more widely distributed; namely, political leadership. The traditional category of 'professional politician' is one that would need to be greatly modified in a thoroughly democratic society; for if men are really to govern themselves (in a collective fashion, not as isolated individuals) then the experience of governing should be widely diffused, and this is incompatible with the concentration of political experience and leadership in a small minority of people who, in Weber's phrase, live 'off' politics. There are several ways of extending more widely the experience of policy–making, especially by the devolution of political responsibilities upon a larger range of regional and other associations and by the development of 'workers' self–management' in an increasing number of organizations, especially business enterprises. The progress of such a movement would be marked by a decline in the numbers of those who made politics their lifetime career, and a considerable increase in the numbers of those who devoted a part of their lives—perhaps a few years—to the exercise of political functions. At the present time, the evident mediocrity of professional politicians in so many countries should allow us to contemplate the prospect of a decline in their function without undue anxiety.

Even in the narrower sphere of occupational specialization Marx's idea of an alternation of activities is not altogether impractical, and indeed it has found some practical applications. 'Work rotation' and 'job enlargement' have been widely discussed in studies of the organization of industrial work and many experiments have been carried out with a view to making routine jobs more varied and interesting.[7] It is true that such experiments have been mainly concerned to raise productivity, by reducing absenteeism, accidents, high labour turnover, etc., but there has also been some element of concern about the effect of monotonous, assembly–line work upon the worker himself, and the experiments do suggest that much more could be done along these lines to improve the situation of the industrial worker without any very adverse effects upon production. Of course, the scope of this kind of job rotation is still quite limited, but I think there would be opportunities for more extensive changes of occupation in a society which actually aimed to organize its production in the rational and humane way that Marx envisaged.

In any case, as we have seen, Marx also proposed two other means of limiting the harmful effects of the division of labour. One was the development of technical education which Marx thought would allow the worker to grasp the nature of the whole process of production in which he was engaged and thus make his own particular task more interesting as well as enabling him to move more easily from one specialised job to another. The second was, quite simply, to reduce the hours of work and increase the amount of leisure time, 'the true realm of freedom'.

Both these lines of thought have been followed by many students of industrial work since Marx's time. In the USSR especially, considerable efforts were made in the 1930s to develop polytechnical education, inspired in part at least by the idea of overcoming the narrowness of subdivided industrial tasks, though this kind of education was also well adapted to the needs of Soviet industrialization during that period. More recently, similar questions have been discussed in the context of a more advanced stage of industrialization, and there is an excellent analysis in the Czechoslovak study by Radovan Richta and his colleagues.[8] The authors describe two main tendencies in the development of industrial work: one is the extension of mechanized industrial production which gives rise to subdivided, monotonous tasks on the assembly line, the other, which they think will become predominant, the growth of automated, computer–controlled production lines, in which the unskilled repetitive operations are performed entirely by machines, while the activity of the workers is directed to the general regulation, maintenance and repair of the machinery. At a still later stage even these functions require fewer workers, and the most important human participation in production becomes the preparation and planning of the whole productive process. Thus, it may be argued, there is a continuing transfer of labour to more creative activities, and this trend can be reinforced by the planned transformation of labour into a scientific activity, in which the producer can experience his work as both a means and an end.

Richta and his colleagues, although they attribute great importance to this scientific and technological progress, which makes possible an entirely new organization of the labour process, also regard its consequences as depending upon the social conditions in which it takes place. From one aspect, it may establish some of the prerequisites of socialism; from another aspect, the realization of its potential benefits presupposes socialist institutions and a socialist culture in which the system of production would be directed not simply by the striving for maximum output and consumption, but also by the desire to provide, in the work process itself, the greatest possible scope for each individual to exercise his judgement, take responsibility, and find satisfaction in the employment of his creative abilities.

In any case, the benefits that are likely to flow from purely technological developments should not be exaggerated. The sphere in which automation can eliminate disagreeable and tedious kinds of work, though it is quite large, is still limited. Moreover, this process is accompanied by an opposite one in which computer–controlled operations encroach upon more skilled occupations—for example, tool–making or industrial design, and a variety of white–collar jobs—and diminish the element of creativity and independent judgement in such work. But on balance the shift from manual to white–collar occupations which is going on in all the advanced industrial societies does probably represent a movement from more routine and irksome jobs to those which are more interesting, require greater initiative, and allow the individual more freedom of choice in the execution of the work.

This trend toward the expansion of more interesting, more intellectually demanding kinds of work, which results directly from technological change, could be reinforced in various ways through political choices. For example, the investment in education could be substantially increased in order to raise the general educational level, and to provide new types of education which might be more directly associated with pro-ductive work, or be made available during periods of leave from work for people of all ages. One important innovation worth considering here would be the extension of an arrange-ment such as sabbatical leave from the universities to all kinds of occupation, so that individuals could pursue their educa-tion, visit similar enterprises in other countries, and generally broaden their experience as well as adding to the variety and interest of their jobs.[9] Another more fundamental change would be to involve employees much more fully in the management of their enterprise, along the lines of the Yugoslav system of workers' self–management; this again would provide the individual with opportunities for a greater variety of activities during working hours and would perhaps enhance the interest of even the most fragmented jobs. Finally, the possibilities of job mobility, discussed earlier, might be greatly enlarged by a policy which set out deliberately to organize production in terms of providing the conditions for maximum satisfaction at work.

William Morris once wrote an essay on 'A Factory as it might be',[10] in which he outlined the character that factory production might assume in a socialist society; but socialists, for a long time, and for various reasons (which I shall examine later), have sadly neglected these issues, while still arguing in an abstract way that the division of labour would need to be modified under socialism.

Even if the changes I have outlined above were successfully brought about, the sphere of production would still remain, in Marx's words, 'a realm of necessity', in which large numbers of people, at least, would not be developing freely their own activities, but would be more or less strongly *constrained* to produce. Hence the importance of Marx's third argument, that the growth of individual freedom in a socialist society would have as its fundamental prerequisite 'the shortening of the working day',[11] This theme has been taken up by many later writers, both socialist and non–socialist, who have seen in the expansion of 'leisure time' a possible compensation for the unavoidable constraints and dissatisfactions of work in an industrial society.

But the relation between work and leisure is a complex one, and we have to consider several different aspects. For some occupations, especially those of a professional or intellectual kind, the division between work and leisure may not be very clear cut; the interests of the occupation are often continued in leisure time, and even the distinction between home and workplace may not be very significant. Equally, in such occupations elements of leisure–time activity may be introduced into the sphere of work; business lunches, conferences, travel on business affairs, all have some features of leisure. On the other hand, for those engaged in routine manual or clerical occupations which are strictly regulated, there is likely to be a sharp distinction between work and leisure; but the extent to which leisure activities in this case provide a 'compensation' for work depends upon a variety of factors. Routine work may predispose the individual to equally routine leisure pursuits, or it may lead him to more active recreations in which he can satisfy a need for self expression. Much depends upon what facilities are available, and how they are organized. It should not be overlooked that in the capitalist societies leisure activities themselves have become a large–scale industry, and the transition from work to leisure assumes to some extent the character of a move from one sphere of mass production to another.

The impact of leisure upon work, however, may be just as important. In so far as individuals do enjoy increasing leisure in which they can engage in freely chosen, self–directed activities, they may become more critical of the authoritarian organization of work, and seek to modify it in various ways. Marx foresaw this possibility when he wrote that:

> Free time—which is both idle time and time for higher activity—has naturally transformed its possessor into a different subject, and he then enters into the direct production process as this different subject. This process is then both discipline . . . and, at the same time, practice, experimental science, materially creative and objectifying science.[12]

During the past decade much stronger demands for participation in the planning of work have been formulated by trade unions (and also in other spheres of activity, such as education), and one of the sources of this movement is probably the experience of greater independence and freedom of choice in leisure time which has accompanied increasing prosperity. In a more general way, material prosperity may have had some effects just the opposite of those which Marcuse outlined so pessimistically in *One – Dimensional Man*, namely, the stimulation of a more widespread critical concern about the quality of life, which necessarily includes a more profound questioning of the quality of working life.

The industrial societies, in the course of the twentieth century, have undergone considerable changes in all those aspects of the division of labour that were of concern to Marx and other socialist thinkers. Job rotation is taken more seriously though the chances of extending it were limited for a long time by the development of assembly–line production;

social mobility has probably increased somewhat as the structure of occupations has changed, so that there is now more congruence between ability and occupation; some of the more unpleasant and monotonous kinds of work have disappeared or are disappearing; above all leisure time has increased, by the shortening of the working week, and especially by the extension of paid holidays.

But the advance in all these directions has been slow, and there are two factors above all that are responsible for this. In the first place, all the industrial societies, whether capitalist or socialist, have concentrated their main effort upon increasing the total output of goods and services much more than upon reducing hours of work or transforming the whole organization of labour. This phenomenon itself has various causes: in the capitalist societies it resulted from the struggle, led mainly by working–class organizations, to escape from the mass poverty of the 1930s, and at a later stage, from the interest of capitalist industry itself in creating ever larger mass markets; in the socialist countries of Eastern Europe it was engendered mainly by the initial poverty of agrarian societies, the requirements of industrialization, and the need—for ideological and political reasons—to approach more closely the consumption levels of the capitalist countries. This element of competition has also a more general significance; high levels of production form one of the essential bases of national power, and international rivalries thus strengthen further the commitment to unrestricted technological advance and ever rising output.

The second factor that has impeded radical changes in the division of labour is the persistence of the class structure based upon property ownership in the capitalist societies, and the emergence of a new type of hierarchical structure in the socialist countries of Eastern Europe. In both cases, a strict and inegalitarian differentiation of social functions is maintained; in society as a whole, between those who direct the process of social development and those who are 'dependent participants',[13] and in the individual enterprise, between managers and workers.

Only in Yugoslavia has there been a sustained attempt to reduce substantially such distinctions, through the system of workers' self–management; and this attempt has revealed some of the difficulties involved in reconciling the aims of technological development, efficient economic administration, and general participation in the planning of production, especially in conditions where the need to raise the overall level of output is very pressing. It seems indeed that a high level of production, such as has been attained only since the war in the more advanced industrial countries, is a crucial precondition for tackling in a radical way the problems of the division of labour, and for making the reorganization of the work process a *major* aspect of socialist policy. Previously, in conditions where a large part of the population was badly housed, undernourished, and often unemployed, the main weight of socialist activity had clearly to be directed toward eliminating mass poverty.

Thus, it may be said that only now are the circumstances favourable, in some parts of the world, for attempting large–scale changes in the organization of work. They are favourable not only in the sense I have just outlined, that the material basis for a comfortable life for all citizens exists at present in many of the industrial countries, but also in another sense; namely, that there is now a widespread recognition of possible limits to economic growth, so that the task of creating a good society can no longer simply be thrust upon a more or less automatic process of endlessly increasing prosperity, which might be expected to provide compensation for the disagreeable consequences of the division of labour—for both the boredom of routine work and the more general inequality of social functions.[14]

The change in attitudes arising from this relative prosperity, and at the same time from the growing doubts about the possibility or desirability of ever increasing consumption, are now becoming very clear in a number of different ways. There has been a marked increase in the scope and activities of egalitarian movements, which have taken shape in a great variety of organizations—in sections of the established labour movement, in ethnic groups, in the women's movement, and so on. The idea of participatory democracy, although it is no longer expressed in the dramatic manner of the 1960s, is still very much alive; and one of its most important manifestations is the growing interest, in the trade unions, in the possibilities of workers' control, or self–management. There is also apparent, especially among the young, a new attitude towards occupations. Many young people, after completing their formal education, are extremely disillusioned by the kinds of occupation that are available to them; some opt out, in communes or in temporary and intermittent work, but many more, while taking their place in the apparatus of production, nevertheless remain critical of a form of society in which, for all its prosperity, there seem to be so few opportunities for enjoyable productive activity. Thus, in one way or another, they express the notion that the division of labour should be made for man, should correspond more closely with his own needs for creative activity, and that man should not be shaped to fit the division of labour. The concern with the environment, and with the 'quality of life', again particularly in the younger generation, embodies a similar outlook; it raises questions about the reorganization of social life as a whole— work, leisure, institutional arrangements and personal relations—in such a way as to satisfy as fully as possible in all spheres the great diversity of human needs. The trends which I have described—the rapid progress of science and technology, and the emergence of a new social consciousness— have already reached a stage where it is reasonable to think about practical policies designed to bring about a radical reorganization of the division of labour. It is not too fanciful to suppose that a socialist Ministry of Employment, sometimes before the end of this century, might be devoting a major part of its activities to developing schemes of self– management and to fostering the variety, interest and human value of work. Indeed, some reorientation of activities toward this end might be undertaken very quickly in many of the industrial countries.

Of course, there will remain very considerable problems. One of the most formidable of these is presented by the enormous gap, in the world as a whole, between the rich and poor countries, and by the tendency of the international division of labour to reproduce and reinforce this distinction. In the long term—the very long term—the problems of industrial work can only be solved on a world scale. But still, the poor countries, just as they can, in favourable circumstances, leap over some of the intermediate stages of industrialization by introducing the most advanced technology, might also be able to avoid some of the most disagreeable features of the division of labour if an alternative model of the organization of production were available for them to follow.

There are other problems arising directly out of technological progress—its enormous destructive potential in military use, its threat to the environment—which can lead one to a very gloomy assessment of the likely future for mankind, such as Robert Heilbroner has recently outlined.[15] Nevertheless, without lapsing into a Panglossian optimism, it may be remarked that this 'oppressive anticipation of the future',[16] induced by the immensity of our problems and the failure to cope with them in any effective way during the past decade, is counterbalanced, to some extent, by the much more widespread awareness of the need to establish a conscious, enlightened human control over the whole process of social life. The question that Marx posed—how men can 'regulate their interchange with nature rationally, bring it under their common control, instead of being ruled by it as by some blind power'—has become the central question of our age for very large groups of people. To work out in detail the meaning of this 'rational interchange', its implications for the organization of production and consumption, for the relations between nations, and for the elaboration of entirely new forms of society, is now the foremost intellectual obligation of social thinkers.

NOTES

1. Quoted from Friedmann, Georges, *The Anatomy of Work* (London, 1961).
2. Marx, Karl, *Grundrisse* (Penguin, 1973).
3. Ibid., p. 488.
4. Durkheim, Emile, *The Division of Labour in Society*. Like much else in Durkheim's sociology this is an elaboration of an idea derived from Comte.
5. Bouglé, C., 'Théories sur la division du travail', *Année Sociologique*, (1903) VI.
6. Friedmann, *op. cit.*, p. 78.
7. See the review of work in this field in Friedmann, *op. cit.*, chap. III. In recent years a number of automobile firms, notably Volvo in Sweden, have

changed over from a system of production involving highly subdivided routine tasks performed repetitively by each individual worker to a system based upon the organization of complete sections of the production line by teams of workers.

8. Richta, Radovan, *et.al., Civilization at the Crossroads.* 3rd edn (White Plains: International Arts and Sciences Press, 1969). See especially Part II on the radical changes in the nature of work, skill and education.

9. Some modest experiments along these lines have been introduced, but I do not think they are very widespread as yet. One case is mentioned in Rubner, A., *Fringe Benefits* (London, 1962), p. 26. In some professional occupations, however, there are already opportunities for periods of leave in order to attend courses, which may last for a month or longer, and this practice could be much more widely adopted.

10. Reprinted as a pamphlet London 1907. In the 1950s I visited a factory which had some of the qualities that Morris envisaged. the *communauté de travail* 'Boimondau', at Valence in France; but so far there have only been isolated examples of this kind of factory organization, though it may be that the numbers have increased since Morris's time.

11. Marx discussed this question at several points in the *Grundrisse*, and in one passage he quoted approvingly the comment of the anonymous author of *The Source and Remedy of the National Difficulties, Deduced from Principles of Political Economy* (London, 1821): 'Truly wealthy a nation, when the working day is 6 rather than 12 hours. *Wealth* is not command over surplus labour time [real wealth], but rather, *disposable* time outside that needed in direct production, for *every individual* and the whole society' (*Grundrisse*, p. 706).

12. Ibid., p. 712.

13. As Alain Touraine describes them in his analysis of the new class structure, in *The Post-Industrial Society* (Random House, 1971).

14. J.K. Galbraith, in one short chapter of *The Affluent Society* devoted to the subject of equality, argued that there had been a 'decline of interest in equality as an economic issue', and that the progressive increase of aggregate output was seen as an alternative to redistribution. This is clearly no longer the case, if it ever was; egalitarian movements have become much stronger and, as they have always done, set the issue of economic equality in the context of a broader discussion of the whole inegalitarian structure of industrial societies. For an analysis of some trends in the USA, see Gans, Herbert J., *More Equality* (New York, 1973).

15. Heilbroner, Robert L., 'The Human Prospect', *New York Review of Books*, XX, 21–22, 24 January 1974.

16. Ibid., p. 21.

10 Socialism and the Working Class

THE PROBLEM

The historical connection between socialism and the working class—however complex and diverse its forms—is quite obvious. Working–class movements produced socialist ideas, and when more systematic socialist theories (in particular Marxism) were elaborated, they found their most responsive public among workers. At the very least one can speak of an 'elective affinity'.

The questions that have been raised more recently about this connection or affinity seem to me to involve the following aspects: (1) The changing economic and social situation of the working class in advanced industrial societies; (2) the factors influencing the political consciousness of the working class; and (3) the capacity of a working–class movement to create a socialist society. I propose to examine these three aspects separately before venturing upon any more general comments.

THE ECONOMIC AND SOCIAL SITUATION OF THE WORKING CLASS

All observers seem to agree that economic developments— the rapid progress of technology and sustained economic growth—in the western industrial countries since the war, have brought about significant changes in the environment of the working class. There is no such agreement, however, about the effects which these changed circumstances have had upon the social role or outlook of the working class.

During the 1950s some sociologists began to write about a 'new working class', meaning by this expression that a part, a substantial part, of the working class was being assimilated into the middle class or as the phrase went, was undergoing a process of *embourgeoisement*. According to this view, rising levels of living, universal welfare services, better educational opportunities, changes in the occupational structure, new residential patterns, increased chances of social mobility, were together tending to break down the barriers between the middle class and a section of the working class, and to diffuse very widely a middle–class way of life. To some extent this process was seen in Europe as a movement towards the American type of society, conceived as being already predominantly middle class, or to put the same point in other terms, as being relatively 'classless'. Such a view was formulated very plainly by S.M. Lipset in an essay published in the early 1960s, when he said that 'instead of European class and political relationships holding up a model of the United States' future, the social organization of the United States has presented the image of the European future'.[1]

The picture thus presented of the emerging society was that of a large middle class occupying the foreground, a more vaguely portrayed small upper class or set of élite groups, and an 'underclass', also regarded as being fairly small (and diminishing in numbers), made up of specific groups in the population (the old, some ethnic groups, workers in declining industries) who were living in relative poverty. This picture is no longer generally accepted as accurate, though it may still be necessary, I think, to consider whether it was not simply drawn prematurely. In considering the objections to it I shall leave aside such matters as that the 'underclass' of those in poverty turned out to be much larger than the more optimistic commentators suggested, and also the problems concerning the social and political significance of the upper class or élites, and shall concentrate on the position of the working class.

What most critics of the *embourgeoisement* thesis have noted is that the working class is still a much more distinctive group, more sharply separated from the middle class, than has been claimed. Although there are 'affluent workers' the general level of income of manual industrial workers is still well below the income level of white–collar and professional workers.[2] Moreover, there are a number of other differences in the work situation which separate the working class from the middle class: less security of employment, more restricted opportunities for promotion, a stricter external control over the conditions of work. Outside the work situation there are other elements of distinction which have been explored particularly by Lockwood and Goldthorpe in *The Affluent Worker*.[3] Do the economic and social changes, which have certainly occurred however much they may have been exaggerated, bring about a change in the social relationships and social outlook of industrial workers? The conclusion at which Lockwood and Goldthorpe arrive is that:

Broadly speaking, our findings show that in the case of the workers we studied there remain important areas of common social experience which are still fairly distinctively working class; that specifically middle class social norms are not widely followed nor middle class life–styles consciously emulated; and that assimilation into middle class society is neither in progress nor, in the main, a desired objective.

And, after quoting Marx's characterization of alienated labour in the *Economic and Philosophical Manuscripts*, they go on to suggest that 'the alienated worker (in the above sense) is, at all events, far more readily recognisable in our research data than the worker "on the move towards new middle class values and middle class existence" '.[5]

Other studies, at various times, have come to similar conclusions; for example the work of Popitz and others,[6] which found that there is still a very strong working–class consciousness in which society is seen as sharply divided between 'them' and 'us', the importance of physical work as the principal creator of value is emphasized, and there is a profound sense of belonging to the community of workers. More recent studies in Germany by Kern, Schumann and others[7] and in France by Andrieux and Lignon,[8] arrive at much the same results.

Another version of the *embourgeoisement* thesis is to be found in Marcuse's *One–Dimensional Man*, though here it is not so much a question of the absorption of the working class into the middle class as of its integration into a national society as a whole, and its pacification as an agent of revolt. According to this view:

changes in the character of work and the instruments of production change the attitude and the consciousness of the labourer, which become manifest in the widely discussed 'social and cultural integration' of the labouring class with capitalist society . . . Assimilation in needs and aspirations, in the standard of living, in leisure activities, in politics, derives from an integration *in the plant* itself . . . The new technological work–world thus enforces a weakening of the negative position of the working class: the latter no longer appears to be the living contradiction to the established society.

Evidently, Marcuse's argument and conclusions are open to some of the same objections as have been brought against other versions of the *embourgeoisement* thesis; in particular, that there is little evidence of the change in consciousness which is the main support of the argument (and a good deal of evidence to the contrary).

Marcuse, however, also gives prominence to another aspect of the situation—the changes in technology and especially the progress of automation—which was not emphasized so much in earlier studies, but which has assumed considerable importance in a different kind of discussion of the future of the working class. This aspect has been presented with particular force by Daniel Bell in some recent writings.[10] Bell's main argument is that there is now apparent a decisive shift in the nature of work in American society; male blue–collar workers, although their *numbers* have continued to increase and will increase up to 1980, will form a smaller *proportion* of the labour force by the latter date. On the other side, the professional and technical occupational category is now 'the central one in the society'. Bell's general conclusion is that while labour issues may become more 'salient and even rancorous' they are unlikely to become ideological or 'class' issues: 'In the economy, a labor issue remains. But not in the sociology and culture of the society, and less so in the polity.' A similar view is taken by another contributor in the same issue of *Dissent*, David M. Gordon, who also points to the tendency to a decline in the proportion of male blue–collar workers, and emphasizes the extent to which there are now quite distinct categories of workers who cannot easily be brought together in a coalition, or engage in what Marxists would think of as a 'class' action.[11] From a different perspective, Alain Touraine has given a somewhat similar account of the changing role of industrial workers, and I shall look at this more closely in the following section.

This kind of argument about the declining economic and social importance of the traditional working class has also attracted criticism. It is suggested that the rate of development of automation (and hence the decline of manual work) has been greatly exaggerated; that even if the worker comes to be employed at a control panel rather than an assembly line this may not significantly change his work situation or his class allegiance; that the balance between white–collar and blue–collar work is misunderstood if it is not recognized that a high proportion of white–collar workers are women (one of the most significant occupational changes in the industrial countries is certainly the rapid increase in the numbers of married women at work) and that many of these women, the wives of manual workers, cannot be regarded in any sense as having moved from the working class into the middle class.

Nevertheless, even taking into account such criticisms, this change in the nature of work is a phenomenon of real importance. At the least, one has to distinguish between the situation which prevailed roughly from the mid–nineteenth century up to the end of the 1930s, with an expanding industrial working class, and in some countries a large peasantry or farmworker class; and the likely situation towards the end of this century, when the industrial working class will have declined as a proportion of the working population, and perhaps in absolute numbers, while the numbers of technical and professional workers will have increased still more. In such conditions it seems probable that the working class, even if it *were* radical and committed to socialism, would have considerably less weight and influence in determining the direction in which society moves.

POLITICAL CONSCIOUSNESS

In any thorough consideration of this aspect it would obviously be necessary to take account of the divergences between countries, resulting from different historical experiences and political traditions. The differences between the American working class and the European working class are evidently great, but there are also differences within Europe between those countries in which the working class is wholly or mainly committed to reformist political parties, and those in which a substantial part of the working class supports parties which claim, at least, to be revolutionary, and in which there is a stronger revolutionary tradition. In what follows I shall consider only some general features of working–class political consciousness, but the variations which I have just mentioned should be borne in mind.

The issue can be approached in two different ways. First, one can examine the historical development of political con-sciousness in the working class, as it is expressed in the doc-trines of working–class movements and parties. Second, one can look at the emergence and prevalence of political doc-trines and preoccupations which do not arise from the working–class movement, but may affect it in various ways.

As to the first: the *embourgeoisement* thesis which I con-sidered above proceeds from an analysis of the economic and social situation of the working class to an assertion of its declining radicalism; and Marcuse's version of the thesis seems to arrive at the conclusion that this radicalism has been totally extinguished. However, there is little evidence to sup-port such views. What needs to be recognized is that no substantial part of the working class in the western capitalist countries has been radical or revolutionary for a long time (roughly since the period from 1913 to 1919); and no working–class party has ever been able to establish itself at the head of a broad revolutionary movement. Thus the situation in the 1950s and 1960s was not that the working class had become politically less radical, but simply that it was as little radical during that period as it had been for the preceding thirty or forty years. Its lack of radicalism appears in all the studies with which I am familiar;[12] and it reappears in more recent studies,[13] in spite of the revival of radical doctrines among intellectuals in the 1960s.

The question to be posed, therefore, is not whether radicalism is declining, but whether working–class radicalism is likely to increase in the future; that is, whether the historical process envisaged by Marx of the formation of a 'class for itself', committed to a radical transformation of society, is likely, in the end, to be accomplished. Leaving aside the kind of answer given by very orthodox Marxists, which involves a large element of dogmatic assertion, there seem to me two more interesting answers, sketched by Serge Mallet and Alain Touraine.

Mallet's argument[14] is broadly that the 'new working class' (comprising the technically–qualified and professional workers employed in the most advanced sectors of production), while it is not revolutionary in the sense of being ready to make a revolution at all costs, especially because it has no desire to see the existing apparatus of production destroyed, *is* revolutionary in the sense that it is led by its situation in the labour process to aim at a fundamental change in social relations. The main evidence brought forward to support this thesis is that workers in some of the most advanced sectors of production have gone beyond wage demands to a more general confrontation over the organization of production in the enterprise and the management of the economy as a whole.[15]

Touraine argues in a similar way, except that he envisages a new structure of classes altogether.[16] In his view, the social conflict between capital and labour is losing its central importance in the capitalist societies of the late twentieth century, but new types of domination (which have also appeared, in more authoritarian forms, in the societies of Eastern Europe) are giving rise to a new social conflicts, between those who control the institutions of economic and political decision–making and those who have been reduced to a condition of 'dependent participation'. Touraine illustrates this change from the events of May 1968 in France, which revealed that

'sensibility to the new themes of social conflict was not most pronounced in the most highly organized sectors of the working class. The railroad workers, dockers and miners were not the ones who most clearly grasped its most radical objectives. The most radical and creative movements appeared in the economically advanced groups, the research agencies, the technicians with skills but no authority, and, of course, in the university community.'[17]

Such a view could, of course, be interpreted along the lines of Marcuse's argument to mean that the working class has now ceased altogether to be a radical element in society. How it is interpreted will depend in part upon conceptual choices—whether the new radical groups are regarded as forming a 'new working class' or a 'new class'—but also upon judgements (influenced also by these conceptual differences) about the degree of continuity between the traditional labour movement and the new social movements. Touraine suggests that there is a large element of continuity, in doctrine and organization; so that the new social groups could be regarded as carrying on a class struggle which is similar in some fundamental respects to that which occurred between bourgeoisie and proletariat. However, there may also be important differences in the formulation of aims and aspirations, in forms of organization, and in modes of political conflict.

But there is a more fundamental question about the development of radicalism in and through the new social movements of the 1960s. The events of May 1968 in France, and the movements of protest and opposition in other industrial countries, may be seen either as some kind of historical accident or aberration, interrupting the smooth upward course of these societies, or as harbingers of a new revolutionary movement, based largely upon the working class or particular sections of it, but also involving other social groups, which will eventually express, in a persuasive and effective manner, the opposition to present social inequalities and to a culture dominated by money, speculation and acquisitiveness. It is still too early to forecast with any confidence the future development of political attitudes in the working class, or in other groups which were involved in recent social movements. In some countries there has been a distinct leftward movement in the trade unions, though a study such as that by Michael Schumann and his colleagues[18] indicates that it has not gone very far, at least in Germany. The renewed interest in workers' control or self–management reveals a change in outlook, but it is still confined to a very small section of the working class. Nevertheless, the events of the past decade do suggest that it may be more realistic to pay attention to the revival of radicalism, and its prospective development, rather than to the decline of radicalism which was the favourite theme of the 1950s.

In taking this view, however, it would still be essential to consider the extent to which there developed, during the 1960s, political doctrines and concerns which were not radical at all, or were radical in a fashion which marked them off very distinctly from the mainstream of working class and socialist politics. I described, in an earlier essay,[19] four styles of political thought and action which seem to me to have little connection with the working class movement: the politics of new élites committed to, and justifying themselves by, the extension of rationality and efficiency in the system of production; those radical movements, especially among students, which attacked bureaucracy and technocracy and broadened out into a general cultural criticism, expressed sometimes in the notion of a counter-culture; the politics of ethnic or national movements in many parts of the world; and the politics of various supranational movements, as exemplified by the creation and development of the Common Market. It is clear that these different styles of politics are still active, that they have affected, and will continue to affect, the working–class movement, and that a profound uncertainty about what are the central political and social problems of the world in the late twentieth century still persists.

THE WORKING CLASS AND SOCIALIST SOCIETY

If the working class were radical, and if it were successful in becoming the ruling power in society, would it establish socialism? In other words, is there a necessary connection between the working–class movement and socialism? One rather crude version of Marxism, which nevertheless has had a great influence, asserts this connection very strongly: the victory of the working class will abolish classes, just as the victory of the third estate abolished estates—and a classless

society simply *is* socialism. Another twist was given to this
doctrine when a political party, claiming to be *the* representative, or vanguard, of the working class, also claimed that *its*
victory, *its* seizure of power, was equivalent to the abolition of
classes and the inauguration of socialism. In a sense Marx
himself gave some plausibility to such an interpretation of his
ideas when he disclaimed any desire to produce 'Comteist
recipes for the cookshops of the future'; which might be taken
to mean that there was no need to think about, or prepare, the
institutions of a socialist society, and that somehow everything would fall into place after the revolution.

The criticism of such conceptions has grown as experience
has accumulated of the difficulties and deficiencies of those
societies in Eastern Europe which call themselves socialist.
Within Marxist thought itself this criticism found expression
especially in the writings of those writers who formed the
Frankfurt School; and it is well summarized in a recent work
by Albrecht Wellmer:

> 'Since history itself has thoroughly discredited all hopes of an economically
> grounded "mechanism" of emancipation, it is not only necessary for a
> theoretical analysis to take into account entirely new constellations of
> "bases" and "superstructures"; in fact, the criticism and alteration of the
> "superstructure" have a new and decisive importance for the movements of
> liberation. In order to reformulate Marx's suppositions about the
> prerequisites for a successful revolution in the capitalist countries, it would
> be necessary to include socialist democracy, socialist justice, socialist ethics,
> and a "socialist consciousness" among the components of a socialist society
> to be "incubated" within the womb of a capitalist order. In short, elements
> that would have to be included are institutions, forms of life, political
> *praxis*, that could become the nucleus of a new, emancipated organization
> of social life'.[20]

This sets out the issues admirably. In so far as the working–
class movement is the principal bearer of the socialist idea we
should expect to see a development, in working–class organizations and through working–class political action, of new
institutions and new forms of social life. To some extent this
has happened, but it has certainly not gone far enough for
anyone to see clearly the outlines of a new society taking
shape within the old one. What conclusions should we then
draw? In the first place, I would say that we have to recognize

that the period of gestation of a socialist society is likely to be very much longer than was envisaged by the early socialists, including Marx. A long, complex and difficult process of development is a necessary precondition of socialism: it must include, especially, the attainment of a sufficiently high level of production of goods and services (so that there are no acute scarcities which would require authoritarian allocation and coercive control of those who are deprived); the achievement of a much higher level of general education for the whole population, and its institutionalization as a normal feature of society (which has not yet happened anywhere); the historical experience, over several generations, of the practice of political democracy, which requires the existence of many autonomous, strongly–established associations able to express the aspirations and defend the interests of diverse social groups, and to contest or oppose the authority of society's rulers for the time being. These preconditions are only now beginning to appear in some of the advanced industrial countries.

Secondly, if there is, as Wellmer argues, no economically–grounded 'mechanism' of emancipation, and if criticism of the superstructure has a new and decisive importance, then the activities of intellectuals, of social and cultural critics, are likely to become more prominent in the movement towards socialism; and this does seem to have been a feature of the recent radical movements. This is not to cast the intellectuals in a Lukácsian role, as party theorists who are able to express the. 'correct class consciousness of the proletariat' by virtue of some privileged insight into the ultimate meaning of history, but only to claim that intellectuals, through their reflection and criticism, can sketch possible new forms of social life, diffuse new outlooks, extend the range of education, and awaken or deepen the capacity for independent critical judgement in ever larger numbers of people, and that through this activity they contribute directly to the realization of socialism.

Thirdly, however, I would say that not only is there no economically–grounded 'mechanism' of emancipation, but there is no such 'mechanism' at all. We have to give up entirely that element in Marxism, and in some other socialist theories, which conceives the transition from capitalism to socialism as a historical necessity. Socialism is only a *possible* future. All the experiences of the twentieth century show how many and varied are the obstacles which the movement towards socialism has to overcome, and which it has so far failed to overcome—the concentration of political power in a party or a bureaucracy (which develops all the more easily where there is public ownership of large scale enterprises), the obsession with economic growth which has corrupted socialist thought itself, the rapid growth of population and of urban congestion, the vast inequalities between nations and the extent of the rivalry and conflict which arise from national sentiment and interests.

It may be that the word 'socialism' has become so corrupted by its association with authoritarian regimes, with centralized planning, with the obsessive pursuit of technological innovation and economic growth, as to be unsuitable any longer to describe the objectives of movements of liberation in the late twentieth century. But until a new term is found we must make do with it, only taking care to interpret it always in such a way that it does adequately express the idea of liberation; that is to say, the creation of a social order in which there is the maximum feasible equality of access, for all human beings, to economic resources, to knowledge, and to political power, and the minimum possible domination exercised by any individual or social group over any others. The striving for such a state of society, it is plain, is not only the concern of the working class, but of many other groups and organizations in present–day society; and the development of such groups—of radical students and young professional people, ethnic groups, community associations, and many others—in relation to the traditional labour movement will have, I think, a profound influence on the outcome of our ongoing social struggles.

NOTES

1. Lipset, S.M., 'The Changing Class Structure and Contemporary European Politics', in Graubard, S.R. (ed.), *A New Europe?* (Houghton Mifflin, 1964), p. 338.

2. There is a useful analysis of the limited degree of affluence even among American workers in Levison, Andrew, 'The Divided Working Class', *The Nation* (1 May 1972), pp. 558–62.

3. Goldthorpe, John H., Lockwood, David, Bechhofer, Frank and Platt, Jennifer, *The Affluent Worker*, 3 vols. (Cambridge University Press, 1968–9).

4. Goldthorpe, et al., *The Affluent Worker*, vol. 3, p. 157.

5. Ibid., p. 180.

6. Popitz, Heinrich, et al., *Das Gesellschaftsbild des Arbeiters* (Tübingen, J.C.B. Mohr, 1957).

7. Kern, Horst and Schumann, Michael, *Industriearbeit und Arbeiterbewusstsein* (Frankfurt, Europäische Verlagsanstalt, 1970); Schumann, Michael et al., *Am Beispiel der Septemberstreiks* (Frankfurt, Europäische Verlagsanstalt, 1971).

8. Andrieux, Andrée and Lignon, Jean, *L'ouvrier d'aujourd'hui* (Paris, Marcel Rivière, 1960).

9. Marcuse, Herbert, *One—Dimensional Man* (London, Routledge & Kegan Paul, 1964), pp. 29, 31.

10. See especially Bell, Daniel, 'Labour in the Post–Industrial Society', *Dissent* (Winter 1972), pp. 163–89.

11. Gordon, David M., in *Dissent* (Winter 1972), pp. 209–11.

12. See the works cited earlier, by Popitz et al. and by Andrieux and Lignon.

13. See, for example, Schumann et al., *Am Beispiel der Septemberstreiks*.

14. Mallet, Serge, 'Socialism and the New Working Class', *International Socialist Journal*, April 1965.

15. See his earlier work, *La nouvelle classe ouvrière* (Paris, Éditions du Seuil, 1963), which reports studies of three modern enterprises in France.

16. Touraine, Alain, *The Post–Industrial Society* (New York, Random House, 1971).

17. Ibid., p. 18.

18. Schumann et al., *Am Beispiel der Septemberstreiks*.

19. Bottomore, Tom, 'The Class Structure in Western Europe', in Bottomore, Tom, *Sociology as Social Criticism* (London, Allen & Unwin, 1975).

20. Wellmer, Albrecht, *Critical Theory of Society* (New York, Herder and Herder, 1971), pp. 121–2.

11 The Political Role of the Working Class in Western Europe

In an earlier paper[1] I discussed, in the context of the revival of radical thought and radical social movements in the late 1960s, some of the changes in working–class and middle–class political orientations, and various sociological interpretations of them. My general conclusion was that a turning point had perhaps been reached 'when the established class parties have attained a peak in their development, while new political forces are beginning to challenge their dominance'; and I suggested that new styles of politics had become apparent in four main directions: the rise of new élites committed to technological progress and economic growth; the emergence of a radical movement, critical of the technocratic and bureaucratic character of advanced industrial societies, in opposition to these élites; the growth of the regional and nationalist movements, and finally the attempts—exemplified by the European Economic Community—to create supranational associations. But I added that it was extremely difficult to evaluate one factor of vital importance for the future development of classes and political movements, namely, the likelihood that economic growth would continue in the rapid and uninterrupted manner which had so far characterized the post–war period.

A decade later the conditions have indeed changed substantially. The radical movements declined during the 1970s and a conservative mood, reminiscent of the 1950s, came to prevail again (although this has been more pronounced in Britain than elsewhere). At the same time, however, an increasingly severe economic recession has developed, with low growth rates and mass unemployment, and there has been a renewal of the nuclear arms race, which now appears to be accelerating. These events may well give rise to a new radicalism, of which there are already some indications; and in this situation it seems appropriate to reconsider the political trends in Western Europe over a longer period, with particular attention to the historical experience and the prospects of the working–class movement.

There are, of course, important differences between the countries of Western Europe to which I shall refer in the relevant contexts (and Britain is in many respects an exceptional case), but for the most part I intend to concentrate upon the common features to be found in party doctrines and policies, the extent of public support for such policies (including voting support), party membership and broad class allegiance. Let us consider first the membership of working–class parties as an indicator of political commitment to broadly socialist policies (either 'reformist' or 'revolutionary'). With very few exceptions the membership of working–class parties has either grown, or has been maintained, in the post–war period. In West Germany the Social Democratic Party (SPD) has increased its membership steadily to over 1 million (higher than it was in Germany as a whole in 1931); the Austrian Socialist Party (SPÖ) has grown ever since 1945, and with some 700,000 members is probably larger than at any time in its history; and the Swedish Social Democratic Party (SAP), which has grown regularly and rapidly since the 1930s, now has over a million members. In France, the Socialist Party (PS) experienced a sharp decline in membership from 1946 to 1950, but it has been growing steadily again since 1970, while the membership of the Communist Party (PCF), after declining from its post–war peak, remained more or less stable until the last few years, though with some fluctuations resulting from political crises in Eastern Europe; and in Italy the Socialist Party (PSI) maintained its membership at around

500,000 from the early 1960s to the mid–1970s, while the Communist Party (PCI) increased its membership.[2] Only the British Labour Party provides a notable exception to this trend, its individual membership having declined steadily, and in the past decade quite sharply, from over 1 million members in 1952 to about 300,000 in 1979.

Voting support shows broadly the same trend as do membership figures. In Germany the SPD increased its votes from 29.7 per cent of the total in 1949 to 42.6 per cent in 1976 and it has been the governing party, in a coalition with the small Liberal Party (FDP), since 1969; in Austria, the SPÖ, which has had a substantial share of the vote since 1945 increased this to 50.4 per cent in 1975 and has been the governing party since 1970; in Sweden the SAP has regularly obtained 45 per cent—50 per cent of the popular vote and was the governing party (or the main party in a coalition) for 44 years from 1932 to 1976; while in France and Italy the socialist and communist parties together have gradually increased their share of the vote. In Italy the total Left vote rose from 39.9 per cent in 1953 to 47.4 per cent in 1976; in France the Left vote for the 'common programme' in 1978 almost reached 50 per cent and the Left might well have achieved a majority had it not been for the disagreement between the PCF and the PS which emerged at a late stage in the election. And in May 1981 the Socialist candidate, François Mitterand, won the Presidential election; shortly afterwards the PS won a large majority in the National Assembly.

Again the British Labour Party provides something of an exception, with its share of the vote reaching a peak of 48.3 per cent in 1951 and then declining fairly steadily to 36.9 per cent in 1979. What is still more striking in Britain is the general decline of electoral support for either of the two main parties (Conservative and Labour). As Crewe *et al.* have noted:

In the general election of 1951 almost nine out of ten eligible electors turned up at the polls, the vast majority (96 per cent) to vote Labour or Conservative, thereby giving them all but twelve seats in the House of Commons. In the quarter century that has since elapsed, the absolute and relative fortunes of the two parties have fluctuated, albeit with increasing volatility. But one electoral change has been unrelenting: the growing, in fact accelerating, refusal of the electorate to cast a ballot for either of the two governing parties.[3]

In fact, the share of the two parties in the total electorate fell from 80.3 per cent (Conservative 39.5 per cent, Labour 40.8 per cent) in 1951 to 56.1 per cent (Conservative 26.8 per cent, Labour 29.3 per cent) in October 1974, although there was a modest increase in the 1979 election when it rose to 61.3 per cent (Conservative 33.3 per cent, Labour 28.0 per cent). Crewe and his colleagues go on to discuss the reason for the loss of support by the two 'class–based' parties, and suggest that it indicates a decline in class alignment: 'only half of the electorate (51 per cent) held an enduring allegiance to the party of their occupational class by the time of the last election' (October 1974).[4] They observe further that 'in no group of Labour partisans have Labour principles lost more ground over the decade [1964–74] than the post–1950 generation of working–class trade unionists',[5] and there was a further loss of support among trade unionists, especially skilled workers, in the 1979 election.

This is very different from the situation in Western Europe as a whole, where the traditional left–wing parties have generally succeeded in retaining working–class support,[6] although this support is divided, in several countries, between rival parties;[7] and it will be necessary to examine the peculiarities of the British case more closely in due course. But even if many of the Western European parties of the Left are solidly based upon working–class support, it may still be asked whether they are any longer socialist; that is to say, whether they express a distinctive, clearly defined class outlook which has been historically associated with the idea of socialism. This question itself has two related aspects: first, whether there is a working–class 'outlook', 'conception of the social world', or 'consciousness', which is fundamentally socialist, or at least anti–capitalist; and second, whether such an outlook is expressed in the doctrines, and above all in the policies, of working–class parties.

The first aspect poses what Hilferding called 'the most difficult problem' of the relation between *class interests* and *class consciousness*.[8] This is too large an issue to be fully examined here, but some of its basic elements need to be briefly considered. The idea of class interests underlies the whole historical development of the modern labour movement, and has been more or less clearly expressed in the constitutions and programmes of working–class parties. Its most precise and vigorous expression is to be found, of course, in Marxist social theory, and the whole conception of a *class* party, with socialism as its objective, has been profoundly shaped by Marxism in almost all the European parties of the Left (though not in the British Labour Party). Marx's theory, as it has generally been interpreted, asserts the existence of *objective* class interests, determined by the position occupied by a group in the social process of production; and further, in the specific case of the working class in a capitalist, commodity–producing society, a *necessary* development of revolutionary class–consciousness which will manifest itself in a political struggle to bring about a radical transformation of society.

This conception raises a number of problems. In the first place it may be questioned whether such a strict separation between 'interests' and 'consciousness' can be sustained, for human interests are always consciously formulated in some way and are matters for reflection and debate (except, perhaps, in the case of the most primitive interest in sheer physical survival). Some recent Marxists have strongly contested such a separation, notably Poulantzas, who argues that 'ideological and political relations . . . are themselves part of the structural determination of class', and hence rejects what he calls 'the Hegelian schema' (though it was clearly set out by Marx) of the distinction between 'class in itself' and 'class for itself'.[9] Unfortunately, like many other recent theorists, he does not go on to analyze the notion of 'class interest' itself. Such an analysis, setting out from Marx (and perhaps reflecting more closely the general tenor of his thought),[10] would begin with a conception, not of objective *interests*, but of objective *conditions* for the emergence of interests in a complex social interaction which involves the practical experiences of the everyday labour process, the confrontations between diverse theoretical and ideological views, and the activities of trade unions, political parties, and other organizations and movements. One possible outcome of the development of interests conceived in this way is the emergence of the working class which—to use Marx's own admirable formulation of its role—arouses

'in itself and in the masses, a moment of enthusiasm in which it associates and mingles with society at large, identifies itself with it, and is felt and recognized as the *general representative* of this society. Its aims and interests must genuinely be the aims and interests of society itself, of which it becomes in reality the social head and heart. It is only in the name of general interests that a particular class can claim general supremacy.'[11]

It is in this sense—as the bearer of a new civilization—that the working–class movement has had a historical importance in the development of modern European society.

But this is not the *only* possible outcome. It may also be the case that, in the later development of capitalist society, ideo-logical debate, political action, and changes in the process of social production bring about a redefinition and reconstruc-tion of the interests of the working–class such that these interests can be accommodated within a modified form of capitalism (which could be described as a 'mixed economy' and/or a 'welfare state'). This means, positively, that working–class interests would now require only a limited control over the labour process (regulation of working con-ditions, hours of work, etc), an assurance of levels of living which for most workers are not very far below the average level in a prosperous society, and hence a certain degree of social equality, all of which can be attained by a combination of trade union action and welfare policies; and negatively, that these interests do not require a transition to a socialist society, in the sense of a 'classless' society where the use of major productive resources and the distribution of the social product would be collectively determined.

Such a conception of working–class interests, which now seems to be held by many trade union and party leaders, is open to several objections, however. In the first place, it may be argued that it is only relevant to a particular historical period, now drawing to a close, characterized by newly–won affluence, sustained economic growth, and full employ-ment. The present economic crisis, and still more the longer–term prospect of stagnation (determined in part by environmental limits to growth), high unemployment, static or declining material levels of living, intensified attacks on trade union power, and deliberate attempts to reallocate the social product in favour of the owners of capital, make the notion of working–class interests which can be adequately satisfied within a capitalist system much less plausible. Second, a more general argument can be advanced to the effect that there is a universal human 'emancipatory interest' (implied in Marx's theory of history) which is embodied, in the capitalist era, in the struggle of the working class to end its subordination to the 'masters of production' by achieving the transition to a classless 'society of associated producers'. From this standpoint, the interests of the working class could never be conceived as being restricted, in a final and definitive way, to the improvements in its economic and social situation gained under a regime of welfare capitalism, even if there were any certainty that such improvements could be maintained.

On the other side, however, it has to be recognized that this notion of the emancipatory interest of the working class, expressed in the ideal aim of a 'society of associated producers', has itself been brought into question by the historical experience of socialist societies. As Touraine has written recently:

Socialism is dead. The word appears everywhere . . . but it is meaningless. Except when it refers to a vast family of authoritarian states . . . Socialism was the theory of the labour movement; in a large part of the world it has become the name of the state power [while] in other countries it amounts only to a defence of particular sectional interests which are less and less the bearers of a general project of human progress. [12]

Undoubtedly, the idea of socialism as the goal of the labour movement loses much of its appeal when it is set against the reality of socialism as a system of centralized planning and one–party rule; and the ideological defence of a capitalist 'free market economy'—and by association, of a 'free society'— has thereby been made much easier and more effective. It seems probable, indeed, that the example of authoritarian socialist states has been a major factor in promoting that transformation of socialism in Western Europe into the defence of sectional interests, or at most a moderate reformist doctrine of the trade unions, to which Touraine refers. More generally, it may be argued that the labour movement, if it pursues the socialist aim, always runs the risk of bringing into existence a new, and perhaps harsher, form of domination, which Konrád and Szelényi, in their study of Eastern European societies, see as the outcome of the intellectuals' rise to class power. They suggest that rational–redistributive society

'can be best described as a dichotomous class structure in which the classical antagonism of capitalist and proletarian is replaced by a new one between an intellectual class being formed around the position of the redistributors, and a working class deprived of any right to participate in redistribution.[13]

Nevertheless, this stark contrast between free market capitalist societies and authoritarian socialist states, which is nowadays so widely current and so readily accepted, leaves out of account the existence of other forms of society which are either socialist or seem to be developing from an advanced kind of welfare state towards democratic socialism, or what Robson called a 'welfare society'.[14] One example, for all its limitations and imperfections, is the system of socialist self–management in Yugoslavia; others are the growth of a more clearly defined socialist political outlook in the Swedish working class, which Korpi has described in a recent study,[15] and the achievements of the SPÖ in Austria, building upon the experience of the Austro–Marxists in their government of Vienna in the 1920s. Hence, in evaluating the significance of socialism as an expression of working–class interests, we should not concentrate our attention exclusively upon the extreme cases of authoritarian rule, but take account also of the continuing vigour and effectiveness of the democratic socialist movement, which is also not without some influence in Eastern Europe as a succession of working–class rebellions there indicates.

But in addition to the general question of the nature of class interests in relation to class consciousness which I have so far discussed, there is a second, more specific and empirical, problem which needs at least briefly to be considered here. The notion of working–class interests assumes or embodies, in much Marxist theory, the idea of the homogeneity of the class itself, which would be progressively realized as capitalism developed, so that eventually the 'two great classes' of bourgeoisie and proletariat would confront each other as two wholly different and incompatible worlds. This model of two 'pure classes'[16] may well seem inappropriate, or at any rate inadequate, in the light of the actual historical development of capitalist societies, which has resulted in a more complex social differentiation, a substantial growth in numbers of the 'intermediate strata', massive state intervention and the creation of a large category of public employees, and generally rising levels of living. These and other factors have produced, or in some cases perpetuated, many differences within the working–class—between workers in different regions or different housing situations, in older and newer industries, in the state, monopolistic, and competitive sectors of the economy, between men and women workers, between groups of immigrant workers and others—and they may also have brought about a greater blurring of the lines of class division in some countries. Hence, the 'interests' of the working class as a whole have to be conceived, in my view, as only *possible* or *potential* interests, which have certainly been clearly expressed in some historical circumstances, but are always a relatively fragile construction, continually challenged, modified, and sometimes dissolved, by the assertion of more limited sectional interests, which may be more easily apprehended and, in some plausible sense, more 'real'.

If, therefore, as I have suggested, interests are not simply 'given' but are constructed through reflection and discussion—although they *are* related to real, objective conditions—the problem of the relation between working–class interests and the representation of those interests by political parties becomes a great deal more complex. We cannot, on this view, simply assert the existence of quite definite 'class interests' and then go on to show that one or other party either promotes or betrays these interests. Rather, we have to say that there are diverse tendencies towards the constitution of class interests in various forms, and that political parties themselves participate in this process by elaborating, giving a more definite shape to, and diffusing, a particular conception of what the 'real' interests are (not overlooking the phenomenon that there is also a process of construction of the interests of parties themselves).

Two examples will illustrate the way in which such a model can be used in the interpretation of political events. One study of the British Labour Party in the post–war era suggests that in the early 1950s, following the victory of 1945 in which it gained its largest ever working–class support, but also its largest share of middle–class support, the party was faced with a choice between two possible strategies: 'Should it seek to maximize the manual working class vote, or should it seek to pursue more strongly a broader social appeal?'[17] In fact, the party chose to follow the second course, and to become what was called a 'people's party' (whatever that may mean), but this did not prove conspicuously successful from an electoral point of view. As the authors of the study just cited observe: 'Certainly on the basis of the evidence of generational displacement and working class fertility it may well have been the case that Labour's movement away from its working class base in the 1950s was a major error of strategy and one whose consequences cannot easily be undone.'[18] Of this particular course of events we might say that the party did misconstrue (for whatever reasons) the interests of the working class, and that this misunderstanding then helped to reconstitute the interests themselves in such a way that they were less and less able to find adequate expression in the policies of the Labour Party. At the present time, however, the party seems to be embarking on a new course as a more distinctively socialist party, and it may be that as a result of another reshaping of class interests it will be possible to overcome the consequences of the 1950s strategy and to achieve much greater electoral success in the future. In Germany the SPD also transformed itself, though in a more formal way, by adopting at the Bad Godesberg conference of 1959 a new programme which declared that: 'From the party of the working class the Social Democratic Party has become a party of the people.' But unlike the British Labour Party it has not lost working–class support, and it has been relatively successful in elections since 1969. In this case it might be argued that the party has construed correctly a change in working–class interests, and at the same time reinforces that change by its own reformulation of interests as those of the 'people' rather than of a 'class'. Undoubtedly, the negative effect of East European socialism, and more specifically that of the German Democratic Republic, has been particularly important in leading the SPD to distance itself from its Marxist past; nevertheless, Marxism in its non–Stalinist western forms is far from having been eliminated as a significant current of thought in German socialism, especially among the Young Socialists, and it seems probable that working–class support for the party is still based to some extent upon its traditional image as a socialist party.

Comparisons of this kind between working–class parties in the Western European countries need to be undertaken in a much more comprehensive and systematic way than has yet been attempted. This is obviously beyond the scope of the present essay, but one feature which I have mentioned at various points—namely, the peculiar situation in Britain—does merit a separate brief comment. The British Labour Party has become one of the weakest and least successful of the Western European parties, and it has always been one of the least socialist. The reasons for this are complex, and I can do no more here than sketch a possible framework of explanation by drawing attention to some of the most important elements in the situation. In the first place, capitalism itself, in Britain, has developed in a very idiosyncratic and incomplete way. Not only have many feudal elements—both structural and cultural—retained an important influence in British society, but the dominant capitalist groups themselves have been those associated with mercantile and agrarian capital; that is to say, with pre–industrial forms of capitalism.[19] And since there has not been a dominant *modern* capitalist class, so there has been no modern working–class movement, given coherence and direction by its own alternative social theory, to combat capitalism; the fundamental issues and the nature of the social conflict have remained permanently blurred. Furthermore, the same factor that helped to ensure the continued dominance of mercantile and financial capital—namely, Britain's position as the leading colonial power—also facilitated in various ways the incorporation of the working class into a national and imperial community. This, in turn, helps to explain why Marxism had so little influence in Britain in the last two decades of the nineteenth century,[20] whereas it became firmly established as the theory of the labour movement in much of continental Europe; and why the Labour Party came to be formed eventually, not as a socialist party, but as a party of the trade unions. As a result the 'class interests' of British workers have almost always been expressed as reformist and sectional interests, and this tendency, far from being counteracted, has been reinforced by the prevalent ideology in the Labour Party, characterized by a persistent, stubborn rejection of the idea of 'class politics'.

However, this situation now appears to be changing. Not only is Marxist thought more widely diffused and more influential than ever before in Britain, but in a much broader sense there is a notable revival of socialist ideas in the Labour Party. This owes much, no doubt, to a growing recognition of the peculiar incompetence of the dominant groups in British capitalism, demonstrated in the protracted, and now accelerating, decline of the economy; but it is also a consequence of more general changes affecting Western Europe as a whole. During the past decade, two of the styles of politics which I considered in my earlier essay have declined substantially in influence. The European Community no longer arouses any enthusiasm, its policies are in disorder, and its character as an elaborate form of customs union which is supported only so long as it serves specific national interests has become increasingly evident. Its survival in its present form is a matter of doubt, and it will perhaps only become viable if it develops eventually as a community of socialist states. At the opposite pole, the various nationalist movements within existing states (except for the Basque movement in Spain) have also suffered a decline.

The style of politics which has shown the greatest vitality, in spite of an apparent eclipse at the beginning of the decade, is in fact that of the radical movements of the late 1960s. Not only have these movements brought into existence new parties which have acquired a significant political influence in some countries (the Green Party in Germany, the Ecology Party in France), and contributed greatly to reanimating the nuclear disarmament movement in Europe which is now growing rapidly; they have also played an important part in the revival of socialist ideas and policies within the traditional working–class parties of Western Europe. In Britain especially it is noteworthy that the new generation of Labour Party activists—those in their early or mid–thirties—who are increasingly socialist in outlook, are in many cases people who were either participants in, or were strongly influenced by, the movements of the 1960s.

In this sense, it is certainly possible to subscribe to Touraine's view of the political importance of the new social movements. What seems to me much more questionable is the idea that new political organizations based upon these movements are likely to take the place of working–class parties, and to become the principal embodiment of a new radicalism. The indications at present are that there is a renewal of socialist ideas in the labour movement; that class politics will continue to dominate political life in Western Europe, and may become even more prominent in the course of this decade; and that the crucial political opposition remains that between a capitalist and a socialist organization of society.

NOTES

1. Bottomore, Tom, 'Class and Politics in Western Europe', in Bottomore, Tom, *Sociology as Social Criticism* (London, 1975).
2. Many of the data on party membership (and subsequently on voting support) are taken from the summaries of party publications and of election statistics given in Paterson, William E., and Thomas, H. Alastair, (eds.), *Social Democratic Parties in Western Europe* (London, 1977).
3. Crewe, Ivor, Särlvik, Bo, and Alt, James, 'Partisan Dealignment in Britain 1964–1974', *British Journal of Political Science* vol. 7 (1977), p. 129.
4. Ibid., p. 136.
5. Ibid., p. 181.
6. See the essays in Paterson and Thomas, *op. cit.*, especially those on Sweden and Austria. In the case of Sweden, Richard Scase remarks that since 1956 the Social Democratic Party has never failed to obtain at least 69 per cent of the votes of industrial manual workers [and] in elections during the 1960s the level of support . . . was around 80 per cent' (p. 327). This illustrates a more general point made by Erik Allardt, and cited in my earlier essay (Bottomore, *op. cit.*, p. 119), that in the Scandinavian countries since the war class membership has become increasingly important in voting

and working-class voters have been more apt to vote for workers' parties.
7. This situation, as is most evident in France, may be a major factor in keeping the left out of power.
8. Hilferding, Rudolf, *Das historische Problem*. Unfinished manuscript (1941) first published, with an introduction by Benedikt Kautsky, in *Zeitschrift für Politik* (New series) vol. 1 (1954): part translation in Bottomore, Tom, (ed.), *Modern Interpretations of Marx* (Oxford, 1981).
9. Poulantzas, Nicos, *Classes in Contemporary Capitalism* (London, 1975), pp. 14ff.
10. Though this would need to be argued more fully. For an illuminating analysis of the concept of 'interest' in relation to Marxist theory, see Benton, Ted, ' "Objective" Interests and the Sociology of Power', *Sociology* vol. 15, 2 (1981), pp. 161–84.
11. Marx, Karl, 'Contribution to the Critique of Hegel's Philosophy of Right. Introduction' (1844) (English trans. in Bottomore, Tom, (ed.), *Karl Marx: Early Writings* (London, 1963), pp. 55–6.
12. Touraine, Alain, *L'Après–Socialisme* (Paris, 1980), pp. 11–12. Touraine seems to conceive a new radicalism based upon the social movements of the 1960s as taking the place of socialism, but this radicalism—as a doctrine and a programme—has not yet assumed a very precise shape.
13. Konrád, George, and Szelényi, Ivan, *The Intellectuals on the Road to Class Power* (Brighton, 1979), p. 222.
14. See Robson, William, *Welfare State and Welfare Society* (London, 1976).
15. Korpi, Walter, *The Working Class in Welfare Capitalism* (London, 1978).
16. See the excellent discussion of this question in Ossowski, Stanislaw, *Class Structure in the Social Consciousness* (London, 1963), chap. 5, especially pp. 73–4, 82–3.
17. Minkin, Lewis, and Seyd, Patrick, in Paterson and Thomas, *op. cit.*, pp. 111–12.
18. Ibid. p. 135.
19. As long ago as 1910 Hilferding, in *Finance Capital* (1910), (English trans. London, 1981), drew attention to the backwardness of British capitalism, which is widely recognized today as a long process of deindustrialization. There is a good account of the pre–eminent position of the commercial and landed élites well into the twentieth century, and the eventual emergence of a single élite 'dominated by the South of England and finance', in Rubinstein, W.D., 'Wealth, Elites and the Class Structure of Modern Britain', *Past and Present* vol. 76 (1977); and an interesting analysis of cultural and political anti–industrialism in Britain in Wiener, Martin J., *English Culture and the Decline of the Industrial Spirit* (Cambridge, 1981).
20. This question, however, needs to be studied much more fully. Few scholars, so far as I am aware, have tried to provide a rigorous explanation; and one attempt, by Pierson, Stanley, *Marxism and the origins of British Socialism* (Ithaca, NY, 1973), seems to me to misinterpret the situation completely, because of its erroneous view of the development of Marxism in general.

Acknowledgements

Several of the chapters have been published elsewhere. I am grateful for permission to include them here, and would like to express thanks to all concerned: Chapter 2, 'Competing Paradigms in Sociology', *Annual Review of Sociology*, vol. 1, 1975 (Annual Reviews, Inc.); Chapter 3, 'Marxism and Sociology,' T. Bottomore and R. Nisbet (eds.), *A History of Sociological Analysis*, 1978 (Basic Books, Inc. and Heinemann Educational Books); Chapter 4, 'Structure and History', Peter M Blau (ed.), *Approaches to the Study of Social Structure*, 1975 (The Free Press); Chapter 5, 'Is there a Totalitarian View of Human Nature?', *Social Research*, vol. 40, no. 3, autumn 1973; Chapter 6, 'A Marxist Consideration of Durkheim, *Social Forces*, June 1981; Chapter 8, 'The Decline of Capitalism', Arnold Heertje, *Schumpeter's Vision*, 1981, (Praeger Publishers); Chapter 9, 'Socialism and the Division of Labour', Bhikhu Parekh (ed.), *The Concept of Socialism*, 1975 (Croom Helm); Chapter 10, 'Socialism and the Working Class', L. Kolakowski and S. Hampshire (eds.), *The Socialist Idea: A Reappraisal*, 1974 (Weidenfeld & Nicolson); Chapter 11, 'The Political Role of the Working Class in Western Europe', A. Giddens and G. MacKenzie (eds.), *Social Class and the Division of Labour*, 1982 (Cambridge University Press).

INDEX

(Note: Marx, whose name appears very frequently, is omitted)